VOLKSWAGEN

CHRONICLE

BY GRAHAM ROBSON AND THE AUTO EDITORS OF CONSUMER GUIDE®

Publications International, Ltd.

Louis Weber, C.E.O.
Publications International, Ltd.
7373 North Cicero Avenue
Lincolnwood, Illinois 60646

Permission is never granted for commercial purposes.

Manufactured in U.S.A.

8 7 6 5 4 3 2 1

ISBN: 0-7853-1599-3

Photography

Special thanks to: **Klaus Parr,** photo archivist with Porsche AG, Stuttgart, Germany; **Tony Fouladpour,** Volkswagen United States, Inc.; **Julia Jansen,** Volkswagen AG, Germany; **Mirco DeCet, Darren Dudley;** BFY Obsolete.

The editors gratefully acknowledge the cooperation of the following people who have supplied photography to help make this book possible. They are listed below, along with the page number(s) on which their photos appear:

Automotive Hall of Fame: 43; **Hot VWs Magazine:** 43; **Vince Manocchi:** 46, 47, 51, 52, 53, 58, 59, 67, 77, 78, 80, 92, 93, 96, 97, 114, 115; **Sam Griffith:** 69, 74, 75, 99; **Mark Bilek:** 106; **Hidden Image:** 109; **Thomas Glatch:** 111, 112, 113, 116, 117; **Mirco DeCet:** 119; **Nicky Wright:** 127; **Bud Juneau:** 133; **Milton Gene Kieft:** 133.

Owners:
Special thanks to the owners of the cars featured in this book for their enthusiastic cooperation. They are listed below, along with the page number(s) on which their cars appear:

Ron Elliot: 43; **Rich Kimball:** 46, 47, 77; **Charles Michelson:** 50, 51; **Michele M. Luby:** 53; **Pedro Sianz:** 58, 59; **Jim Miller:** 67; **Ken Dedic:** 69, 74, 75; **Lorenzo Pearson:** 78, 92, 93; **Julie Byer:** 80; **Stephen Nye/Ken Leighton:** 93, 97, 114, 115; **David Worden:** 96, 97; **Jerry Spellman:** 99; **John Benz:** 111, 116, 117; **Scott Hiss:** 112, 113; **Andrew Holmes:** 119; **C.A. Stoddard:** 127; **Michael F. Hartmann:** 133; **P. Garvey:** 133.

Acknowledgement: Ronald Davis, Kultur/Whitestar Films.

Contents

Foreword

For nearly half a century, Volkswagen has been a gigantic international corporation based in Germany. But it was very much a piece of Americana during the 1960s.

This was, of course, because of the Beetle and a brilliant North American advertising campaign that turned the simple, rugged Bug into the darling of intellectuals, youngsters, and anyone who wished to express individuality. By the middle of the decade, Beetles were omnipresent on American roads. If you didn't drive one, you knew two or three people who did.

The Beetle's reputation for simplicity and sturdiness was enhanced by its unchanging appearance; to American buyers, the willfully old-fashioned shape—"retro" before retro was faddish—was a source of delight. Owners swore by them, and even the uninitiated couldn't resist a smile as one puttered by, giving off the distinctive, resonant growl of its rear-mounted, air-cooled engine.

Obviously, the Beetle is just one part of the Volkswagen story. The company has offered dozens of models over the years, and although the Beetle continues to be produced for Third World markets, other, more sophisticated Volkswagens now account for the lion's share of VW profits. And those profits are significant. Volkswagen, which owns Audi, Seat of Spain, and the Czech automaker Skoda, sells more cars in Europe than any other manufacturer and ranks behind only General Motors, Ford, and Toyota among the globe's largest automakers.

A backdrop to this prosperity is an epic reversal of fortune.

North America is the world's biggest automobile market and from the mid 1950s to the early 1970s, VW dominated its import segment. But as the Beetle aged, VW could not deliver a replacement that matched the little Bug's appeal. Succeeding Volkswagens succumbed to Japanese brands that offered more creature comforts at unbeatable prices. To blame VW's alarming American decline solely on Japanese competition, however, is to ignore the corporate miscalculations that helped seal VW's fate on these shores.

Stolid, unexciting styling was a problem. So was a decline in assembly quality and in marketing inspiration. VW had become irrelevant to a large portion of potential American buyers. So while its cars were generally well-engineered and fun to drive, VW spent much of the 1980s and '90s bumping along the bottom of the sales charts. Only now, as a new century approaches and Volkswagen seems intent on reinventing itself, do U.S. sales show signs of resurgence.

If VW's American decline is dramatic, the company's birth in the 1930s and '40s was practically high opera. The principals included Ferdinand Porsche, Adolf Hitler, and the Beetle as a tool of Nazi propaganda. Slave laborers died building machines of war in Volkswagen's plants. And it survived as a carmaking enterprise only by the will of a small group of British soldiers. It is a fascinating journey, one that is far from finished, and it unfolds in all its dimensions, in *Volkswagen Chronicle*.

KdF-Wagen—Hitler's "People's Car" Project

When Ferdinand Porsche's new enterprise opened in Stuttgart in December 1930, its founder was taking a great gamble. The world already was one terrible year into the Great Depression. In Germany, the economic collapse was magnified by political instability. In a county of 65 million people, six million were unemployed. Currency inflation was chaotic. A desperate citizenry was beginning to take stock in the radical promises of a nationalist agitator named Adolf Hitler. In such a climate, automobiles were a low priority with most Germans. This highly industrialized nation produced only 189,000 cars during 1930. The United States, with a population of 119 million, built 2.8 million passenger cars that year. All told, there were fewer than one million cars on Germany's roads.

Any sensible engineer would have sought security, taking shelter in whatever work a big corporation could provide. But Ferdinand Porsche would no longer accept that. In three tempestuous decades at the top of both the Austrian and German motor industries, he had always been a part of a corporation. It had been 30 years of answering to boards of directors, to shareholders, and worst of all, to bankers he did not respect. Now, at 55 years of age, Porsche would start his own business. It would be run his way.

"We found premises for the offices and design department of the new company at 24 Kronenstrasse, in the north of Stuttgart," recounted his son, Ferdinand Anton Ernst "Ferry" Porsche. "We moved in at the end of 1930, and on 25 April 1931 the new company was entered in the commercial register." The title of the enterprise told its own story: *Dr. Ing. h.c.F. Porsche G.m.b.H, Konstruktionsburo fur Motoren-, Fahrzeug-, Luftfahrzeug- und Wasserfahrzeugbau,* (Doctor Engineer honoris causa F. Porsche, Incorporated, Design Office for Motors, Motor Vehicles, Aircraft and Ships).

That Porsche himself had never worked on aircraft or ship design did not seem to worry him. With thousands of qualified engineers out of work, Porsche knew he could easily bring in whatever expertise he needed. Nor was he bothered that there was no space to assemble cars at the Kronenstrasse offices. Porsche had faith that with a strong professional core, all else would follow.

Indeed, the new business was small, but highly qualified. Chief designer was Karl Rabe, a colleague from Porsche's days at the Austrian automaker Steyr. The body designer was a young aerodynamisist named Erwin Komenda. In total, Porsche persuaded 12 Austrian engineers to join him in Stuttgart. Ferry, then 21 years old and an engineer in his own right, was the youngest recruit. Legal affairs were managed by Dr. Anton Piech, who had married Ferdinand's daughter Louise. Their son, Ferdinand Piech, would control VW in the 1990s.

Porsche's reputation and that of his new team preceded him. Even before the doors opened, Wanderer, the German maker of medium-priced cars, commissioned Porsche for a design of a small sedan. It was given the name Type 7 to imply that others had already been completed. This original "Porsche" Wanderer, named the W17/W20 series and introduced in 1932, kept the Bureau busy for a time, though it did nothing for its technical reputation. It was a very staid car, with a separate chassis frame and conventional, forgettable, styling. The rear wheels were driven by a front-mounted overhead-valve six-cylinder engine.

Still, sales of the W17/W20 were relatively healthy and Wanderer commissioned a larger model with a supercharged 3.2-liter eight-cylinder engine. Soon, however, Wanderer merged with Audi, DKW, and Horch to form Auto-Union. Horch already had an eight-cylinder model and the new Wanderer car was quickly dropped after construction of just one prototype. The prototype did hint of the future, however. Shaped by Komenda, its body was an aerodynamic two-door with integral headlamps and a sloping tail.

Luckily, *Porsche Konstruktionsburo* was busy with additional projects. It completed a swing-axle rear-suspension layout for Horch, and patented a new type of independent front suspension with transverse torsion-bar springs. Through it all, Porsche and Rabe nurtured the idea of designing a highly efficient small car that would put the common man on wheels. They began serious conceptual work on their dream in September 1931. They didn't have

Adolf Hitler's political aim of a car for the common man fused with Ferdinand Porsche's plan for a uncommonly good small car to produce history's most successful automotive design. More than 22 million have been built since the end of World War II. Before the war, only a handful of test and demonstration models were assembled. This is one of those—a 1937 KdF-Wagen, or "strength through joy" car. Its name came from a Nazi motto, but even from the start, most referred to it as the German people's car: the Volkswagen. The more endearing Beetle nickname was prompted by the shape of the body. The locale is VW's giant Wolfsburg factory.

to wait long to begin actual development.

Zundapp, the respected Nuremberg motorcycle manufacturer, was keen to expand into the car business, but had no established automotive designers. In November, 1931, Zundapp chief Fritz Neumeyer commissioned Porsche to design a prototype. On the road by mid 1932, this Type 12 was the true forerunner of the Beetle. Neumeyer christened it *Volksauto*—people's car.

Porsche had suggested using an air-cooled horizontally opposed engine, but Neumeyer insisted on a five-cylinder, water-cooled, radial of 1.2 liters. Porsche put it in the extreme tail, driving the rear wheels, with the gearbox ahead of the differential. The Type 12 featured a backbone chassis frame with all-independent suspension incorporating a transverse leaf spring at the front and a transverse leaf with swing axles at the rear.

Though it had a conventional front radiator and its headlamps were only partly faired into the front fenders, the Zundapp car's body—again influenced by Komenda—was another glimpse of the future. It had two passenger doors and four seats. The shell featured generous curves and few straight lines. Running boards were eliminated, and the tail swept down smoothly over the radial engine.

The design was completed early in 1932. Three body shells were finished in April by Reutter in Stuttgart, and three prototypes were assembled by Zundapp at Nuremberg. Testing began soon afterward. Problems were immediate, and severe. They included engine oil boiling after just a few miles, and teeth snapping off gears. The crunch came when Neumeyer discovered how much it was going to cost him to buy tooling to build the Type 12 in quantity. He cut his losses, killed the project, and severed links with Porsche after paying him 85,000 reichs marks, about $31,000.

His dream deferred, Ferdinand withdrew to lick his wounds. German car production had slumped to a miserable 43,448 in 1932, and he could see little opportunity at home. But again, his reputation opened a door. Communist dictator Joseph Stalin invited him to Russia on a "fact-finding tour" of automobile plants, tractor factories, and aircraft works. In Moscow, Porsche was offered the remarkably attractive post of National State Designer. Along with all the advantages a privileged person in the Soviet Union could expect, he would have a free hand to oversee all vehicle activities and was invited to name his own salary. Porsche would be asked to bring his family to Soviet Russia, and would be offered a luxurious villa in the Crimea.

It sounded wonderful, but Porsche was cautious. He knew he would face a language barrier, which might never be conquered. More importantly, once settled in Russia, he knew he might never be allowed to leave. Returning to Stuttgart, he sent his apologies and turned Stalin down.

In the meantime, the Porsche Bureau had grown short of business, so as a speculative venture, designer Josef Kales was set to work on the layout of a Grand Prix racing car. The resulting P-Wagen featured a tubular chassis with a supercharged 295-horsepower 4.4-liter V-16 engine mounted behind the driver. In the Porsche spirit, it had a trailing arm front suspension sprung on torsion bars and a swing axle rear suspension.

Though it was a diversion from Porsche's overriding people's-car scheme, the sleek silver P-Wagon was nonetheless a product of his automotive passion and was an enormous success. Campaigned as an Auto-Union beginning in early 1934, it and its descendants (culminating in the 6.3-liter 545-horsepower Type C of 1937) waged a series of classic battles with Alfa-Romeo and Mercedes-Benz for world racing dominance until the very start of World War II.

Through it all, the small-car dream was percolating. Soon after Zundapp killed the Type 12 project, one of Germany's most successful motorcycle manufacturers, NSU, came calling. NSU had recently sold its car-making plant to Fiat of Italy, but now wanted to resume automaking. Baron Fritz von Falkenhayn of NSU commissioned Porsche to produce a new design for a low-priced, high-volume small car. Falkenhayn knew of the Zundapp debacle and saw to it that this time, things would be different.

"Fritz von Falkenhayn...laid down no limits on our technical ingenuity," Ferry Porsche wrote, "which meant that we were able to put our own ideas into practice, provided, of course, that we kept within the agreed budget."

The Porsche Bureau began work in August 1933, finished its drawings five months later, and by early 1934, had delivered to NSU the three requested prototypes. The new car was christened the Type 32. For the first time, Porsche had been able to build what he wanted rather than what a client bound him to. Type 32 was somewhat larger than the Zundapp Type 12, though it was similar in many ways. As before, it was built on a backbone chassis, which was now forked at the rear to support an air-cooled, horizontally opposed, four-

(continued)

The true forerunner of the Beetle was the Type 12 of 1932 (top and, in concept-drawing form, middle right). It was a Porsche design with which Zundapp, a German motorcycle manufacturer, hoped to enter the car business. Antecedents of the Bug are clear in its overall shape and rear-mounted engine position, though only a few examples were built. Contrast it with the wholly conventional Type 7 (bottom right), also of 1932. Porsche paid the bills by designing the Type 7 for Wanderer; at the wheel is his son, Ferry. An exciting variation on Porsche's design ideal was the mighty P-Wagen mid-engine race car of the 1930s (bottom left). Campaigned under the Auto-Union banner and with a succession of ever-stronger V-16 engines, it had torsion-bar front springing and a swing-axle rear suspension—a setup later used on the Beetle.

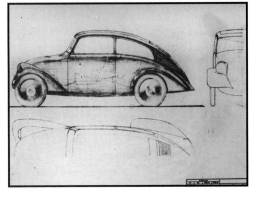

Ferdinand Porsche

Ferdinand Porsche did not "invent" the Volkswagen Beetle so much as he crystallized thinking about the design of a small, lightweight European car. This is not to discount Porsche's responsibility for the most successful automobile ever. Indeed, the Beetle as the world came to know it would not have been possible without his unwavering devotion to its central idea, his engineering expertise, the power of his personality, and the fashion in which it all fit into the grand plan of Adolf Hitler.

Porsche was born in 1875 in a small village in Bohemia called Maffersdorf, in what was then the Austro-Hungarian Empire. His father was a metalsmith, but young Ferdinand disappointed him by gravitating toward engineering and the new science of electricity. After taking a course in electro-technology at Reichenberg state technical school, Porsche joined an electrical equipment company in Vienna.

Vienna coachbuilder Jacob Lohner, who wanted to build an electric automobile,

hired Porsche in 1898. Ferdinand developed a coach with electric motors in the front wheel hubs (making it the world's first front-drive motorcar). Unveiled at the Paris Salon in 1900, it changed Porsche's life, turning an interest in electricity into a passion for automobiles. He followed up with a hybrid electric car in which power was generated by a small onboard gasoline engine. It won an Austrian prize for "best construction of the year" in 1905.

Then, as later, the stocky, intense Porsche was a restless spirit. As a colleague, he was prickly and dogmatic. Negotiation was to be endured, not embraced. And if he sensed himself losing an argument, he would storm away, sometimes never to return. When Lohner resisted further development of Porsche's cars, the engineer resigned, and almost immediately was hired as technical director of Austro-Daimler, Austria's most important car manufacturer. He was 30 years old.

Over the next 17 years, Porsche designed a string of stirring machines for Austro-Daimler. These included the seminal 90-mph "Prinz Heinrich" sports-racers of 1910, which used lightweight construction and low-drag body shapes to outrun stronger, heavier competitors. When World War I came, Porsche was assigned to the armament company, Skoda, for whom he designed hybrid electric tractors capable of hauling huge mortars that fired one-ton shells. He also designed self-steering electric carriages that could be driven independently or coupled together to form a land train. Porsche's education did not include a formal advanced degree, but in 1917, in recognition of his war work, he was granted an honorary doctorate from the Vienna Technical University and thereafter was justified in using "Dr." before his name.

By 1919, Porsche had risen to managing director of Austro-Daimler. His interest in the high-efficiency auto was rekindled when Count Sascha Kolowrat, a rich Austrian filmmaker, engaged him to design a lightweight sports-racer with a 1.0-liter engine. Called the Sascha, the two-seat, overhead-cam roadster was competitive in its racing

class. But more importantly to Porsche, it underscored the new reality of postwar Europe, in which the need for efficient, low-cost motor transportation was far greater than the desire of the established automakers to build large, expensive automobiles.

Porsche admired Henry Ford's success with the Model T and his co-directors at Austro-Daimler were aghast when he suggested they start building small cars. Already chafing at financial policies enforced by the bank that controlled Austro-Daimler, the rejection of his small-car idea was the final straw. Porsche lost his temper, hurling boardroom ornaments around as he swept out. As at Lohner years earlier, he had walked away from a conflict in which he would not compromise. And again he rebounded quickly, joining the German automaker Daimler in Stuttgart as technical director in 1922. Daimler was then building Mercedes cars, and the merger with Benz was still four years ahead.

The 47-year-old Austrian and his family settled into a newly built villa in Germany and began a turbulent six-year stay at Daimler. It was a stodgy company and the arrival of a blunt-talking technical director with a strange accent shocked its culture. Here was "...a prim little man with an amiable moustache and a sharp twinkle that could become a bolt of electricity when he chose," American author Walter Henry Nelson wrote of Porsche in this period. "His attire was almost a trademark. He would wear a loose-fitting tweed suit with giant patch pockets and a cloth cap pulled down to his ears. At races, a pair of binoculars would dangle from his neck and a pair of goggles would be perched on top of his cap. His demeanor was one of intense dignity and concentration...."

In his first years with Daimler, Porsche's team designed a series of large, complex, and extremely effective sporting automobiles, the classic K, S, SS, SSK models. They won speed events across Europe. Porsche also worked on Daimler's existing medium-sized cars, but could not keep in check his desire to take the company toward smaller, cheaper, mass-market machinery.

Daimler merged with Benz in 1926 amidst Germany's catastrophic economic downturn. It was a painful marriage. Daimler was in Stuttgart, Benz was in Mannheim. Daimler seemed to have the better engineers, but Benz seemed to have stronger connections with the financial establishment. Porsche again found himself at odds with two old nemesis: the banking class he had come to mistrust, and an employer resistant to his small-car ideas. Ferdinand had proposed several small-car designs, including a rear-engined concept. Daimler allowed him to build some compact-car prototypes, but when the machines proved difficult to start in cold weather, management issued a challenge: Porsche was asked to start any one of 15 left sitting out overnight. He couldn't. But he wasn't contrite. Instead, he quit on the spot.

Back to Austria he went, becoming technical director of his homeland's Steyr motorcar company. Porsche promptly began work on the magnificent new "Austria" limousine. Its success was thwarted, however, when the bank controlling Steyr collapsed, only to be rescued by the same financial institution that controlled Austro-Daimler. With so much enmity between Porsche and Austro-Daimler, he had no future in the revived company and left after less than two years.

In April 1930, at 55 years of age, the distinguished engineer was out of work. Though still unwilling to compromise his ideals and known throughout Europe's auto industry as difficult to work with, he apparently received several lucrative job offers, including one from Skoda in Czechoslovakia, and one from General Motors.

But Porsche was disillusioned, and left Austria yet again. Back in Stuttgart, he brooded. He was not ready to retire—financially, he could not afford to retire. But he recognized that he was probably too old, too set in his ways, to take another corporate position. He decided to set up as an independent design consultant. The result was *Dr Ing. h.c.F. Porsche G.m.b.H.,* and eventually, the birth of the Beetle.

Porsche and his colleagues spent the war

An elderly Porsche on 1950 Alpine road trip with nephew Ghislaine Kaes.

years bound up in the KdF-Wagen project, and in designing tanks and other armored weapons. Porsche has been described as politically naive, seeing Adolf Hitler only as a sponsor, not an adored leader. Slave laborers were used at Wolfsburg, and documents uncovered in the 1990s indicate that Porsche did recruit some of these workers. German historians hired by VW said there was evidence that Porsche contacted SS leader Heinrich Himmler directly to obtain labor from the Auschwitz concentration camp. Porsche was never tried for war crimes, however, and was not a member of the Nazi party. After Porsche was arrested by the British following the war, Albert Speer, Hitler's state architect, testified that the engineer neither knew nor cared anything about politics and was not a Nazi.

After his release by the British, Porsche was invited to France to consult on a "people's car." The French arrested him instead, charged him as war criminal, and imprisoned him in an unheated Dijon dungeon—though not before consulting him about the design of the new rear-engine Renault 4CV. Porsche was never brought to trial on the charges. His son, Ferry, raised a one-million franc "bail" by signing a design contract

with Cisitalia, and his father was freed in August 1947.

Porsche was 72 years old. His spirit and health were broken, and he returned to Gmünd in Austria, where the first VW-based Porsche sports car was being designed. In September 1950, on a trip back to Wolfsburg, Porsche saw the autobahns awash with new Beetles. He broke down and wept. On his 75th birthday, the family presented him with a Porsche sports coupe, but he was too frail to enjoy it. A month later he suffered a stroke, and on January 30, 1951, Ferdinand Porsche died.

The 1900 Lohner-Porsche with electric front-wheel hub motors.

cylinder engine. Front suspension was by trailing arms and torsion bars. The rear swing axles also used torsion bars, though these were placed longitudinally, alongside the main backbone. The engine itself was a 1.47-liter "boxer" similar in design to the VW engine that would follow. And though the Type 32 was considerably larger than the Beetle—wheelbase was 101.4 inches, to the VW's 94.5—all of what we would now call the styling cues for the Beetle were in place.

Improving on what he had already done for Wanderer and Zundapp, Komenda produced rounded, modestly decorated, but fully individual styling. Fared-in headlamps were mounted low on each side of the nose, and the long, sloping tail had cooling louvers pressed into the panels above the engine. One questionable decision was the use rear-hinged "suicide" doors.

Two NSU Type 32s were built with Reutter bodies, a third with a Drauz bodyworks shell. The claimed top speed was around 56 mph, and though the cars were initially thought to be noisy, it was considered a flaw that could be addressed as development progressed. A more serious problem was that suspension torsion bars kept breaking. Considerable changes were needed in the steel specification to make the material pliable.

All was going well until NSU abruptly cancelled the Type 32 project. Some accounts hold that Fiat activated a protective clause in its contract that barred NSU from building cars under its own name. Others say NSU, like Zundapp, retreated after calculating the investment realities. Ferry Porsche added that NSU, faced with a heartening upturn in demand for its motorcycles, simply could no longer find factory space to build cars.

Once again, Porsche's plans had been frustrated, and once again he found a savior. Jacob Werlin, a politically connected Mercedez-Benz dealer, visited Porsche in Stuttgart. What were the Porsche Bureau's current projects, he wanted to know, and what were its plans?

Porsche was puzzled. Werlin, a member of the Mercedes board of directors and an industry insider, likely knew what was going on in the Bureau. Porsche suspected Werlin was fishing for information about the latest P-Wagen, which would compete with Mercedes-Benz on the racetrack. Soon, however, Werlin admitted that he was seeing Porsche on behalf of Germany's new Chancellor, Adolf Hitler.

Hitler had first met Werlin in Munich in 1923, when as a struggling young politician, the future führer had bought a Mercedes out of Nazi party funds. In the early 1930s, as his power grew, Hitler had apparently suggested that mighty Mercedes-Benz build a line of small cars. Werlin's colleagues turned down that idea without discussion.

In January 1933, Hitler and the National Socialist Party swept to power on promises to restore prosperity. Any overt military buildup was still constrained by the 1919 Treaty of Versailles that punished Germany for World War I, so Hitler was not openly talking of military adventures. Instead, he forecast huge public works projects, including an unprecedented system of new highways. Thus were Germany's autobahns born. They were billed as high-speed motorways for civilian and commercial travel. That most of the original two-lane sections were built from Berlin toward Germany's boarders, and then along those borders, was not lost on those who thought in terms of military advantages. An enticing corollary to the autobahn scheme was Hitler's vision of a mass-produced, German-built, low-priced "people's car."

One of the dictator's first big speeches was at the Berlin Motor Show in February 1933. "Without motor cars, sound film and wireless...there is no victory of National Socialism," Hitler proclaimed. "A nation is no longer judged by the length of its railway network, but by the length of its highways." He went on to praise the propaganda value of motor racing. Taking the cue, Auto-Union invited Porsche to lobby Hitler for the same $250,000 in racing support the new Chancellor had just granted Mercedes-Benz. Hitler was swayed by Porsche's impassioned confidence in the P-Wagon and granted the state subsidy.

Porsche was just as passionate about his own ideas for a small people's car. He had shared his hopes with Werlin at the initial Stuttgart meeting and Werlin knew that one of Hitler's populist platforms included such a car. The intermediary approached the Füehrer, who summoned Porsche to a Berlin hotel to discuss the people's-car concept. Hitler requested from Porsche a memorandum on the subject. Dated January 17, 1934, the engineer's memo spelled out in terms agreeable to Hitler the basic specification of a people's car for the German public:

- It must be designed to be space-efficient and very durable, even if that meant developing new materials and production methods.
- It must be capable of 100 kph (62 mph), have the ability to climb hills, and average seven liters of fuel per 100 km (about 40 miles per gallon).

(continued)

As early as 1904, automakers were building cars with elements later found on the Beetle, including a central-tube frame, a rear mounted and air cooled boxer engine, swing axles, torsion-bar suspension, even streamlined bodywork. But Porsche brought these ingredients together at the right time in history. An important evolutionary step was the Type 32, (opposite page) which the engineer created for NSU in 1933. It was larger than the Beetle, but included all of the aforementioned design features, plus transverse leaf springs. Only three prototypes were built before NSU cancelled the project. Porsche's ideas had attracted attention at the highest levels of power, however.

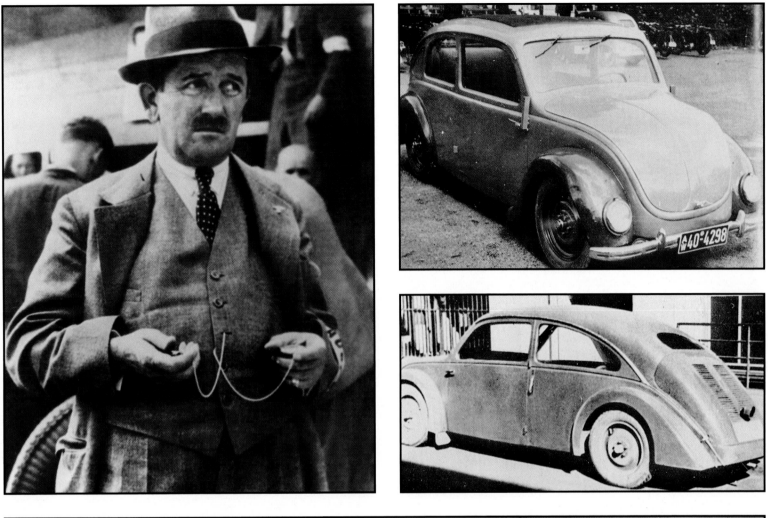

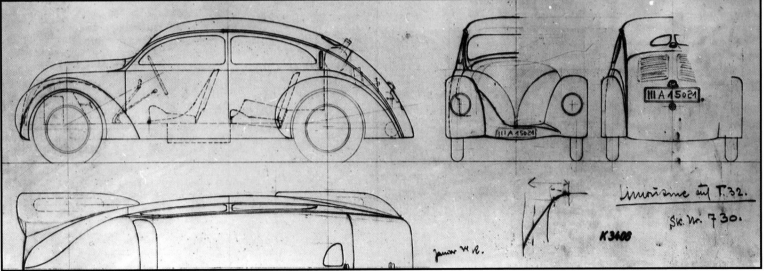

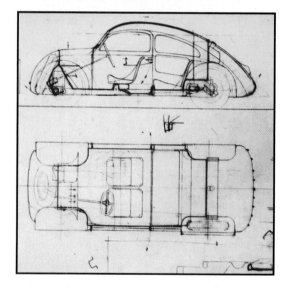

By 1934, fellow Austrian Adolf Hitler had ordered Germany's motor industry to cooperate in the development of Porsche's design. The Beetle took shape via prototypes based on Porsche's Type 60 concept. These included the V2 cabriolet and V3 sedan of 1935 and '36 (top four photos, this page). They were followed in 1937 by the VW30. The bottom photos on both pages illustrate some differences; a V30 is on the left and a late-model V3 is on the right in both views. That's Porsche's villa at Stuttgart in the background on page 17, and Ferdinand himself standing with a VW30 (opposite, top right). Road tests took place out of a Nazi storm-trooper barracks (opposite top left). Note that all these cars had rear-hinged doors. A rear window would not be added until 1938.

• It should have an air-cooled engine for reliability in all climates, and be very cheap to repair.

• It must accommodate a family of two adults and three children and their luggage.

• Its basic platform should accommodate several uses, including transport vehicles. (This point grew from Porsche's sense of sound engineering, but also spoke nicely to Hitler's agenda for military versatility.)

Hitler agreed with these basic specifications, but then threw Porsche a curve. The car, said the Führer, must sell for no more than 1,000 reichs marks, about $360. Porsche knew it would be impossible to produce such a car at a selling price under RM1,550 ($560), though he conceded that if Hitler could force down the cost of raw materials, the selling price could be brought down.

Memorandum in hand, Hitler addressed the 1934 Berlin Motor Show: "So long as the motorcar remains only a means of transportation for especially privileged circles, it is with bitter feelings that we see millions of honest, hard-working, and capable fellow men...cut off from the use of a vehicle which would be a special source of yet-unknown happiness to them...." Within months, Hitler was promoting a state-controlled project to produce a cheap, private car. The Porsche Bureau had already begun the design of yet another rear-engine, air-cooled car, the Type 60. Hitler studied the drawings in May 1934, and chose to back it.

He ordered the *Reichsverband der Deutsche Automobilindustrie* (RDA), the German Automobile Manufacturers' Association, to support the Porsche project. Understandably, there was resistance. Some companies, such as General Motors-owned Opel, for example, thought they could build a better people's car. Others balked at supporting a competitor. But in Hitler's Germany there really wasn't much choice, and on June 22, 1934, the association granted Porsche a development budget, albeit a ludicrously small one. The Bureau was guaranteed RM20,000 ($7,200) per month for ten months. Out of that, Porsche would have to pay salaries and all development costs. The association clearly was setting up the venture to fail. Wilhelm von Opel snidely counseled Porsche to look on the bright side: "It's a wonderful contract, Herr Porsche. Ten months on good pay and then you tell our leaders their project is impossible." But Porsche, stubborn and proud, accepted the challenge, and inspired his workers to do the same.

Except for some detail revisions, the original design laid down for the Porsche Type 60 concept was retained in the pre-production car. The Type

60 family was essentially a linear development of the NSU Type 32 project. The Type 60 had a 98.5-inch wheelbase, a 47.3-inch track, and a dry weight of 1,435 pounds. An air-cooled 985cc flat-four engine was mounted in the tail.

All the best features Porsche had proved on previous project cars were brought together: A backbone/platform chassis; a rear-mounted engine geared so the 62-mph top speed was also the cruising speed; a trailing link/transverse torsion-bar independent front suspension; and the swing axle, transverse torsion-bar rear suspension.

Though Porsche had dabbled with the idea of building two-stroke engines, he settled on a four-stroke for the prototype. The overhead-valve, flat-four, air-cooled "boxer" was designed for Porsche by Franz Reimspiess and was very similar to the Beetle engines that would later be manufactured in the millions.

All design work was completed at 24 Kronenstrasse—with the reluctant assistance of the German auto industry's component suppliers. Assembly of the prototypes was carried out at Porsche's villa in the Feuerbacher Weg. His garages had been turned into workshops, and Frau Porsche's laundry room was appropriated for the lathe and power drills. By 1935, using little more than rudimentary hand tools, the team had turned out two cars: the V1, a sedan, and the V2, a convertible. "V" stood not for Volkswagen, but for *"Versuch,"* or experimental.

The Bureau built three additional prototypes in 1935—what became known as the V3 cars—but needed an extension of the contract to get the job done, and in particular to refine the flat-four engine. The impossible-to-meet RM990 selling price had become somewhat of a moot issue and was brought up only when Hitler or his cronies were within earshot.

Hitler was optimistic. Opening the 1935 Berlin Motor Show, he announced: "I am pleased that the outstanding designer Porsche, with the assistance of his staff, has succeeded in drawing up the preliminary designs for the German people's car; the first versions will be available for trials in the middle of this year." Britain's *The Motor* magazine put two and two together—Hitler's auto-show announcement and Porsche's design patent—and published an article in December 1935 entitled "Hitler's 'Volkswagen.'"

"Is this Germany's National Car?" it asked, praising the "interesting" lightweight, rear-engine layout. "German car makers...have shown marked initiative in design," the magazine said. "The

Hitler presided over the cornerstone ceremony for the Volkswagen factory at Wolfsburg, near the village of Fallersleben, on May 26, 1938. He had become Chancellor of Germany in 1933 and viewed an inexpensive mass-produced motorcar as a showpiece of the Nazi state. Part of the plan was a brand new factory town in which workers would live and labor in National Socialist harmony. Hitler did not live to see Wolfsburg mass-produce Volkswagens, and in 1959, the cornerstone was buried in the foundation of a bridge at the nearby Mittelland Canal.

encouragement which they receive from the German government, both directly and in respect of the national road-building programme, is in sharp contrast with the anti-motoring policy of most British politicians."

It took until mid 1936 to complete the revised V3 cars. Two had a mixture of structural wood and sheet-steel body panelling, the third had an all-steel body shell. Although these Komenda-revised cars were close to the shape that would later become so famous, they still did not have head-lamps in the fenders, and none had a rear window. The rounded shape—especially the way in which the roof flowed gracefully into the tail—was distinctly insect-like and spontaneously, it seemed, the prototypes gained a nickname: the Beetle.

On October 12, 1936, all three V3s were handed over to a skeptical RDA for testing. A harsh schedule was imposed, originally covering 18,000 miles, then 30,000. The test route started and finished in Stuttgart, taking in roads in the Black Forest, the Alps, and long stretches of autobahn just opened between Stuttgart and Bad Neuheim.

Each car was expected to complete more than 465 miles per day at the hands of drivers and observers provided by the RDA. There were teething problems, including crankshaft, gearlever, and torsion-bar breakage, and even some engine failures. But each of the three cars completed its assigned mileage by the end of the calendar year.

The RDA's technical report—painstakingly prepared to meet the scrutiny of Hitler's top advisers—was generally in favor of the Porsche Bureau's design. Once again, though, the RDA argued that the new machine could not possibly be sold at less than RM1,000, and once again the Association tried to muscle in on what, to it, was a threatening project.

The RDA suggested that its own members take over further development, and that the Porsche-designed cars be tested against their own best offerings. Hitler's advisers finally lost patience. Scenting an RDA plot—which was real and being encouraged by the dominant GM/Opel and Ford-Germany interests—the government decisively ended the controversy. Sweeping the Porsche contract into its all-powerful bosom, the Nazis instantly converted the effort into a state-funded project. Because its members were so dependent on the goodwill of the state—and, with war clouds already gathering, there was a great deal of business to be gained by staying in favor—the RDA reluctantly accepted the move in May 1937.

Within days, an office was set up at Porsche's Kronenstrasse premises by the *Deutsche Arbeitsfront* (DAF), or German Labor Front. The DAF was effectively the state labor union. One of its first decisions was to build 30 pre-production test cars, which became known as the VW30 series. To rub salt in the RDA's wounds, the DAF directed Mercedes-Benz to construct the cars, with Reutter contracted to provide bodies. The DAF also took testing out of the hands of the RDA. It arranged for performance evaluations to be carried out by young soldiers based at an SS barracks outside Stuttgart. For its part, Porsche expanded into new workshops in Stuttgart-Zuffenhausen.

The VW30 cars were closer to final specification, but they still lacked rear windows and wouldn't lose their suicide doors until Porsche returned from a fact-finding trip to Detroit and accepted that rear-opening doors, while not matching the structural or ingress-egress benefits, were safer.

This was the period in which the VW design proved itself. The initial fleet completed 850,000 test miles by the spring of 1938, and a final batch of 44 more prototypes, coded VW38, took up the endurance tasks in 1938. This was testing and evaluation on an unprecedented scale. No motor manufacturing organization before or since has developed a car by testing as many prototype and pre-production models for as many miles.

It was time to name the new car. "Volkswagen" had actually been applied formally or informally to several earlier German small cars. The state felt something new was in order. The project was being managed by the recreational and leisure section of the DAF, whose motto was *Kraft durch Freude* (Strength through Joy). To the bureaucratic ear, KdF-Wagen must have sounded fine, so KdF-Wagen it officially became. Those who scoffed at the odd name scoffed in private. Nobody was willing to tell Hitler it sounded silly. Most civilians simply continued to use Volkswagen, and especially its diminutive, "VW."

And there was plenty of talk. Once the German state became involved, and the propaganda machine began to detail every successful test mile, public enthusiasm—and sales forecasts—soared. Even in the mid 1930s, Porsche talked of an annual production of 100,000 cars, higher than the output of any individual member of the German motor industry. Before the end of the decade, wild estimates of 500,000-unit annual production runs were being bandied around.

But with the average monthly salary of a middle-class worker at around RM300 ($105), even a low-priced car was unaffordable for most

KdF-Wagens in production-ready form were part of the chilling pageantry at the cornerstone ceremony. Hitler rode in the cabriolet with Ferry Porsche and shared a satisfied moment with Ferdinand. Although they accepted the Fuhrer's sponsorship, the Porsches were not members of the Nazi party and by all accounts did not share Hitler's politics. Instead, they considered him a means to achieving their automotive goals.

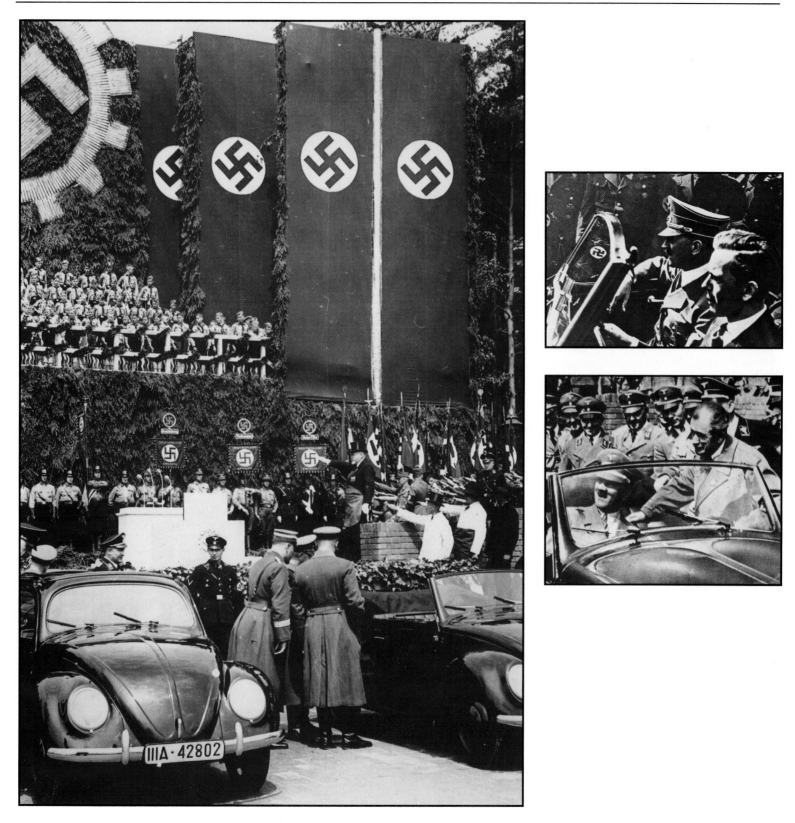

Germans. The Nazi solution was to impose on the public a method of purchasing KdF-Wagens. Loyal party members were directed to save for a new car by buying a stamp for RM5 (about $1.75) and sticking it into a savings book on a regular basis, preferably monthly. When enough stamps were saved to meet the retail price (still publicly tabbed at RM990, about $343), the card could be redeemed in exchange for a new car. In the topsy-turvy world of Nazi Germany, you paid for the car first and took delivery later. Of course, the only guarantee behind the whole scheme was the word of the Nazi state. But by 1938 Germany had become totalitarian, the nation's economy was being directed from Berlin, and few individuals or groups who openly questioned the party survived to do it twice. The stamp-book scheme not only made Germans feel part of the people's-car project, but generated a huge cash flow for the government. More than 336,000 Germans obtained savings books before war broke out, many filling them fully with stamps. And not one ever got a car in exchange.

But as the cash flowed in, the focus turned to a production site for the car. Now anxious to get its hands on such a sure thing, the RDA offered to build VWs in four of its member plants. It pledged to sell them at RM1,000, but to do so would require a state subsidy of RM200 per vehicle.

Hitler was infuriated. He reasoned, wrote Ferry Porsche, "that instead of paying a subsidy per car the money would be better spent on constructing a factory in which to build the new car. If it were assumed that a million units were to be built, then a state subsidy of RM200 per vehicle would provide RM200 million of investment capital." Thus, in May 1937, *Gesellschaft zur Vorbereitung des Volkswagens*—Company for the Development of the Volkswagen—was established to find, design, and build a new factory. It had three directors, one of them Ferdinand Porsche.

Hitler, acting out his favorite role as a visionary, told the trio to pick a greenfield site. It had to be in central Germany, with good road, rail, and canal links. Understated but understood was that it should be far from the established motor industry complexes. The site should not only accommodate the factory, but a town where all its workers would live. Find the site, Hitler said, and worry about ownership afterward.

An aerial search turned up several possible locations, with the most suitable one about 40 miles to the east of Hanover in northern Germany. In its favor was proximity to transportation links, including rail lines, the still-unfinished Mittelland

Canal, which connected Hanover with Berlin, and the new east-west autobahn from Berlin to the Ruhr. It was in a part of Germany that desperately needed jobs, and it would also be close to the new Hermann Goering steel works at Salzgitter.

The parcel was near a small village called Fallersleben and most of it was owned by the Count of Schulenberg, whose family had occupied Wolfsburg castle for generations. The Count learned of the state's interest in his land only after observing unexplained surveys being taken of his grounds. His protests went for naught, and he soon sold out at the state's price. A young architect, Peter Koller, a protegee of Nazi-party architect Albert Speer, was commissioned to design the new complex. The factory would be a vast complex on the north side of the Mittelland canal, while a new town would be constructed on the south. It was a model of Hitler's vision of the future: He would not graft a factory onto an existing town, nor would he expect workers to travel to the factory from other locations. Instead, the entire complex would be built to operate as a unit. Work and pleasure would be close-knit—a true statement of *Kraft durch Freude*. It would be, in Speer's phrase, "the mother town for National Socialism."

Because this was such a colossal enterprise, getting the KdF-Wagen into showrooms would take time—a long time. Hitler himself laid the cornerstone of the new complex with much fanfare in a ceremony on May 26, 1938. The town itself was officially designated in July (though without a formal name). The first main assembly plant complex was not ready until the following spring. The very first cars of any type—still pre-production machines—were not cobbled together until April. By July, 1939, the last series of test cars, 50 near-production standard machines known as VW39s, were completed. Photographs and general specifications of the cars were widely published in Europe and Britain, but since no independent road tests were allowed, all the outside world knew about the performance of these cars was what Nazi propagandists told it. No matter. Production forecasts were already set: 150,000 in 1940, rising to an incredible 1.5 million two years later. The latter figure was unbelievable to anyone with an educated, objective view of Europe's motor industry.

The design of the 1939 production-standard KdF-Wagen was already several years old. It was not complex, but simplicity is often the product of very sophisticated thinking.

The platform chassis, with its central backbone and its sturdy cross-members supporting the sus-

The VW38 prototype was not much different from the millions of Beetles that would follow. It had a 94.5-inch wheelbase, a four-seat cabin, and an all-alloy horizontally opposed four-cylinder engine of 985cc and 24 horsepower. The dashboard's only instrument was a speedometer flanked by lighting switches. The panel displaying the shift pattern could be removed if a radio was ordered. The knob at top center is the control for the semaphore turn signals. Two glove boxes were provided. Under the front "hood" were the spare tire, fuel tank, and a small luggage area. The doors by now were hinged in front. Above: This brochure helped lure Germans into the state-run stamp-saving scheme that promised—but never delivered—a new KdF-Wagen.

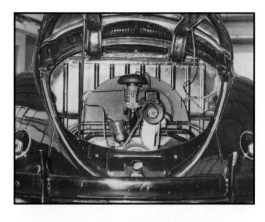

pension pivots, was much as conceived by the Porsche Bureau in 1934. The air-cooled engine was in the tail and the four-speed gearbox was ahead of the rear axle, nearly under the rear seat.

Two-door sedans and two-door convertibles were scheduled, with the only option a roll-back sunroof for the sedan. As with Ford's famous Model T of an earlier generation, there was no choice of color: All the original cars would have blue-gray paintwork.

Hitler himself was said to have asked for changes around the nose. In a period when he was building up military forces, turning Germany into a one-party state, and annexing countries to the east, south and west, it would have been remarkable that Hitler also found time to indulge in artistic trivia. Such is propaganda. Nonetheless, the headlamps were now fully fared in and there was a small split rear window.

For the 1940 model year, the engine, which had started life as a 985cc unit making 24 horsepower at 3600 rpm, was enlarged to 1,131cc and made 24.5 horsepower at 3300 rpm. It was a horizontally-opposed boxer with a bore and stroke of 2.95 inches x 2.52 inches and would maintain this displacement until 1954. Most of its bulk was taken up by the cooling fan and the surrounding cowling. It already ran with the familiar clatter that would become so unmistakable worldwide.

By 1930s standards the suspension was not only advanced, but expensively specified, as all four wheels were independently sprung. At the front there were trailing arms with transverse torsion bars, while at the back there were swing axles located by trailing arms themselves sprung on transverse torsion bars.

Automotive journalists got their first drives in prototypes during February 1939, and were impressed with both the car and the new autobahns on which much of the testing took place. "A drive in the car on the occasion of the recent Berlin Show demonstrated clearly that the vehicle has been designed with particular brilliance by Dr. Porsche to fit the German market and German roads," said *The Motor*.

As promised, the car cruised near its 60-mph top speed, throttle wide open. At 50 mph, where the engine in the typical one-liter British car was winding at 3500 rpm, the VW's boxer was turning a relaxed 2500 rpm. But the small displacement required frequent downshifting to produce anything like sufficient passing power. Acceleration was abysmal by today's standards—0-35 mph took 17 seconds, as clocked by the German maga-

zine *Motor Kritik*—but not bad against entry-level rivals. Curb weight was 1,510 pounds and fuel consumption was 41.5 mpg at 43 mph.

The air-cooled engine was noisy, though most journalists didn't find it excessive and some credited Porsche's rear-engine layout for providing a rather quiet passenger compartment. Though cabin appointments were crude by most standards, the KdF did come standard with a feature not offered on other low-priced European cars: a heater. Simple chambers captured engine heat and fed it through vents into the passenger compartment. Overall, testers were so taken with the car's seemingly efficient shape and rugged design that problems like tail-happy oversteer and sensitivity to side winds were played down. And in those days it was still normal to expect cable-operated brakes in this class.

A second test-drive session was held in mid 1939, with journalists treated to rides around the Nurburg Ring, Germany's demanding 14-mile road-racing course. A writer for Britain's *Light Car* magazine was aboard a KdF-Wagen with two other journalists; at the wheel was a German test driver identified as "Herr Deine."

"We sat in simple comfort on cloth-upholstered seats," the British writer said, "and we had excellent all-round visibility." There was praise for the little engine's ability to rev and to climb hills, but it was the suspension that got most of the credit for getting the car around the circuit at a speed competitive with anything in its class. The KdF-Wagens were averaging a laudable 42 mph over the course, which included 89 left turns and 85 right turns. (Herman Lang's Mercedes won the '39 Grand Prix at the Ring at an average speed of 84 mph.) "We left Herr Deine with a profound respect for both his driving and his car," said *Light Car*.

Just 135 "Beetles" of all types had been built since that 1932 Zundapp Type 12. But at a promised list price of RM990/$343, the production KdF-Wagen looked sure to sell in huge quantities—as well it should, for there was no other European car that could match that price. In America, the least-expensive 1940 Chevrolet, the 6-cylinder business coupe, started at $659, while Ford's entry-level counterpart (with a standard V-8) retailed for $619.

Then, on September 1, 1939, Germany's world changed—permanently. Hitler's Panzer armies rolled in to Poland. Britain, France, New Zealand, and Australia declared war on Germany two days later. Life at Wolfsburg, indeed life everywhere in Europe, would never be the same.

KdF-Wagons spent much time on public display, including this 1938 lineup along a Berlin boulevard. Automotive journalists got their first test drives in January 1939, and even British writers were impressed. By 1940, the engine had been enlarged to 1,131cc and made 24.5 horsepower. At a promised price of RM990, about $343, the government-controlled automaker looked to sell millions of these people's cars. Though a convertible model was part of the original run of KdF prototypes, it was eased out of the picture because it would have cost more and taken too long to build. Sedans with huge foldback canvas sunroofs took its place. KdFs were geared to cruise Germany's new system of high-speed autobahns. In reality, years of terrible destruction lay ahead.

War and Peace— VW's Struggle for Survival

Signs of war were evident well before 1939, even to those who preferred not to think the unthinkable. They were there for Ferdinand Porsche, the engineer who rarely thought about anything except his work.

As early as 1934, when defining the specifications of the new "people's car," the RDA considered its adaptation as a utility and cross-country vehicle—and suggested that it should have space for three men, ammunition, and a machine gun. In 1937, the military modified one of the spare VW30 chassis with a crude open body and a gun mount.

Porsche could have had few illusions about such developments. While the factory was being built at Wolfsburg, he noticed the way the wooden floors were being banded and recognized that this was to reduce the fire risk after a bombing raid. He saw that windows were placed to avoid reflecting moonlight, lest they give enemy bombers a target.

Was this to be a car plant, Porsche asked, or a war-machines factory? Hitler replied it was a VW facility, nothing more. If there were a war, added the Führer, it would be in the East, and the KdF plant would be well out of aircraft range. In any case, the factory site was still so new it did not appear on most maps. The town being built on it didn't even have a name. If Hitler and his cronies had not spent so much time boasting about the project, the Allies might not have known it existed.

Germany's first year of World War II was fought largely at sea and on fronts far from Wolfsburg. Plans for the production of civilian VWs proceeded virtually as planned. But as the first Beetle, or Type 1, rolled off the assembly lines in August 1940, the Luftwaffe was being stymied in the Battle of Britain. And on August 25, the Royal Air Force executed its first bombing raid on Berlin. The planned flood of Beetles was reduced to a trickle. Hitler and his planners realized what they needed from Germany's motor industry was not passenger cars. Thus, the first vehicles churned out by the KdF factory in any numbers were ugly, open-top machines called the VW Type 62. Just as the original Beetle quickly acquired a nickname, so did the super-spartan Type 62. "Kubel" is German for bucket, so this gawky-looking device was tagged the Kubelwagen—a "bucket-car."

The first proper Type 62 Kuebelwagen was drawn up by Franz Reimspiess in 1938. Reimspiess had designed the definitive VW flat-four air-cooled engine. Despite retaining rear-wheel-drive, the Type 62 was designed as a cross-country vehicle, capable of linking troops at the front with each other and with headquarters. It was in essence a German Jeep—but without as much capability or panache.

Early Type 62s retained the already-familiar backbone chassis and air-cooled 985-cc boxer engine, though the structure was substantially reinforced. The ultra-utilitarian bodywork of ribbed steel panels was augmented with canvas doors and a canvas soft top. Ground clearance was enhanced by increasing wheel diameter to 19 inches, from the Beetle's 16 inches.

Drawing on data gathered from the road-car prototypes and spurred by the war effort, the design was refined again in mid 1939. Four waist-level steel doors and a limited-slip differential were added, though the Kubel was still mechanically similar to the road cars. The bodies, incidently, were provided by Ambi-Budd of Berlin. Since Budd was an American corporation, there was at first an arm's-length North American connection.

The German army used early examples in the Polish campaign of September 1939. The boxer proved reliable, but at only 985cc, it lacked the torque to carry full loads. At the same time, the military groaned that the Kubelwagen was actually too fast and too high-geared for some work. (This may be the only recorded complaint that a Beetle-based vehicle had too much performance.)

A quick revamp produced the Type 82, and the Kubelwagen design was set for the rest of the war. Though the 1,131-cc engine was fitted, lack of power was a flaw that dogged the bucket-car. To give it better "crawling" ability—the Kubel had to be able to move along at the speed of a column of marching soldiers—the transmission was re-designed with rear-hub drop gears. Along with simple changes to the stub axles to elevate the front end, this increased ground clearance to 11.4 inches and allowed the less-expensive 16-inch wheels to be restored.

Factions within the German military were cool

Nazi bureaucrats named the site of the VW factory KdF-Town and geared up to produce the people's car. Instead, they were forced to retool to assemble the weapons of war. Between 1940 and 1945, the plant's 16,000 workers, which included concentration-camp slave laborers, manufactured aircraft components, camp stoves, and V1 flying bombs. Amid deadly air raids by American and British forces, they also built some innovative vehicles, such as this amphibious Schwimmwagen.

to the Kubelwagen. It wasn't a fighting vehicle from the ground up, after all. Others in the professional-soldier class opposed it simply because it was a Hitler favorite. But the Kubel did beat a prototype four-wheel-drive rival in field tests. That, and the Führer's support, settled the issue.

The Kubel had its advantages. Its flat bottom allowed it to skid over most soft obstacles. It had simple bodywork that could be repaired in the field. There was no cooling radiator to be holed by a stray bullet. And the engine proved as adaptable to the heat of the African deserts as to the cold of the Russian front. Kubels were less expensive and more maneuverable than rival scout cars, and with their lighter weight, could survive treks across fields of mines fused to detonate under heavier machinery, such as tanks. It could be manhandled on the battlefield, even righted by hand.

Serious production of the Kubel began at Wolfsburg in February 1940, just about the time British bombers first targeted the factory. Production was largely unaffected by these early raids, however, and the 1,000th Kubel was driven off the assembly line on December 20, 1940. Deliveries increased rapidly. Mass production was achieved in 1941, and by 1945 the Kubel had become the most-numerous of the VW Beetle-type derivatives built at Wolfsburg. Total wartime production exceeded 50,000, and hundreds more were assembled from available parts under British military control in 1945 and 1946.

By the time the war was in full swing, though, production of wheeled vehicles took up only a portion of Wolfsburg's massive, still-unfinished facilities. Wings and complete fuselages were produced for twin-engine Junkers 88 bombers, spare parts were manufactured for BMW aircraft engines, and a huge number of stoves were made for the soldiers on the Eastern front. Beginning in 1943, the plant assembled the V1 pilotless aircraft, the pulse-jet powered "doddlebug" that started indiscriminate attacks on London in June 1944.

Some 16,000 workers labored at the factory during the war. Coming to grips with its past nearly 50 years later, Volkswagen acknowledged that up to 80 percent of those workers were slave laborers. VW in 1990 hired German historians to investigate the period, and they confirmed the plant's use of concentration-camp inmates and Soviet prisoners of war, which was not a crime in the Third Reich. In October 1991, the company dedicated a granite memorial at Wolfsburg to the slave laborers. "We owed it to the victims who suffered here," said VW board member Peter Frerk.

Of the wheeled vehicles built at Wolfsburg during the war, just 630 were outwardly standard-looking Beetle sedans, and those were mostly Army staff cars or for use by Nazi officials. The main thrust was to design and assemble variations on the Beetle and Kubelwagen theme, sometimes with amazingly effective results. The Type 82E, for example mated the near-standard body of the Beetle saloon with the high-ground-clearance Kubelwagen chassis. Several hundred were built, mainly for use by the officer class, which did not like to ride in Kubels. After that there was a four-wheel-drive version of the Kubelwagen, known as Type 86. Then the Type 82E was mated with the Type 86 to produce the ultimate in closed Beetles, the four-wheel-drive, high-ground-clearance Type 87. Again, several hundred were produced.

The most-successful oddity to come out of the plant during the war was an amphibious device known as the Type 166 "Schwimmwagen"—the swimming scout car. More than 14,000 were built between 1942 and 1944.

The idea of a small, handy amphibious craft had appealed to the world's military for years, but had never been turned into efficient hardware. The need was obvious: In modern, mobile, warfare, troops often had to get from one side of a river, estuary, or lake to the other, even though all bridges had been destroyed. Using boats meant transporting the craft to the shore by truck, then abandoning them on the far shore. The ideal solution was to drive to the shore, engage a propeller, ferry across, clamber up the far shore, reengage the road-going mode, and drive ahead.

In 1940, the Porsche Bureau was asked to peruse this ideal by developing an amphibious version of the Kubel. The result was the Type 128, which was based on the Type 87's four-wheel-drive chassis. It was not successful, being too large, too heavy, and underpowered. Two improved versions followed, but after a number of unsatisfactory tests, the team started over. Their work resulted in the Type 166. First shown to Hitler in August 1941, it was so much better than the Type 128 that it was immediately committed to production.

The Type 166 performed so well that for a time it was being produced in greater numbers than any other vehicle at Wolfsburg. Particularly happy was the Waffen SS, the combat arm of Hitler's shock troops, which had long sought a go-anywhere scout car. So pleased was the SS with its Schwimmwagens that its boss, Heinrich Himmler, nominated Ferdinand Porsche as an honorary SS officer. Porsche was said to have been embarrassed

Porsche's designers based a variety of vehicles on the Beetle platform, the most notable being the Type 82 scout car. Viewing the crude open bodywork, soldiers quickly dubbed it the bucket car, or Kubelwagen. Some 50,000 were built during the war; most were rear-wheel drive. Though they were no match for the four-wheel-drive Jeep, their light weight and simple, rugged construction served well. One advantage was the air-cooled engine. It wasn't powerful, but ran well in all climates and had no radiator to be shot up.

at the "commission," and he found it difficult to disclaim after the war.

The Type 166's secret was in its construction: It was a boat that could be driven on roads, rather than a car that could float. The purpose-designed hull was smaller than the body of the Kubelwagen, but engineers nonetheless found space for the four-wheel-drive powertrain of the Type 87. It had four seats, but was devoid of creature comforts or sidescreens; a skimpy canvas top was the only weather protection.

After the Army demanded that it have at least 25 horsepower, the Type 166 became the first Wolfsburg product to be fitted with the 1,131-cc flat-four engine as standard. Rounding out its drivetrain was a five-speed gearbox and a four-wheel-drive system that could be disconnected to provide rear drive.

At the tail was a proper marine propeller assembly on a hinged cradle. On dry land, the propeller shaft was not engaged to the transmission. For aquatic use, the cradle was lowered and the propeller powered via a clutch that linked its shaft to the transmission. There was no rudder; steering was by alignment of the exposed front tires.

Technically it wasn't elegant, but it worked, and it was more than a match for its jerry-rigged Jeep counterpart. After the war, the British officer placed in charge of the Wolfsburg complex, Major Ivan Hirst, confirmed the Type 166's operational success. "We all admired the Schwimmwagen greatly," he said. "It was the right approach to the amphibian problem, a real boat hull with Volkswagen front axle outside. The U.S. model was a horror, just a leaky hull around a Jeep chassis."

The Porsche Bureau proposed many other special vehicles during this period, including half-track versions of the Kubelwagen, four-wheel-drive conventional Beetles, diesel engines, and automatic transmissions. None of these passed beyond the prototype or idea stage, however. Meanwhile, Ferdinand Porsche himself was busy with several important war designs. During World War I, while with the Skoda armaments firm, Porsche had drawn up an innovative tractor capable of pulling a mammoth 420mm mortar. Now the German military called upon his expertise again and Porsche designed one of World War II's most effective weapons, the Tiger tank, a 56-ton fighting machine. His plans for an upgraded Tiger II were rejected, but he convinced the military to use its chassis as the basis for the *Jagdpanzer Elefant,* a heavily armored tank destroyer fitted with an 88mm cannon. Ninety Elefants were built in 1943.

Porsche also had a hand in some of Hitler's "secret weapons," including a 20-foot high mobile fort improbably named the *Maus.* Unveiled in 1944, the "mouse" proved immobile on soft ground and only three were built.

In late 1944, the German High Command ordered the Porsches and their crew to evacuate to Czechoslovakia, where they would be safe from bombing. Instead, Ferry Porsche secreted some of the tooling at the family estate at Zell am See, Austria, and moved the personnel to the Austrian village of Gmünd, where work continued.

The village in which the VW complex was located still was not well-enough established to have a formal name; it was unenthusiastically called KdF-Town. By the end of 1943, the plant had already delivered 60,000 vehicles, all stemming from the original Porsche Bureau VW design. Hitler visited the facility in May 1944 and gave it his seal of approval. But the tide had turned. The factory had already been bombed several times, and once the Allies discovered it was constructing not only Kubelwagens and Schwimmwagens, but V1 doodlebugs as well, attacks intensified. During the day, American B17s and Liberators, escorted by Mustang fighters, plastered the vast site. British Bomber Command's Lancasters added their heavy loads of high-explosives at night. By the end of 1944, two-thirds of the factory had been flattened and more than 70 workers had lost their lives.

By the spring of 1945, Allied armored columns were pounding across the northern plains of Germany and were close to meeting Russian forces coming the other way. America's Ninth Army, 102nd Division, reached Fallersleben, near Wolfsburg, on April 10. The VW factory guards fled in panic, and some slave laborers set about destroying what equipment they could. Troops of the advancing 102nd, however, didn't continue into KdF-Town; it wasn't on their field maps. The inhabitants were quite ready to surrender—but not to the Russians fast approaching from the east.

Included among the KdF workforce were a few German-Americans who had been recruited by Porsche during his Detroit visits in the late 1930s. Some of these English-speaking expatriates joined a hastily formed delegation that set out across hostile territory to find the Americans. The little band encountered a forward column of U.S. tanks and convinced its surprised young commander that fellow Yanks were in danger in this place called KdF-Town. The officer pressed on and on April 11, 1945,

(continued)

Wartime variations on the Beetle theme included the mating of a sedan body with the four-wheel-drive Kubelwagen underpinnings to create the all-terrain Type 87 (opposite top). For officers who considered the Kubel uncouth, there was an open four-seat command car (opposite bottom). Faced with a shortage of gasoline, Wolfsburg converted a few sedans to run on charcoal and mounted a wood-burning boiler in place of the fuel tank (above).

As early as 1937, army engineers considered the fighting possibilities of Porsche's people's-car platform. One experiment outfitted a VW30 chassis with machine guns (above). Perhaps the most successful iteration was the Type 166 Schwimmwagen (right and opposite page). Loosely based on the four-wheel-drive Kubel, this "swimming scout car" had a water-tight hull and a fold-down boat propeller that enabled it to navigate streams, rivers, and lakes. Rudder action was provided by turning the front tires. More than 14,000 were built between 1942 and 1945.

four weeks before the end of the War in Europe, the remains of the VW project and its decimated factory fell into American hands.

It stayed under Allied control even after the partition of Germany following the war. If the VW factory had been erected just ten miles east, it would have been in the Russian zone, and its fate might have been much different. After all, BMW's 1930s headquarters at Eisenach was just five miles into the Eastern Bloc side of the Iron Curtain, and within a decade it was making horrid, two-stroke, Wartburgs instead of high-class BMWs.

Still, KdF-Town didn't look like much of a prize. It was a smoldering ruins, and the central concern of its inhabitants was survival. They didn't know where their next meal would come from, whether the water supply was disease-ridden, or how they would be treated by the occupying powers. In the midst of all this, the provisional Town Council found the strength to decide an important issue. It eradicated the now-hated KdF-Town name and on May 25, 1945, the town of Wolfsburg officially came into existence.

Gradually, the Americans were withdrawn from the region, replaced as an occupation force by the British Second Army. A detachment of the Royal Electrical and Mechanical Engineers under the command of Major Ivan Hirst assumed control of the VW plant. Coincidentally, one of the officers to whom Hirst reported, Colonel Mike McEvoy, had driven a KdF-Wagen prototype in 1938.

Hirst was given a free hand make some order of the chaos. Theoretically he had to worry only about the state of the Wolfsburg factory and what could be done with it. But in reality, he and his men also had to look after the thousands of inhabitants, whose spirit was broken and whose prospects were grim. Food and shelter were immediate concerns, then restoring electrical power, and finally, setting up a motor-vehicle repair facility. At the same time, British troops were badly in need of light transport to match the Jeep, and Hirst was asked to see if a few VW products could be assembled at Wolfsburg.

This request was a blessing, for it gave the town a purpose and some hope. The factory, of course, was a blasted hulk. When it rained, everyone and everything got wet. Water pooled on the floor. There was no heat. Wisely, the Brits quashed an initial plan to ship the remaining machinery to the west as war reparations. Much of the tooling was rusty and neglected, spattered with dust, buried in rubble, but equipment that had been dispersed and hidden was painstakingly reassembled.

Hirst found technicians in the town who were desperate to get back to work. Undamaged parts and sections of cars and military vehicles were located and a few Kubelwagens were cobbled together. Even a Beetle that had been assembled during the war was reconditioned, sprayed up in British khaki green, and driven to the headquarters of the British 21st Army Group as a demonstration model.

By the end of 1945, a rudimentary assembly line had been set up. The factory was gradually beginning to look more like a building than an open bomb site, and Hurst's team had begun a long love affair with the Beetle. After demonstrating the Beetle to his own officers, Hirst was delighted to get an order for no fewer than 10,000 of them from British and French occupation forces.

What VWs and how many VWs were built in 1945 is in dispute. Some sources maintain that 1,785 Beetles were produced that year, others say factory records show 2,490 vehicles were assembled. According to these records, most were military-type Kubels and Kubel-chassis sedans, with only 58 Beetles built (all sedans). For a time, Kubelwagen bodies were even being shipped in from the surviving facilities at Ambi-Budd in Soviet-occupied Berlin, suggesting there was some East-West trade before the Iron Curtain was slammed shut. What is not in dispute is the way the VW workforce expanded, from 450 when the American tanks arrived, to 6,033 by the end of 1945, to nearly 8,000 by mid 1946.

Still, there was debate over the long-term future of the enterprise. Hirst was encouraged by the potential of both the plant and its product. But there was opposition within his own ranks. Some of it was based on a disdain for any remnant of the Third Reich. There was skepticism about the car, as well. "The vehicle does not meet the fundamental requirements of a motor-car," concluded the head of one British commission that considered the issue. "As regards performance and design it is quite unattractive to the average motor-car buyer. It is too ugly and too noisy...a type of car like this will remain popular for two or three years, if that. To build the car commercially would be a completely uneconomic enterprise...."

By the end of 1945, however, the British administration had the bit between its teeth. Wolfsburg increased production of Beetles not only for use as British military transports, but for supply to the German Post Office as auxiliary delivery vans and for other official uses. Once the autobahns were repaired, Beetles turned out to be ideal long-dis-

Bombed into rubble, saved from capture by the Russians, then put under Allied occupying forces, the Wolfsburg plant and its workers stumbled into an uncertain postwar existence. Guiding their recovery was British Major Ivan Hirst, seated at the rear to the left in this picture of the English officer's mess. While others scoffed, he discerned the Beetle's design integrity and got the British and French military to order 10,000 of them. Production resumed from spare parts and bartered components. The 1,000th VW came off the line barely 14 months after the end of the fighting and by late 1946, the 10,000th had been built. These cars were identical to the prewar KdF-Wagen sedans.

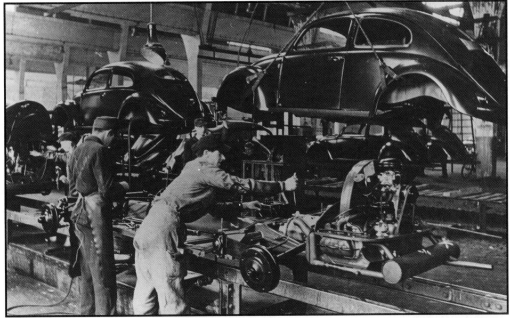

The VOLKSWAGEN built during MARCH 1946 coming from Assembly Line

tance cruisers—which was exactly what Ferdinand Porsche had intended more than a decade earlier.

By 1946, the specifications of the Beetle had stabilized. Although it was not quite the same car that had been finalized by testing in 1938 and 1939, it was demonstrably the same type of car the Porsche Bureau had laid down in 1934.

The rear-engine layout, with a platform chassis incorporating a stiff center tube and torsion-bar independent suspension, was unchanged. Making 25 bhp at 3,300 rpm on a compression of just 5.8:1, the 1,131-cc overhead-valve engine was on a par with European and British entry-level cars of the day, though by American standards, it was puny. The first postwar Fords, for example, had 226-cubic-inch six-cylinder engines of 90 horsepower.

VW's transmission and braking systems were relatively crude. The Beetle's transmission was an all-indirect four-speed assembly joined to the floor-mounted gearshift lever by a long linkage, and there was no synchromesh. Where the suspension—particularly at the front—was complex, carefully detailed, and therefore costly to produce, the braking system was simplicity itself, being cable operated. Cost, of course, had much to do with these oddities. A hydraulic braking system would cost more than the cable system, as would the inclusion of synchromesh in the gearbox. Use of this elementary hardware made the presence of the expensive torsion bar suspension all the more difficult to understand.

All the original civilian Beetles were two-door sedans, with that familiar slope nose, rear widow separated by a center "spine," and long tapering tail. The fuel tank, spare tire, and a small luggage bay were all under the forward bonnet. Once the production engineering bugs were sorted out, the high quality of the body design became clear. Against almost every other car of the day, the panel gaps were smaller, the sealing better, and wind-noise levels lower.

The interior was spartan, but well-assembled. A speedometer offset to the right of the driver was the only real instrument, though it did contain an odometer and was augmented by a selection of warning lights. The only way to keep track of fuel consumption was to maintain a careful log or to run the engine dry, then reach below the dashboard for a lever that tapped a one-gallon reserve supply. The gearshift was between the seats and the clutch, brake, and accelerator pedals sprouted from the floor. Ignition was via a starter knob hung under the instrument panel. The meager heating system was controlled by rotating a knurled knob mounted on the tunnel between the front seats.

On the road, the Beetle's merits and disadvantages were soon clear. It could climb icy gradients that had other cars spinning in vain. It could forge through deep water without leaking into the cabin. And it ran on the most awful grades of fuel.

With only 25 horsepower in a car weighing perhaps 2,000 pounds with a couple of passengers, it was certainly no racehorse. But widely spaced gear ratios gave it useful versatility. First gear was good for climbing hills, while overdrive fourth allowed it to cruise wide-open at 60 mph without fear of blowing the engine. Second and third gears were tall, as well, so the engine was understressed and promised a long life. Taking on long grades or simply keeping up with fast-moving traffic demanded aggressive use of the shifter. The suspension kept the car planted over rough surfaces, though bumps turned the ride bouncy.

Borrowing the new Beetle of a Royal Air Force aviator home on leave, *The Motor* in June 1947 published one of the first tests of a VW driven on English soil. "The 1947 Volkswagen is a modern-looking car, neat in appearance and handy in size," said the magazine. "Lacking some of the refinement which British cars show, the German 'people's car' that was to have been, strikes the driver as a sound job which should give long years of service with the minimum of professional attention. It is sturdily built, mechanically simple, and the main components seem readily accessible. It will carry four people anywhere in adequate comfort, and, given a driver prepared to use the gears in the manner intended, it can complete any journey in a creditably short time."

Note that the magazine's editors referred to the car as the Volkswagen "that was to have been." This was entirely accurate, for in 1947, civilian production of the Beetle was not at all a certainty. VW was in effect on life-support. The only task was to find the parts and supplies to build as many as possible. There was no corporate plan to advance past this stage simply because there *was* no corporation—no board of directors, no shareholders, in fact no financial and industrial infrastructure behind the project. With the Third Reich smashed, ownership of the VW project had gone into limbo. Cars weren't even being offered to the hundreds of thousands of Germans holding KdF savings cards.

The Wolfsburg plant itself held substantial promise. It had its own presses to make body panels, its foundry could be refurbished to produce non-ferrous castings, and the machinery to build air-cooled engines had been repaired. The major

Of 9,962 automobiles built in Germany during 1946, nearly 8,000 were Beetles, though they were not sold to private buyers. Designed to provide the most basic transportation, the exteriors were devoid of brightwork and used mechanical semaphores to signal turns. The early postwar dashboard had no glovebox doors and no shift-pattern outline. The speedometer face was made of bakelite plastic and its needle rotated counterclockwise. Directly below the speedometer is the ignition key receptacle.

stumbling block was a shortage of outside component suppliers. The British Army management team used its own trucks and even some early Beetles to scuttle around devastated Germany searching for coal stores, for fabricators to build carburetors, and for companies to supply glass, paint, and trim materials—in fact, for anything needed to complete Wolfsburg's painful jigsaw puzzle.

In many cases parts were acquired via the barter system, rather than purchased. There was no consideration of bringing in parts from other countries, even if this had been politically possible; the discredited reichs mark was virtually worthless in Germany, let alone in the nations that had helped to bring about its collapse.

Fortunately, there was little threat of a full disintegration of the VW project. Hirst's small team showed that Wolfsburg could still build cars and that given time and investment, it could be restored to its original purpose as a mass-production plant.

Slowly, the enormous obstacles to producing private cars were being overcome. Once Hirst and the highly motivated workforce sorted out a snag, it tended to stay sorted, so as the factory became weatherproof and as the parts-supply shortage eased production increased. The last of the military-type vehicles—the high-ground clearance Beetles with Kubel chassis—were built early in 1946, after which the ever-growing team concentrated on Beetles. Nearly 8,000 VWs of all types left the building during 1946, with a one-month high of 1000 during March. To put this in perspective, only 9,962 cars (plus about 20,000 trucks, buses, and tractors) were built in all of Germany during 1946.

Coal shortages during an extraordinarily severe European winter limited the plant's ability to generate power, so only 8,987 VWs were assembled during 1947. But by the end of the year, 2,500 cars were produced in a single month for the first time. Still, the military market for VWs was finite, and few civilian Germans could afford a new car. Exporting Beetles became the key to survival.

Few countries wanted to do business with Germany, however. The reluctance went beyond political revenge for starting the war; the reichs mark had no value. Then, on June 20, 1948, the German currency was reformed. A new deutsche mark replaced the reichs mark (the exchange rate was DM4 to the dollar). The controlled market was dissolved, a free market instituted, and each German citizen was given DM40. Germany's economic recovery had begun.

Hirst and his Royal Electrical and Mechanical Engineers had worked wonders. They not only provided employment for thousands of Germans, but helped them survive the terrible postwar period. But they were not professional motor-car builders. Heinrich Nordhoff was. Hired by Hirst himself, the former Opel executive took over at Wolfsburg in early 1948, insisting on and being granted authority to make all decisions. The outlook brightened immediately.

One of Nordhoff's first moves was to reestablish formal ties with the Porsche Bureau, which now was under the direction of Ferry Porsche. The younger Porsche, in his autobiography, recounts that he visited Wolfsburg several times before Nordhoff's arrival in an attempt to have VW honor its prewar contract with the design firm. But none of the Brits had the authority to renew the relationship.

"In the summer of 1948, I had a preliminary discussion with Nordhoff, and we very quickly agreed that the relationship between the VW factory and the Porsche company needed clarification," wrote Ferry. "On 16 September 1948 I met Heinz Nordhoff...with the minimum of discussion, we negotiated a new contract between Volkswagen AG and Porsche...we were to act as design consultants to VW. Since Nordhoff was unable to give me any guarantee about the scope of future development contracts, I said: `In that case, I want a license fee for the VW that we designed!' As a result, it was written into the contract that we would receive a license fee of DM5 (about $1.25) for each Beetle produced...." Importantly, Nordhoff also got Porsche to agree not to peruse a small-car development program of its own.

Clearly, the outlook for VW had changed dramatically. The largely repaired factory was poised for long-term growth. Nordhoff would later be criticized for staying too long at Wolfsburg and for relying too much on a one-model policy. But statistics tell their own story. In 1947, VW turned out 8,987 Beetles. In 1948, the same factory produced 19,244. Annual production leapt to 81,979 in 1950 and only four years later the rejuvenated buildings churned out 202,174 cars. If the 1940s had been about destruction, survival, and a crawl back to life for VW, the 1950s would be about expansion and colossal sales.

As for Major Hirst, he was demobilized from the British army and stayed on at Wolfsburg until mid 1949 as an adviser, then moved back to England, never again to be involved in the motor industry.

VW was still a government-run company in late 1947, when it finally put cars on sale to the public. "Yesterday a dream...today a reality," said the initial brochures. Though the early 1,131cc engine had only 25 horsepower and would seldom last more than 30,000 miles without a major overhall, it could push the Bug to 60 mph and keep it there all day. The early Beetles were noisy and had primitive cable-operated brakes, but boasted a sophisticated suspension and decent interior space. Build quality was a major virtue, though a rudimentary tool kit was provided, just in case. As this '47 model demonstrates, jaunty two-tone paint and chromed bumpers were now a commercial necessity.

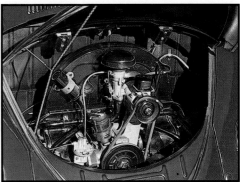

Building a Legend: The Rebirth of the Beetle

After four years of rebuilding Germany's infrastructure and economy, the Allies turned to helping their former enemy set up a civilian-controlled democratic government. On May 23, 1949, American, British, and French authorities established the Federal Republic of Germany. The Fatherland was now divided into Democratic West and Communist East.

Among the first acts of West Germany's new federal government was to transfer ownership of Volkswagenwerk GmbH to the State of Lower Saxony. In September 1949, the VW business, which had been in a military limbo since 1945, became a state-owned business whose directors were democratically elected Saxony officials.

Even before VW was turned over to the state, its new director, Heinz Nordhoff, had mapped out a long-term master plan: He would concentrate on a single basic model and expand by opening export markets. In Europe, Nordhoff shrewdly laid a foundation of VW service centers. Then he touted the car with a sophisticated campaign that included high-quality brochures in several languages and no-nonsense advertisements that outlined the low cost of buying and maintaining a Beetle. Finally, he offered buyers auto insurance through VW dealers. Orders poured in. Exports to European markets climbed to 23 percent of VW's total production. Inside Germany, 64 percent of the new cars purchased were Beetles. By May, 1949, VW had built 50,000 postwar Beetles.

That was the year America got its first two Beetles. They were brought over by a Dutchman, Ben Pon, who had been importing VWs to the Netherlands, and appeared in New York at a German industrial trade show. Attending the show was an American auto dealer named Maximilian Hoffman, whose Park Avenue showroom reflected his taste for imported cars. Hoffman expressed an interest in the VW and Nordhoff reportedly offered to sell him the entire company for $2 million. A surprised Hoffman turned him down, instead accepting sole importation rights for the odd-looking little car. Shipments began in July 1950, but despite Hoffman's enthusiasm for the Beetle and base prices of less than $1600, annual sales languished below 1,000. In late 1953, Hoffman relinquished his import agreement, a move he latter recognized as the mistake of a lifetime.

Undeterred, Nordhoff, who firmly believed that America was VW's most important export market, secured the services of an import-export expert named Arthur Stanton. Stanton expressed optimism about the car's prospects and recommended that VW divide the U.S. into Eastern and Western sales territories. Stanton was the head of the Eastern district out of Long Island, while an established sports-car dealer named John von Neumann ran the Western region. To oversee national operations, Nordhoff chose Will van de Kamp, an associate whose wild enthusiasm for selling VWs was well known around Wolfsburg. In June 1955, Van de Kamp set up Volkswagen United States, which in turn became Volkswagen of America Inc., the company's exclusive national importer headquartered in Englewood Cliffs, N.J.

The earliest Beetles in the U.S. were clearly a breed apart from the behemoth American cars of the day, both in styling and in performance, which was tailored to European driving. *Road & Track* recognized the car's particular strengths in a February 1952 test of a "Deluxe" sedan provided by von Neumann's Competition Motors in North Hollywood, California.

"How would you improve on a car which will cruise effortlessly all day long at top speed? What changes would you suggest in a vehicle which will seat a driver and three passengers in adequate comfort and which will handle 'light as a feather'? Could you ask a 94 inch wheelbase automobile to give any more than 30 to 35 miles per gallon...on regular gasoline? These are questions for which *Road & Track* is hard pressed to find answers."

The magazine clocked a 37.2-second 0-60 mph time for the 1,860-pound sedan, and recorded a top speed of 66 mph on a flat road. But to their surprise, the editors found that accelerating away from a stop, the 25-horsepower Beetle could easily stay abreast of normal traffic. They showed their sports-car mindset in advising drivers to "drift" the car through fast corners to counteract its rear weight bias, and counseled that a stiff ride at low speeds was just compensation for the independent suspension's fine control on bad pavement.

Guided by a conservative manager and girded by products of exceptional value, Volkswagen took on the postwar world. During the 1950s, it would make inroads into the American market and grow into a major automotive force in Europe, all the time relying on the humble Bug as its sole mainline product. The only variation on the Beetle theme was a cabriolet, here represented by a 1950 version of the Karmann-built four-seater.

Overall, they were quite impressed with the $1,740 Bug. "The car was pounded unmercifully through traffic and absolutely floorboarded on the open road. At no time was there any sign of distress.... It is difficult to attach negative criticism to the little German Volkswagen. When you consider what it is supposed to do, and that it does just that admirably, you come away from a Volkswagen weekend well satisfied."

By 1955, the Beetle had taken hold in America. Of 51,000 cars imported to the U.S. that year, 35,851 were Volkswagens. Sales would breach 50,000 in 1957, and threaten 90,000 by 1959. But while VW was the import sales leader, all foreign makes accounted for just five percent of the U.S. market in this period. To most Detroit auto executives, the Beetle wasn't much more than a novelty. Many Americans knew differently.

"There is no longer any doubt about it," said *Road & Track* in its October 1956 Beetle test, "enough figures are in to confirm that Dr. Ferdinand Porsche's little 'people's car' has done what no other vehicle manufactured outside the U.S.A. has ever been able to do: it has gained an unmistakable wheel-hold in the garages and hearts of the American car-buying public.... The only mystery is: how did it happen? Especially with practically no national advertising?

"Of the various explanations, probably the simplest is that the Volkswagen fulfills a need which Detroit had forgotten existed—a need for a car that is cheap to buy and run, small and maneuverable yet solidly constructed, and perhaps above all, utterly dependable and trouble-free."

The '56 Beetle sedan tested by *Road & Track* had a list price of $1,495 and a curb weight of 1,640 pounds. Horsepower had climbed to 36, and 0-60 mph times had dropped to 28 seconds.

Helping boost VW's prospects in the U.S. was arrival of the first variation on the civilian Beetle sedan—a four-seat convertible. There had been a drop-top model in the original KdF-Wagen program, and several test ragtops had appeared in public, notably when Adolf Hitler laid the factory cornerstone in 1938. A two-seat convertible also was hand-built in the late 1940s. But none of these cars made it to production.

Initially, VW's Wolfsburg operation was neither capable of nor interested in building its own open Beetle, and a 1946 proposal from Karmann coach-builders to do the work was turned down by the British. The picture changed after Nordhoff arrived. In 1948, he authorized two factory-approved cabriolets: a two-seater built by the Josef

Hebmuller coachbuilder of Wuelfrath, and a four-seater from Karmann.

The original Hebmullers were hand-converted sedans. First displayed at the Geneva Motor Show in March 1949, they looked remarkably similar to the stillborn two-seater of the late '40s. Hubuellers used the production Beetle's platform chassis, running gear, and inner body panels. They retained the roll-down side windows, but cut off the roof aft of the windshield. To restore overall structural stiffness, hefty longitudinal Z-profile steel pressings were installed on each side of the platform under the floor, the windshield surround was beefed up, and reinforcement was added in and around the tail and engine bay.

Hebmullers looked sportier than Beetle sedans. Their roof was constructed of canvas, coated in rubber for moisture protection, and stuffed with horse hair to provide some sound insulation. Erected, the top's rakish lines gave the car a racy coupe look. Folded down, it fit into the area formerly occupied by the rear seat, leaving the body-line undisturbed. Of course, with the added weight of the structural reinforcements, the Hebmueller was even slower than a VW sedan.

Production had been underway just one month when a July 1949 fire in Hebmuller's factory crippled the conversion work. By 1950, sales had almost dried up, and the company itself collapsed financially in 1952. Only about 750 of these two-seat ragtops were produced between 1948 and 1953. Most were built between June 1949 and March 1950, with the final examples actually completed by Karmann.

While the Hebmueller two-seater was a short-lived commercial failure, the Karmann-produced four-seat ragtop became the most-successful convertible in history. It was launched in July 1949, at the same DM7,500 price as the Hebmueller, and would continue as a modified Beetle until 1980, with a total production of 331,847.

Though it too was basically a VW with the top chopped off, Karmann's convertible was much more closely related to the Beetle sedan than had been the Hubmueller car. It used the sedan's four-seat cabin layout and offered the same standard equipment. More panels were retained around the tail and engine bay, though Karmann welded sturdy longitudinal girders under the body sills and also beefed up the inner structure to restore stiffness sacrificed in the loss of the steel roof.

That these cars weighed as much as 200 pounds

(continued)

Legendary New York auto dealer Max Hoffman (above) *was the first Volkswagen retailer in the U.S.; he unwisely abandoned his involvement in 1953.* Opposite, top right: *The very first VW brought to America is unloaded in New York in January 1949. The gesturing fellow is Ben Pon, the Dutch importer who pioneered VW's U.S. arrival. With its quaint split rear window, the tiny Beetle sedan was an odd sight among the bulbous domestics then dominating American roads. The 1,800-pound 1950 model* (color photos) *listed for $1,480, had 25 horsepower, and took nearly 40 seconds to reach 60 mph. Just 328 were sold. Note the lack of sound-deadening material in the engine compartment. In 1955, Volkswagen established its national headquarters, renting the first floor of a two-story brick building in Englewood Cliffs, New Jersey* (opposite, top left).

Heinz Nordhoff

Heinrich "Heinz" Nordhoff ruled Volkswagen for two decades, but it was his rock-solid stewardship in the 1950s that ensured the company's future. He refused to change, disfigure, or drop the Beetle, faithful to the little car as a father to his only child.

Nordhoff was born near Hanover, Germany in 1899. His father was a banker and his family moved to Berlin in 1911 when the business failed. Nordhoff fought in World War I and was wounded. After the war, he studied mechanical engineering in Berlin, then was hired by BMW to work on airplane engines.

He explored joining Nash in the U.S., but the Wall Street crash of 1929 redirected him to Opel, where he wrote service manuals, and then worked in customer service. By the late 1930s, he was a member of the Opel board of directors, and in 1940, was appointed to run the Opel truck plant at Brandenburg.

Nordhoff was too old to fight in World War II, but he didn't escape its misery. The Opel plant was seized by the Nazi party for war work, then bombed persistently by the Allies. By 1945, Nordhoff and his family were living in a cellar and he had contracted pneumonia.

After the war, the family survived precariously as Nordhoff scraped by on a series of menial jobs. The British who had been operating the VW plant were looking for a German engineer to pilot the Wolfsburg facility. Their search led them to Nordhoff and at the end of 1947, he was invited to run the business. Nordhoff actually had wanted to return to Opel, but agreed to the VW challenge. He was almost 49 years old.

Moving to Wolfsburg meant living apart from his family, and for the first six months, VW's new chief slept on a cot in the near-derelict factory.

"When I came to Wolfsburg, I was as poor as a churchmouse," he later wrote. "I was hungry too, and about 60 pounds underweight. All the people I met in the factory were not only as poor and hungry as myself, they were desperate and without hope...."

But Nordhoff's demand for a free hand to make what changes were needed had been granted. He was a confident fellow and did not hide it.

Gunter Hellman, a Canadian VW executive, remembered the change Nordhoff inspired. "Everybody was in a rut before Nordhoff came. We had no food and no materials to speak of and no one had any real idea of where we were heading. When Nordhoff came and took charge, he just quietly got everyone moving."

Nordhoff's self-assured bearing, along with the 1948 launch of the new deutsche mark, was the springboard VW needed. His status grew along with sales of the cars, and he basked in his reputation as the savior of VW. His authoritarian ways were tolerated, welcomed even, because the company was a success.

Still, by the early 1960s, his one-model strategy was being criticized. What the public didn't realize was that starting in the 1950s, Nordhoff had commissioned Porsche to examine a Beetle replacement. Time and again prototypes were delivered from Stuttgart to Wolfsburg, tested, rejected by Nordhoff, and stored away in secret. In 1967, irritated by complaints about VW's stubborn faith in an old car, Nordhoff sprung upon an unsuspecting world no fewer than 36 prototypes, most of them Porsche's handiwork. The variety spanned four-wheel-drive models with two-cylinder engines, to a rear-engine car with a 2.0-liter six-cylinder.

But by then Nordhoff was 68, and ready to retire. His health had not been good for some time—he had undergone surgery for stomach ulcers as early as 1958—and by the mid 1960s, he had begun to size up other executives as potential successors. But until he was sure that someone of his stature could take over, he would struggle on.

During 1967, he announced his choice: Kurt Lotz, deputy chairman of VW's managing board. Lotz would work alongside the patriarch until the two were in harmony. Nordhoff's plan was to allow Lotz to run the business while he stayed on as elder statesman, adviser, and general top-level sounding-board for the younger man's agenda.

It was a good idea, but one that never came to fruition. Within weeks of Lotz's ascension, Nordhoff was felled by a sudden heart attack. He died on April 12, 1968, at age 69.

October 5, 1950: Nordhoff (near left in white tie) *celebrating the 100,000th postwar VW.*

The first postwar effort at a Beetle cabriolet was the one-off "Radclyffe convertible," (above) which was cobbled together in 1946 for Colonel C.R. Radclyffe, an officer of the British contingent occupying Wolfsburg. In 1948, VW chief Nordhoff authorized the first production cabriolet, the charming two-seater designed by the Hebmuller coachbuilder (top). It was assembled at the Hebmuller works (right) until a fire crippled the operation. Only about 750 were built through 1953.

more than the equivalent sedan did nothing for acceleration, but no one seemed to mind. Neither did the bulky hump of the folded soft top cause much of a fuss; in fact, it became something of a trademark. Karmann made its folding top of the same material as Hebmueller, but presence of the standard rear seat meant the top could not be hidden away when folded. It stowed instead in a big pouch above the engine bay, where it obscured the driver's rear visibility. On early models, the folded roof also blocked the engine-bay louvers, which made it necessary to relocate the vents from below the rear window to the engine cover itself.

The convertible quickly became an integral part of the Beetle range, and over the next 30 years, every change to the Beetle's powertrain, chassis, cabin, or trim was made to the Karmann cars. As popular as they were, however, convertibles were never more than a fraction of Beetle sales.

As demand for its cars increased, the Wolfsburg factory was enlarged, expanding along the Mittelland canal. By 1950, when it turned out 81,979 Beetles, the complex consisted of four assembly-line halls each about one mile long, other large buildings and offices, a railway siding, a test ground, even a power station. The town of Wolfsburg grew in proportion. Tens of thousands of Germans and an increasing number of immigrants—"guest-workers" as they were called—moved there to work. Most walked or bicycled to their VW jobs from their VW-owned houses. That the threatening Eastern Bloc boarder was almost within sight of the plant never seemed a worry.

While the 1950 introduction of the Transporter (see Chapter 6) was the boldest outward sign of change in the VW line, the Beetle had all along undergone detail revisions under the skin. VW's method of fine-tuning mechanical and chassis components while leaving the body appearance virtually untouched would become central to its corporate identity and a key to the car's cult-like popularity. While shoppers focussed on a new badge or trim piece as the only visual change, for example, VW engineers were relentlessly laboring to improve body sealing so the car eventually was so air tight that it was difficult to slam a door unless one of the windows had first been cracked open.

Under Nordhoff, so many engineering changes in so many areas of the car were progressively introduced that it was sometimes impossible to differentiate model years. This is especially true when comparing German-market cars to Export models, which often received changes at different

times. Here is a sampling of important modifications made during Nordhoff's first decade:

• 1949: The Export model was officially launched in July, with a wider range of colors, more trim, better sound-deadening, and more-complete equipment. The dashboard featured white panels in a KdF-Wagen style instrument panel and only two prominent gauges, a speedometer and a clock. Double-acting telescopic front suspension dampers were fitted from August of this year.

• 1950: In April, Export models got hydraulic brakes in place of cable brakes, and a canvass sunroof became an option. (Cable brakes were retained for German-market models until 1954.)

• 1952: In October, a new gearbox was introduced with synchromesh on second, third, and fourth gears. Wheel diameter was reduced to 15 inches from 16 inches, but rim width was increased to four inches from a puny three. Tire width also increased, from 5.25 inches to 5.6. The dashboard was redesigned and the speedometer was relocated to a position within the driver's line of sight.

• 1953: In March, the original split rear window was replaced by a single-pane oval piece of glass. VW said this increased rear visibility by 23 percent. It was a monumental change in the unchanging world of Beetle styling, and many owners modified their older cars with the new single-pane window. Split-window Beetles came to have greater collector appeal, however.

• 1954: In January, the engine was enlarged from 1,131cc to 1,192cc (69 cubic inches to 73). This was accomplished by a simple increase in cylinder bore, from 75mm to 77mm. Larger valves, redesigned cylinder heads, and a higher compression ratio accompanied the increase in bore. Such a change might sound trivial today. But in VW terms, this was another earth-shaking event. Since 1945, Wolfsburg engineers had continuously improved engine reliably and assembly quality. But this alteration gave the car more muscle. Peak power increased from 30 horsepower at 3,400 rpm to 36 at 3,700 rpm—a 20 percent boost.

These advances, and other improvements to come, were made possible by the foresight of engineers who in the 1930s deliberately designed the little four-cylinder boxer to be understressed, under-powered, and with smaller-than-necessary breathing passages. This is one reason the engines lasted so long, and why the design was so successful for so many years. The motor's potential was

(continued)

This 1951 Beetle sedan is a Deluxe model, as evidenced by the bright running-board trim and white instead of black control knobs. Front-fender ventilation flaps were added to Deluxe models in January 1951 and were gone by October 1952, when all Bugs got vent wing windows. The Wolfsburg crest was new on all Beetles for '51. A fuel-level gauge was still an option, however, so the cars came with a floorboard lever that tapped a one-gallon reserve tank when gas ran low. This sedan has the available extension arm (opposite, middle right) marked "A" for Auf (on), "Z" for Zu (off), and "R" for Reserve. Mechanical semaphore turn signals (above) were used until 1955 on U.S. models and until 1960 on European VWs.

Denied annual styling changes, VW's early brochures highlighted technical features. This 1954 example displayed the three body styles (right). A drawing illustrating the central-backbone platform chassis detailed the independent front suspension, in which two eight-leaf torsion bars enclosed in tubes acted via trailing arms on the front wheels. Art from 1955 on the opposite page revealed the inner workings of the boxer engine, which was enlarged to 1,192cc and boosted to 36 horsepower for '54. A phantom drawing of the sedan explored its "swinging half axles" and independent rear suspension. Note the oval rear window, a momentous new feature for '53. A revamp of the dashboard in 1952 moved the speedometer in front of the driver and introduced a steering-column turn-signal lever.

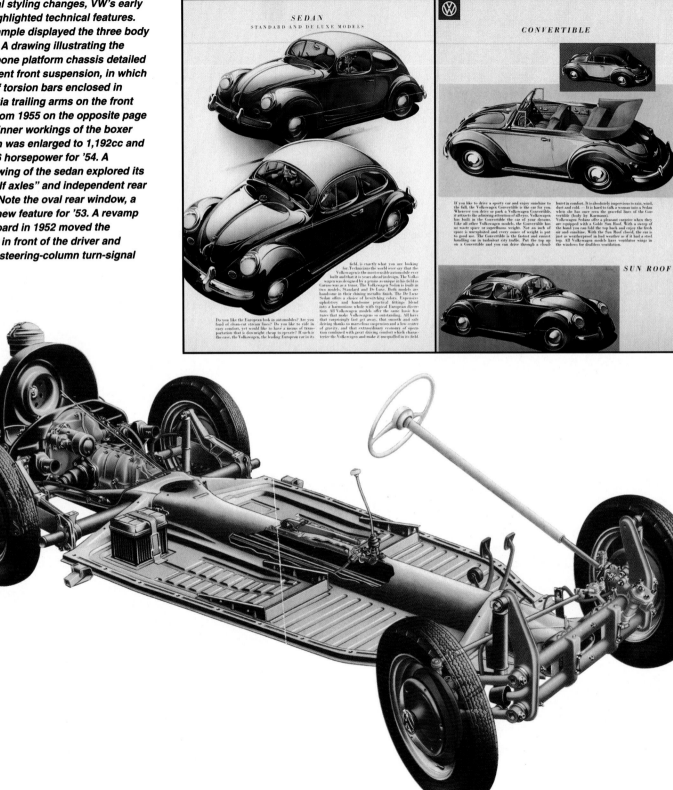

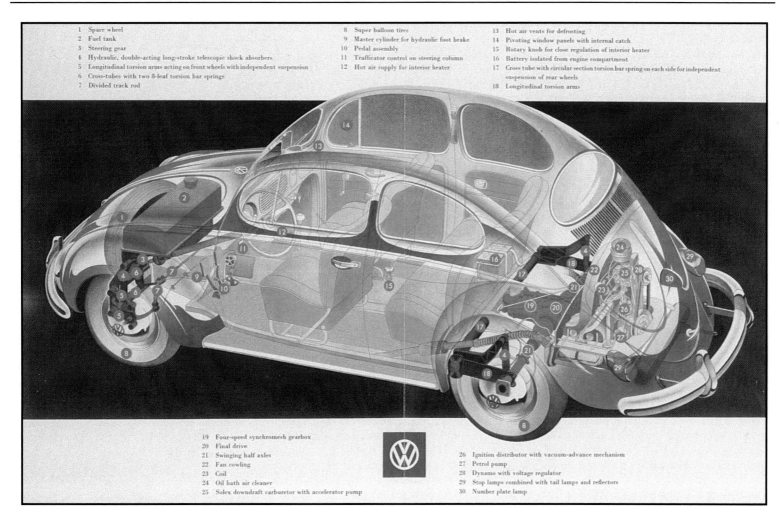

1　Spare wheel
2　Fuel tank
3　Steering gear
4　Hydraulic, double-acting long-stroke telescopic shock absorbers
5　Longitudinal torsion arms acting on front wheels with independent suspension
6　Cross-tubes with two 8-leaf torsion bar springs
7　Divided track rod

8　Super balloon tires
9　Master cylinder for hydraulic foot brake
10　Pedal assembly
11　Trafficator control on steering column
12　Hot air supply for interior heater

13　Hot air vents for defrosting
14　Pivoting window panels with internal catch
15　Rotary knob for close regulation of interior heater
16　Battery isolated from engine compartment
17　Cross tube with circular section torsion bar spring on each side for independent suspension of rear wheels
18　Longitudinal torsion arms

19　Four-speed synchromesh gearbox
20　Final drive
21　Swinging half axles
22　Fan cowling
23　Coil
24　Oil bath air cleaner
25　Solex downdraft carburetor with accelerator pump

26　Ignition distributor with vacuum-advance mechanism
27　Petrol pump
28　Dynamo with voltage regulator
29　Stop lamps combined with tail lamps and reflectors
30　Number plate lamp

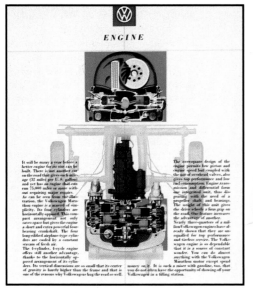

ENGINE

It will be many a year before a better engine for its size can be built. There is not another car on the road that gives such mileage (32 miles per U. S. gallon) and yet has an engine that can run 75,000 miles or more without requiring major repairs. As can be seen from the illustration, the Volkswagen Marathon engine is a marvel of simplicity. Its four cylinders are horizontally opposed. This compact arrangement not only saves space but gives the engine a short and extra powerful four-bearing crankshaft. The four long-ribbed airplane-type cylinders are cooled by a constant stream of fresh air.
The 4-cylinder, 4-cycle engine offers still another advantage. Its vertical dimensions are so small that its center of gravity is hardly higher than the frame and that is one of the reasons why Volkswagens hug the road so well.

The aerodynamic design of the engine permits low piston and engine speed but coupled with the use of overhead valves, also gives top performance and low fuel consumption. Engine transmission and differential form one integrated unit, thus dispensing with the need of a propeller shaft and bearings. The weight of this unit gives the drive wheels a firm grip on the road. One feature increases the advantage of another.
Nearly three-quarters of a million Volkswagen engines have already shown that they are unequalled for top performance and tireless service. The Volkswagen engine is so dependable that it is a source of constant wonder. You can do almost anything with the Volkswagen Marathon motor except speed money on it. It is such a miser with gasoline, too, that you do not often have the opportunity of showing off your Volkswagen in a filling station.

recognized even before VW made its 1954 change. Private engine tuners had already begun to increase displacement. As early as 1951, Porsche had developed a 1,286-cc version with an 80mm bore for its 356 sports cars. A year later, Porsche added a 1,488-cc version, complete with longer stroke (see Chapter 8).

• 1955: Fender-mounted lamps replaced the semaphore turn signal arms, and the fuel tank was reshaped to increase cargo capacity.

• 1957: VW made the biggest alteration to body appearance so far by fitting a much larger, rectangular-section rear window. It made headlines around the world. This signaled the start-up of the 1958 model year for North American Beetles.

By now, there had been several thousand modifications to the original KdF-Wagen design and very few parts remained from the original Porsche bureau days. These advances were accompanied by enormous sales gains. Total postwar production reached 100,000 Beetles in March 1950, and had climbed to 250,000 by October 1951. By July 1953, 500,000 had been built and by 1957, the total was more than 1.5 million. And in many ways the car was just hitting its stride.

A main part of its appeal, of course, was that the VW's character didn't change, but developed, and seemed to connect with more and more people. The look and feel of the car were unique. Even its sound, with the engine thrumming away in the tail, was a noise no rival could—or wanted to—imitate.

One more problematic constant was the car's handling. Owners soon found that Beetles had phenomenal traction in slippery conditions, but the chassis could also bite back if they went around a corner too fast. A typical American sedan reaching the limit of tire adhesion in a turn would begin to plow, nose first, toward the outside of the curve. This was called understeer, and a even novice driver could easily regain control by easing back on the throttle. A Beetle might actually sustain traction to a slightly higher cornering speed. But when its limit of adhesions was exceeded, it didn't understeer—it oversteered. The rear-end weight bias would quickly snap the tail toward the outside of the turn and the car could fly off the road backwards. VW tinkered continuously with front and rear torsion-bar settings, and though it never went away, oversteer was less of a problem as the Bug design matured.

Another constant was the Beetle's instability in crosswinds. A sudden gust could blow the car into the next lane, and at freeway speeds on windy days, drivers had to continuously correct the steering to maintain a heading. The problem was in the basic design. Here's how the editors of *Car Life* magazine explained it: "With 57.6 percent of its weight on its rear wheels, the VW has a center of gravity rather far behind its center of wind pressure—something similar to placing the arrowhead behind the feathers. Thus side winds try to spin the front of the car around the rear wheels. Front-end-heavy cars (usually any car with its engine mounted forward) demonstrate the opposite condition: Because the center of gravity is ahead of the center of pressure (arrowhead in front of the feathers), wind gusts try to pivot the car on its front wheels. This latter condition is dynamically more stable and requires less driver attention."

Poor directional stability in windy conditions, like oversteer, and for that matter, weak acceleration, engine noise, and assorted other compromises, was something Beetle buyers obviously were willing to live with, for sales continued to climb.

In fact, increasing demand threatened to overwhelm Wolfsburg, which in the early 1950s was the sole VW assembly facility (a satellite factory in Brunswick concentrated on component production and toolmaking). The rebuilt plant was already unmatched in Europe as a self-contained auto-building complex, but it was clear that it could not cope with Nordhoff's long-term ambition.

"We stand at the beginning of development without peer," he declared in August 1955, celebrating production of the one-millionth Beetle. With the concurrent birth of VW of America, Nordhoff and his Saxony bosses agreed a second assembly plant was needed.

They settled on a site in Hanover, about 50 miles west of Wolfsburg. Transporter assembly was transferred from Wolfsburg to the new complex in 1956, followed shortly by the relocation of engine manufacture. Even with this expansion, Wolfsburg was still extremely busy. In 1957, it churned out 380,561 Beetles, sometimes well over 1,500 per day. By 1958, VW had opened a third assembly plant, this one in Kassel. It was 150 miles from Wolfsburg, but close to a new autobahn than ran to Hanover. Kassel also was ideal for German political purposes. VW redeveloped a complex that still was mostly a pile of war-damaged rubble, while at the same time tapping into the region's ready pool of labor. Kassel's initial task was to recondition mechanical components, and it was soon rebuilding 150,000 engines and transaxles annually. Manufacture of new transmissions was moved out of Wolfsburg to this factory, as well.

Karmann coachworks began building cabriolets based on the Beetle sedan in 1949. Unlike the two-seat Hebmullers, which stowed their folded top neatly into the space formerly occupied by the rear seat, Karmanns were four-seat ragtops, so their folded roof hung over the tail. Note that the air vents were in the engine cover rather than below the rear window, as on the sedans. This 1957 model retailed for $1,995, $500 more than the sedan. VW had replaced the semaphores with fender-mounted "bullet" turn signals for 1955. For '56, all Beetles got bumper overriders, chromed dual tail pipes in place of a single pipe, and a curved gear shift lever. Americans happily bought 47,446 Beetle sedans and 2,613 cabriolets during 1957.

By the end of the 1950s, therefore, Wolfsburg was by no means the integrated car-building plant that had originally been conceived, but merely a vast complex where Beetles were being screwed together. By the early 1960s, with engines coming in from Hanover, transmissions from Kassel, and other components from Brunswick, there was a constant and fascinating two-way flow of trucks and trains in the area.

As if the expansion of its markets, production facilities, and model line weren't enough, Volkswagen had another diversion during this period: one of the longest-running legal disputes of all time. It had its roots in the infamous KdF savings scheme launched way back in 1938.

A group of savings-stamp holders had in 1948 formed the Self-Help Association of One-Time Volkswagen Savers. Its members were participants in the original scheme who had bought their savings stamps, filled out their cards, and now wanted to exchange those cards for a new Beetle. There was, of course, one major snag. They had saved reischs marks, which were now long gone, and they wanted to buy a late-1940s Beetle at the price quoted in 1938, postulating that one reichs mark was worth one new deutsche mark. It wasn't.

Many of the original savers had died—some were killed in the war—but by 1949, the association had attracted 1,000 members, a figure that rose to 3,000 by 1951. Lawsuits were filed demanding delivery of cars, plus the original two years of insurance that had been promised. The claimants soon dropped their demand for Beetles at the original KdF price, but later asked for cars to be delivered at DM2,475, which was less than $500, and clearly a ludicrously low figure.

From the start, Nordhoff's Volkswagenwerk AG maintained it had no connection with the original KdF enterprise, which had gone up in flames along with Hitler's regime. VW pointed out that it never received any of the proceeds of the KdF savings scheme, and was not therefore accountable.

True enough, but not at all satisfactory to the claimants. In January 1950, a Saxony court ruled against the saver's association on grounds that a contract no longer existed, but an appeals court did suggest there might still be a contract with VW. The association sensed hope, and its legal machine ground relentlessly on. The German supreme court ruled that VW was still involved, and that the company should pay the costs of legal action so far. Nordhoff gritted his teeth and complied. In 1954, a subsequent ruling absolved VW of involvement in the original savings plan. Undeterred, the associa-

tion filed another suit. When it was rejected in 1955, VW sought to settle the matter once and for all by offering all savers DM250 in cash, or a credit of DM500 toward the purchase of a new Beetle. An Export-specification Beetle cost about DM5,000 at the time, so the offer was attractive.

But the savers association rejected it, choosing instead year after year of mind-numbing legal quibbling. Finally, in October 1961, the courts established a sliding scale of rebates depending on how full the savings cards actually were. Association members would get a maximum of DM600 off the price of a new car. It took VW until 1970 to sort out every one of the 120,573 prewar savings-card "contracts." With legal costs, the savings-card scheme ended up costing the company around $12 million.

That, though, was just about the only bad news VW had during the 1950s. Counting only Beetles built in Germany, annual production had climbed from 81,979 in 1950 to 279,986 in 1955 to 725,927 in 1960. By the end of the decade, Beetles were being shipped in CKD (Completely Knocked Down) form to several other countries for assembly at factory-authorized plants. Volkswagen do Brazil had progressed even further. Setting itself up with a genuine manufacturing facility, it built its first Beetles in 1959 and expanded output steadily over the next 15 years.

The VW enterprise, and Wolsburg in particular, was unrecognizably different from the battered, grubby, patched-up business that had ended the 1940s. The mushrooming town finally got a city hall in 1958. The Beetle was Europe's fastest-selling car ever, and demand was increasing, particularly in the U.S., where annual sales topped 100,000 for the first time in 1960. Three thousand cars were being built every day, and Beetle number three million was produced in 1960.

Nordhoff and his democratically elected bosses now began to face the decade ahead. For a start it seemed as if Nordhoff, and particularly his engineers, had been listening to critics of the Beetle's handling. The sedan gained an anti-sway bar for the 1960 model year, and the engine position was altered a tad to allow the swing axle pivots to be lowered. New colors joined the catalogue, the heater was improved, an automatic choke was fitted, and a steering damper was added up front.

In the 1960s, VW would hit the acquisition trail, build a new factory specifically to assemble Beetles for North America, go through major financial changes, and add new models. It was going to be a busy decade.

In its biggest appearance change yet, the Beetle got a larger, rectangular rear window for 1958. The windshield was enlarged slightly, as well. Also in evidence on this coral red '58 are other alterations made that year, including turn signals mounted on top of the fenders and a redesigned dashboard that put the radio speaker behind a grille to the left of the steering column. This was the first Beetle with a flat gas pedal; previously, it had used a roller accelerator. As early as 1952, sedans had rear quarter windows that hinged open. With U.S. sales of the Beetle reaching 55,482 in 1958 and 88,857 in '59, VW was poised to begin a string of 15 years in which it would sell more than 100,000 Bugs annually. America was smitten.

New Models, New Problems

Although its growing legion of buyers loved the Beetle precisely because it was a model of design stability, there was pressure to make sweeping changes in VW's mainstay product.

Traditional automobiles rewarded customers, dealers, and marketing people each autumn with a festival of fresh features. VW might grudgingly alter a badge, modify a seat style, or maybe enlarge a rear window. Swayed by an ingenious advertising campaign that portrayed this inertia as a virtue, Americans considered it part of the cute little Bug's charm.

But in Germany, influential observers of the auto industry openly questioned Volkswagen's commitment to future products. Dire predictions of the company's demise were published. Wholly dependent on an archaic vehicle, warned the naysayers, the company would wither while competitors raced ahead with modern designs.

Heinz Nordhoff deflected the charges with little response, infuriating his critics. His concern of the moment was to see Volkswagen turned from a state-owned business into a conventional enterprise with shareholders, profits, and dividends. Indeed, the German federal government and the State of Lower Saxony had argued for years over VW's destiny. In the early 1950s, they would have been content to practically give the business to another car maker. But by the end of the decade, there was no way this would have been acceptable.

Finally, in June 1960, the German Federal Parliament privatized the company. Volkswagenwerk GmbH was created as a joint stock corporation and 3.6 million shares were issued on January 1, 1961. Sixty percent of the stock was sold to private shareholders, 20 percent was retained by the State of Lower Saxony, and 20 percent was held by the federal government and its agencies. The private shares were snapped up and the stock quickly began a steep climb in value. On January 7, 1961, 7,000 stockholders jammed Wolfsburg for the first annual meeting of Volkswagenwerk AG.

But the faultfinding continued, both in the press and to Nordhoff's face at company meetings. The VW chief would smile patiently, point out the company's financial performance, and remind all of ever-escalating production. What was wrong, he challenged, with a company that could do this?

Undeterred, critics began to talk about the "Model T phenomenon," after the Ford debacle of 1927. It referred to a company whose prosperity was tied to one model, and which appeared to have nothing in the pipeline.

However, VW's situation was different from Henry Ford's. When sales dried up for the aged Model T, Ford crippled his dealers and dealt a blow to the nation's economy by closing down his factories to tool up for the Model A. But there was no sign that Beetle demand was softening—it was in fact on the rise. Second, dictatorial Henry Ford had allowed virtually no development work to go on behind closed doors, complicating the transition to the new model. At VW, there was always something happening in private, even if Nordhoff never boasted about it.

Since the end of the 1940s, the Porsche Bureau had been designing and building prototype after prototype—some smaller than the Beetle, some larger, some similar, some radically different. The ultra-conservative Nordhoff had turned them all down—but not without carefully recording their advantages and faults.

By the late 1950s, the pressure was getting to the Volkswagen chief. Nordhoff was not looking to replace the Beetle, but he was finally ready to supplement it with another mainstream model. His main export market, North America, was happy to buy huge numbers of Beetles, but elsewhere there was a clear demand for a larger and more powerful car from Volkswagen.

In March 1958, the Porsche Bureau was commissioned to build two new body shells. Both were based on the existing Beetle platform, with the bulkhead and pedals moved forward 3.1 inches to help provide a larger cabin. Both were fitted with Porsche's latest "underfloor" 40-horsepower four-cylinder engine. This was a development of the Beetle unit, but different in detail and much more space-efficient, capable of being mounted "under" the rear floor section rather than in a vertical cavity behind the passenger compartment as on the Beetle. One of the Porsche development cars was the Type 726/1, a fastback, the other was the

Volkswagen's crop of Beetle alternatives was far less successful than the original. As variations of the basic Bug, they were rooted in a design that dated to the 1930s. It was an insurmountable handicap against modern rivals that were more space-efficient and had better performance. Nonetheless, VW engineers made the best of it, producing cars such as this 1970 Fastback, the sportiest exploration of the Beetle theme.

726/2, a notchback.

What the Porsche people didn't learn until later was that their prototypes were part of a design competition. Ghia and VW's own development department had also been invited to create design studies. Nordhoff viewed these offerings in a line-up, but couldn't make up his mind which he preferred. He asked all three contenders to go back, cooperate, and produce a definitive proposal. The job got done, but not without great deal of pride swallowed on all sides. Years later, Ferry Porsche was still uneasy about the process and its outcome. "The compromise proposal requested by Nordhoff turned our very advanced design into a car like any other," he wrote.

The compromise style was a squared-up two-door sedan that had lost all traces of Beetle ancestry. It was a "three-box" design. There were no sloping headlamp housings, no separate fender bulges, no vestigial running boards. One of the main differences from the Porsche proposal was a higher waistline, which made it possible, among other things, to locate the headlamps in a position that would satisfy American headlight-height regulations. Most remarkably, except for louvers in the deck behind the rear window, there was no indication that this was a rear-engine car—until the air-cooled power unit under the tail gave away its location with that familiar rattle.

VW called its first new car in 27 years the Type 3, and to prepare its customers and dealers, Nordhoff made sure it was previewed extensively before it went on sale. Introduction was set for September 1, 1961, but VW leaked the first pictures of the new car in early 1961, and released the initial technical analysis before mid-summer.

When the Type 3 made its official bow, a number of critics had already rushed to complain that it was no more than a Beetle chassis with a larger engine and a more-modern body style. True, the general layout and chassis principles were the same, but almost every detail was different.

As before, there was a floorpan that doubled as the chassis platform to which the body shell was bolted. The engine/gearbox/transaxle installation was familiar, as was the torsion-bar, radius-arm-and-swing-axle rear suspension. At the front, the Type 3 had a new version of the trailing-arm and torsion-bar setup in which round torsion bars replaced the laminated bars of the Beetle, and there was an anti-roll bar connecting the top links.

The Type 3, which was more familiarly known as the VW 1500, shared the Beetle's 94.5-inch wheelbase, but its body was 166.3 inches long overall, about six inches longer than the Bug's. It was slightly wider, too, with an advantage in track of 0.2 inches in front and 2.3 inches in the rear. At about 1,950 pounds at the curb, the 1500 was around 300 pounds heavier than the Beetle.

The new car's interior was roomier overall, with four inches more hip room in front and two inches more in back. Front leg room was about the same, but the identical wheelbase meant both cars shared only adequate rear leg room, and the 1500's lower roof gave it about one inch less head room than the Beetle. The cabin was more modern and less austere, however, with a padded dashboard, front-door armrests, a pull-down rear center armrest, and front seatbacks that adjusted through seven positions of back rake compared to the Beetle's three positions. The heating and ventilation system was more effective. And larger windows gave the 1500 driver greater outward visibility.

Unlike the Beetle, the 1500 sedan had no storage area behind its rear seat, and its rear seatback. didn't fold to increase luggage capacity. But with a trunk at either end, the 1500 had more overall cargo room (the front compartment held 6.3 cubic feet, the rear 7 cubic feet).

Presence of the rear compartment was made possible by the new "underfloor" engine. In time-honored VW tradition, it was a four-cylinder boxer with overhead valves. But by relocating the cooling fan from above the transaxle area to the nose of the crankshaft (which was actually at the extreme rear of the car itself), VW lowered the height of the new powerplant by a full 16 inches. The 1500's engine was located below an insulated cover that made up the floor of the rear trunk, isolating it much better than the engine in the Beetle. A portal allowed engine oil to be checked and added without lifting the insulated cover.

The Beetle's formal name at this point was the Volkswagen 1200, befitting an engine displacement of 1.2 liters (1,192cc, 72.7 cubic inches). Enlarging the bore and stroke for the new model boosted displacement to 1.5 liters (1,493cc, 91.1 cubic inches) and begot the 1500 name. The Beetle's 1.2-liter increased from 36 horsepower to 40 for '61, while the 1500 debuted with 45 horsepower. VW introduced its first all-synchromesh four-speed gearbox for '61, and both the Beetle and the Type 3 got it that year.

Would the new car sell? Nordhoff and his acolytes—who now seemed cocky about every VW's merits—were certain it would. Many

(continued)

Unknown to the public, VW had been studying alternatives to the Beetle throughout the 1950s. Finally forced by market demand to seriously consider a companion model, it commissioned Porsche in 1958 to build two concept prototypes (opposite page): the Type 726/1 fastback and Type 726/2 notchback. Both were rear-engine cars and, to Porsche, very advanced designs. But Wolfsburg ordered Porsche to cooperate with VW's own designers and with Ghia to combine elements of the 726 prototypes into a new production sedan. The result pleased hardly anyone.

VW's first new car in 27 years debuted in 1961 as the Type 3. It was launched as a notchback sedan on the Beetle's 94.5-inch wheelbase, but its body was longer and wider, and offered more luggage space. The Type 3 shared the Bug's air-cooled flat-four powerplant, but mounted the cooling fan differently. This allowed for a shallow rear trunk over the engine. The front cargo bay still held the spare tire. The Type 3's interior was more modern than the Beetle's, and it offered more width, though no more leg room. A convertible prototype was built, but didn't meet VW's structural stiffness standards and never went into production.

observers were not so sure. After all this time, surely VW could have been more adventurous. Had it really ignored all the criticism of noisy air-cooled engines, rearward weight bias, and mundane styling?

As it turned out, the doubters' arguments had merit, particularly where the European market was concerned. The 1500 debuted at a price about one-fifth higher than the Beetle's, but advanced orders were relatively healthy; VW sold about 10,000 Type 3s through 1962. A two-door station-wagon model called the Variant had been added to the 1500 range in September 1961, and would eventually account for nearly 40 percent of Type 3 production.

But sales never reached the pace VW had hoped. Nearly half the 1500s built during the first year required unscheduled service. This wasn't unusual for a completely new model, but it was outrageous to VW customers, who had come to expect outstanding reliability. The maintenance problems seemed to open the door for complaints that this essentially rebodied Beetle was not as good a value as more-modern competitors in the same price class. Neither was performance that much better than the Beetle's, given the price differential. The 1500 could approach 80 mph, to the Bug's usual 60-65 mph, and while it was maybe six seconds quicker 0-60 mph, the 1500's 26-second clocking was still slower than most small-car rivals.

The 1500 had less engine noise and less wind noise than the Beetle, and its wider track made it more stable in changes of direction, though the new car still would oversteer in a fast corner. Ride quality was about the same, but the 1500's added weight hurt fuel economy slightly.

None of these flaws seemed to matter much to the North American market, which greeted the 1500 eagerly. Exports were initially confined to Canada. In the United States, Beetle sales were still so strong—288,583 sedans and 7,848 convertibles in 1965—that VW waited until 1966 to bring in the Type 3. In the meantime, a thriving gray market had developed, with more than 12,000 Canadian Type 3s finding their way into the States.

Motor Trend compared one of these gray-market 1500s to a U.S. Beetle 1200 in its August 1963 issue. It listed the 1500 as having 53 horsepower at 4000 rpm and 83 pounds/feet of torque at 2000 rpm, compared to the Bug's 40 at 3900 and 64 at 2400. The magazine timed the 1500 at 20.8 seconds 0-60 mph with a top speed of 85 mph. The Beetle took 32 seconds to 60 mph and maxed out at 74 mph.

"The 1500 is just a little bit more of everything—faster, bigger quieter, and more deluxe through-

out," said *Motor Trend*. "It's loaded with features that distinguish it from the smaller VW.... If the 1500 is imported, it should find its own group of fans, but we expect the less expensive 1200 to continue its import dominance."

That prediction was spot on. While the wagon seemed to find a niche—being quieter and more versatile than the sedan—Americans never seemed to get very enthusiastic about the rather anonymous 1500. Beetles were quirky, Beetles were strange, Beetles were dead reliable, Beetles were family pets, and Beetles could be bought as convertibles. 1500s? They were just cars.

VW had in fact considered a convertible 1500. Karmann-Ghia showed a four-seat 1500 drop top at the Frankfurt auto show in September 1961. VW judged the structure insufficiently rigid, and the open car was never produced. Karmann-Ghia did build a sporty coupe based on the 1500, but it sold slowly due to awkward styling (see Chapter 7).

Nordhoff soon realized that one way to boost the 1500's image was to give the car more performance. In late 1963, the original sedan, wagon, and Karmann-Ghia coupe were joined by twin-carburetor 1500S counterparts with 54 horsepower. By previous VW standards this "Sport" was a road burner with an 85-mph top speed and a 19-second 0-60 mph time. By most other standards, it was still a very ordinary car.

In 1965, VW released a second version of the engine, enlarged to 1,584cc. In Europe, this new "1600" engine had the same power ratings as the 1500, but made more of its torque lower in the rpm range. In addition, the Type 3 models got front disc brakes as standard equipment.

The new engine was at first exclusive to a new two-door fastback body style, the 1600TL, which some VW fans took to calling the poor-man's Porsche. Cynics suggested the sloping roofline was meant to ape that of the Beetle, which it did to a degree. But the TL also was the most-expensive model in the line, which opened it for more criticism in light of its middling performance.

The U.S. finally got Type 3s for the 1966 model year. VW imported the TL, which it dubbed the Fastback, and the Variant wagon, which it called the Squareback; the three-box sedan was not imported. The '66 Fastback tested by *Car Life* listed for $2368, $705 more than that year's top Beetle model. The export 1600 engine had 65 horsepower at 4600 rpm and 87 pounds/feet of torque at 2800. The 2,450-pound Fastback turned in a credible 0-60 mph time of 17.7 seconds with a top speed of 83 mph. It was slightly more stable in crosswinds

Beetle sales were so strong in the U.S. that VW didn't introduce the Type 3 in America until 1966. The only models imported were the station wagon, called the Variant in Europe and the Squareback in the U.S., and the slope-roof 1600TL, here dubbed the Fastback. The Squareback pictured is a 1969; the Fastback is a 1970 and displays that year's minor front-end facelift. These cars were marketed as the 1600 Series, for their 1.6-liter engine. It had 65 horsepower and pushed them to 60 mph in about 17.7 seconds. The 1600s were VW's costliest cars—the '70 Fastback started at $2,339—and sales languished behind those of the Beetle.

than the Beetle, and had more useable power throughout the rpm range.

"Doubtlessly the 1600 is better looking, and far more efficient in shape and space utilization," said *Car Life*. "The 1600 is a Volkswagen with the bug taken out."

For 1967, the 1600 engine was made standard in all Type 3 models, the rear suspension gained "double-jointed" semi-trailing arm geometry, and a fully automatic transmission made its VW debut. This optional automatic did even more to harm performance, however, sapping what excess power the 1600 engine had. U.S. models got Bosch fuel injection (it was an option in Europe) in 1970, and all Type 3s got a minor front-end restyle that increased the front trunk by 1.6 cubic feet.

U.S. sales were steady, if not sensational, but there were no further innovations as the Type 3 soldiered on into the new decade. The end came early in 1973, when the last of 1,813,600 Type 3-based cars rolled off the Wolfsburg assembly line to make way for VW's first water-cooled, front-engine cars. VW didn't step into the universe of the water-cooled, front-engine automobile without one last detour, however.

Though the Type 3s were a moderate success by Volkswagen standards, they weren't enough for the company's dealers—especially in Europe—who by the mid 1960s were screaming for bigger, faster, and more up-market models to sell. Nordhoff might originally have thought that the Audis could fill that role (see Chapter 9). But during the mid 1960s, he was persuaded by his consultants, by Porsche, and by the many traditionalists on his staff, that the vehicle VW needed was bigger and better—and more of the same. By the time Nordhoff's successor, Kurt Lotz, took over in May 1968, the new car, internally known as Type 411, was almost ready for launch.

More of the same turned out to be a 1960s-style restatement of the traditional VW Beetle layout, complete with a rear-mounted, flat-four, air-cooled engine. In fairness, almost every other detail of the Type 411's chassis was new, there was a new monocoque/platform, new front and rear suspension, new engine and transmission, and of course, new styling.

But industry observers and rivals could not understand why VW persisted with the rear-engine layout while competitors were abandoning it. Chevrolet was preparing to retire its Corvair after the 1969 model year, ending a 10-year affair with rear-engine, air-cooled design. Fiat, having sold millions of rear-engine 500s, 600s and 850s,

was also changing over to front-engine/front-wheel-drive cars.

By the late 1960s, the only worthwhile rear-engine virtues seemed to be good slippery-surface traction and the fact that such cars tended to leave their engine racket behind: A VW sounded much noisier to its occupants when it was sitting at a red light than it did cruising along a freeway. But no matter how much work went into developing the layout, it was impossible to avoid the rear-heavy weight distribution that compromised handling, and no amount of wind-tunnel testing could stop rear-engine cars from feeling sensitive to cross-winds. (In Germany, where VWs accounted for nearly half the market, autobahns displayed signs warning of *Seitenwind*, or sidewind.)

If Porsche had not continued to be the major influence on VW's mechanical design, perhaps Wolfsburg would have made the change to a front-engine design earlier. But Ferry Porsche and his team were committed to mid- and rear-engine layouts for all their new designs, and there was pressure on VW to do the same.

Interest in the new model was high. This was the first production car from VW's own development center at Wolfsburg, and many observers also felt it was the first truly postwar VW automobile. Although Volkswagen's new and very-secure test track at Ehra had been used throughout the Type 411's development, spy photographers in the German press shot the new car long before it went on sale in August 1968. As it turned out, the 411, as it was officially badged, looked better in photographs than it looked on the road.

Pininfarina was credited with the styling, but not even the premier Italian design house could produce a startling shape given the car's engineering parameters. This was to be the first VW passenger car with a choice of two or four doors, and there was no escaping the fact that the engine was in the tail and that it had to be kept cool. The result was a very conventional, rather rounded fastback sedan. Its weakest aesthetic feature was the nose, which was marred by a large front overhang and goggle-eyed headlamps. At least the overhang provided a generous luggage bay, for unlike the Type 3, the 411 had no rear "trunk."

The 411's platform was completely new and its wheelbase, 98.5 inches, was four inches longer than that of the Beetle or Type 3. The engine was no more than a reworking of the 1600TL's, the principal difference being increased displacement, to 1.7 liters (1,679cc, 102 cubic inches). The new boxer's compression ratio was only 7.8:1, so it

Relocating the cooling fan reduced the height of the engine by 16 inches, making possible the Type 3's rear trunk. The insulated panel that served as the trunk floor quelled engine noise, so these cars were quieter than the Beetle. They also were built with VW's renowned assembly quality and were the first Volkswagens to offer disc brakes and a fully automatic transmission. But rivals were beginning to market front-wheel-drive small cars that made the rear-engine Type 3 feel dated. Production ended in 1973 after 1.8 million had been built.

The spare tire sits in front of the forward luggage compartment. You don't have to unload to change a flat. Also up front: easy see-through plastic containers for the brake fluid and windshield-washer water.

Pull out the ashtray in the dashboard and a metal guard pops up. A neat touch that protects the finish and upholstery.

Recessed door handles won't catch your clothing. A light one-finger touch opens them. And you don't need a key to lock up. Just push the small lever closed.

The button on the turn signal lever controls the high and low headlight beams. To dip your lights for an approaching car, just squeeze. No more fishing around on the floor with your foot to find a button.

The bucket seats adjust in seven positions, front to rear. The seat backs recline at seven angles. 49 possible seating positions in all.

A sliding sunroof gives you 390 sq. in. of sunshine overhead. Plus the protection of a steel roof when you crank the sunroof closed. An optional extra.

The engine is under the floor of the 10.5-cu.-ft. rear luggage compartment. To check the oil without unpacking the trunk, unscrew the oil cap. (It sits underneath the back door.) A dip stick's attached.

The 4-cylinder engine is cast of light aluminum and magnesium alloys to eliminate dead weight. Pistons travel a short distance at slow speeds to cut down engine friction, lengthen engine life.

You get even stops, less brake fade with front wheel self-adjusting disc brakes. They're standard equipment.

The Fastback is a five-passenger sedan with headroom, legroom and elbowroom to spare. Everything inside—upholstery, door panels, side trim, dashboard padding—hair cord carpeting, steering wheel—matches everything else in color. (You choose what the color will be.) Safety notes: seat belt mounting points are installed for both frontseats and rear bench seat. Once the doors are closed, the frontseat backrests automatically lock to prevent them tilting forward. So if you make a sudden stop, backseat passengers and/or luggage can't push the frontseat passengers forward.

could run on regular-grade fuel, and it had incredibly mild camshaft timing, but its 68 horsepower was the most yet of any VW engine.

Otherwise, technical innovation was everywhere, though it was well hidden beneath the skin. Both front and rear suspensions were totally different from those used on previous VWs. There were two reasons for this: one was to reel back the high costs of earlier systems, the other was a general attempt to improve roadholding. Much of the impetus for the change had in fact come from VW's accountants, who had finally convinced the engineers to reconsider suspension details, pointing out that torsion bars, even when made in the millions, were too expensive, and that simple coil springs would do a better job.

The 411 was the first VW to use a MacPherson strut front suspension. This system, named after the American engineer who invented it, combined the spring/suspension strut units and fixed the top of the struts directly to the body shell. It was a compact and efficient layout gradually being adopted by many of Europe's automakers. At the rear, VW took the latest Beetle setup a step further. There were semi-trailing swing arms allied to double-jointed half-shafts, as on the latest Bugs, but for the 411, coil springs with co-axial shock absorbers provided the suspension. The rest of the chassis was a mixture of tradition and innovation. Recirculating-ball steering was new, though the gasoline-fired auxiliary heater was familiar. Front disc brakes were standard, as were radial-ply tires.

The air-cooled flat-four breathed mostly though a long line of cooling slots in the decklid below the rear-window glass. The engine mated to a new four-speed, all-synchromesh manual gearbox that featured VW's first direct-drive top gear. Automatic transmission, as pioneered on the 1600TL, was optional.

In many ways this was a much better car than any previous VW, but it was certainly no hellcat in either character or performance. The distribution of weight—53 percent over the rear wheels, compared with 62 percent in a Beetle—and the more-precise geometry of the new suspension made this the most neutral-handling car in the VW stable. In fast turns, the 411 would plow toward the outside of the curve, understeering where previous VWs risked tail-happy oversteer. Still, the 411 was none-too-powerful and, at around 2600 pounds, rather heavy compared to rivals. Summed up the British magazine *Autocar* upon the 411's European launch: "Performance seems average for the 1,600cc class, and below standards for the 2-liter class that this

car will have to fight....it shows all the signs of being too slow, and certainly too expensive." The press duly reported that the 411 was now the only car in its class to retain air-cooling and a rear-mounted engine, and that it was less economical than any of its competition.

The public wasn't fooled. Type 4 assembly began in the summer of 1968, but at just 150 cars per day, not the 500 that was possible. VW was confident demand would rise rapidly, particularly for the automatic-transmission version, which management believed finally had an engine that wouldn't be sapped of most of its power. Sales did increase, but slowly, and never to VW's expectations.

The lukewarm enthusiasm toward the 411 was reminiscent of the response that greeted the Type 3 in 1961. VW's dismay was evident. All the effort that had gone into producing a new platform, new suspensions, and a more-powerful engine seemed to have been wasted. If ever a manufacturer should have been persuaded to change its philosophy, this was it. But instead, VW encouraged Porsche to produce yet another anachronism—the Type EA266 mid-engine sedan (see Chapter 10).

Trying a quick fix of the 411, VW in late 1969 gave the engine new heads and pistons, slightly more compression, and electronic fuel injection. It renamed the car the 411E, the E for Einspritz (injection). The move infuriated first-year customers and dealers who still had original 411s to sell. But while 411Es had to use premium fuel, they did have 80 horsepower and could cruise at 90 mph.

These were the first 411 models to come to the U.S., debuting for the 1971 model year with a rating of 85 horsepower at 5000 rpm and 99 pounds/feet of torque at 3500. America didn't immediately receive the two-door station wagon recently introduced for Europe, but the slightly altered quad-headlamp nose that came here was universally adopted.

For the 1973 model year in Europe, VW made one last stab at the Type 4, replacing the 411E with the 412 range. Although the model name had changed, the only real alteration was a new nose with a flatter body line. The two-door version also got larger doors. It still wasn't enough, so from the autumn of 1973 (and just in time to be hit by the Energy Crisis), the 412E turned into the 412LS. There were no visual changes, but the engine was both enlarged and simplified. Out went expensive fuel injection, in came twin carburetors, and up went displacement, to 1.8 liters (1,795cc, 110 cubic inches). Horsepower declined to 75 in Europe, but torque was up.

Kurt Lotz (above) replaced tradition-bound Heinz Nordhoff as VW's director in 1968. He liked front-engine/front-drive designs, but didn't arrive in time to thwart the Type 4, which bowed in Europe for 1968. It was VW's largest, plushest car yet, the first with four doors and MacPherson strut front suspension. But as a product of Porsche's influence, it retained a rear mounted air-cooled flat-four engine. The Type 4 came to the U.S. for 1971 as the 411 (blue cars). For '73, it got a new nose, fuel injection, and new name: 412 (yellow car). Just 355,200 Type 4s were built before VW halted their production after the '74 model year. It was VW's last rear-engine automobile.

The 412 came to the U.S. for the 1973 model year, but retained fuel injection. The two-door sedan carried on with the 1.7-liter engine, which had a 76-horsepower rating, while the four-door sedan and two-door wagon got the 1.8; it had 72 horsepower at 4800 rpm and 91 pounds/feet of torque at 3000. These were Volkswagen's most-expensive cars. U.S. base prices for this final Type 4 ranged from $3,775 for the two-door to $4,200 for the wagon. That was higher than the new, larger, front-wheel-drive VW Dasher that had debuted for '74. And Americans could buy a Pontiac Catalina four-door sedan with a standard V-8 engine for less; its list price was $3,952. Sales of the 412 were terrible and VW stopped production after the '74 model year. In all, 355,200 Type 4s had been built, which about equalled the number of Beetles VW sold in an average year in the U.S. during this period. Though VW's station-wagon bus would carry on with a rear-engine, air-cooled layout, the Type 4 marked the end of Wolfsburg's infatuation with the design. Except, of course, for the Thing.

VW may have been controlled by sober, engineering-minded Germans, but the success of its best-selling car, the Beetle, owed much to the sense of whimsy that it conjured in buyers. The Thing took whimsy a step further: it was downright absurd. The Thing name was of North American origin; in Germany, it was the Type 181.

Planning for the Type 181 began in the 1960s, though there is little to suggest that the Old Guard under Nordhoff would ever have approved production. It was the new regime, under Lotz that gave it the nod.

The Type 181 was originally designed to a German military specification as a cross-country vehicle. Building to military requirement meant VW could use a host of expensive chassis features, with little regard for civilian sale, though four-wheel drive was not part of the specification. The first Type 181s rolled off the assembly line late in 1969, but only 2,000 were ever sold to the German military. Others were supplied to the Belgian and Dutch armed forces, and VW did begin offering them to the public, but being rear-wheel drive only and at roughly the price of a Type 4 sedan, orders were rare. In America, meanwhile, it was said that people so loved the Beetle they would buy almost any derivative. So the Thing was added to VW's 1973 lineup.

For civilian production, VW opened a Type 181 assembly line at the Hanover factory. The vehicle shared the Beetle's 94.5-inch wheelbase, but its platform was based on that of the Type 1 Karmann-Ghia, which had a squarer floorpan than the Bug's. It retained torsion-bar suspension, and like the Kuebel of old, the first Type 181s had swing axles, modified front hubs, and Transporter-style reduction gears in the rear hubs to provide eight inches of ground clearance. Later models got VW's more-conventional underpinnings, including the double-jointed rear suspension.

Styling of civilian and military models was very similar. Reminiscent of the Kuebel, it was sharp-edged simplicity itself. There were four flat-sided doors, all heavily ribbed to make them more rigid and less likely to drum in sympathy with engine vibrations. The doors could be quickly removed without tools, and simple wet-weather protection was provided by plastic sidescreens and a canvas soft top. Overall length was just 148.8 inches, some 14 inches shorter than a Beetle, though the Thing was about two inches wider and with the soft-top erected, it was taller. Curb weight was just 1,995 pounds, about the same as a Beetle.

The four-place interior was a study in painted metal and minimal amenities. It had split front bench seats and a one-piece fold-down rear bench. There was a small luggage area behind the rear seat, though cargo space could be expanded by folding down the rear seatback, which was backed with steel to form a sturdy deck.

Early Things used the Bug's 1.5-liter flat-four engine, but later ones, including those that came to America, had a detuned version of the 1.6-liter. U.S. versions were rated at 46 horsepower at 4000 rpm and 71 pounds/feet of torque at 2800. To compensate for the lack of four-wheel drive, Things got higher numerical gearing than Beetles, enough to climb a 55-percent grade in the lowest of the four forward gears. Tall gearing, along with the wind-blunting shape, helped limit top speed to 68 mph. Neither was fuel economy great.

With prices around $3,000, the appeal of the Thing was limited to individualists who really needed to make a statement. VW optimistically marketed it as a go-anywhere vehicle, and offered a host of factory options, including chrome wheels, a roll cage, even a fiberglass hardtop. But the Thing was more a curiosity than a sales success and it wasn't imported to America after the 1975 model year. It continued for a short time in Mexico, where it was built and sold as the "Safari." Production ceased in 1976.

VW veered into near absurdity with the Type 181, known in North America as the Thing. It was conceived during the 1960s as a scout car for the German military and its design consciously recalled World War II's Kuebelwagen. Civilian models were offered beginning around 1970, and The Thing came to the U.S. for 1973. It used a Beetle platform but its body was 14 inches shorter. The rear-mounted, air-cooled 1.6-liter flat-four made just 46 horsepower and drove the rear wheels; four-wheel drive wasn't available. Bare metal panels lined the four-seat cabin. Even a host of dress-up options couldn't hide the fact that the Thing was little more than a crude novelty, and with base prices of around $3,000, a rather expensive one. Production ceased in 1976.

From People's Car to Icon: The Beetle Matures

While the Type 3 and Type 4 ranges struggled to find a broad audience during the 1960s, the Beetle kept marching, confounding its critics and amazing even its admirers. As in the 1950s, there was almost imperceptible change in specification from year to year. But to VW fans, the changes made a difference.

For example, the addition of the hydraulic steering damper for 1960 improved directional stability on bad roads. The following year's boost from 36 horsepower to 40 and the new all-synchro gearbox was accompanied by the introduction of an automatic choke and a pump windshield washer.

"When driving the new VW, one soon discovers that the changes made for 1961 definitely have made it a better car, in spite of the way that they have been underplayed," said Road & Track in its December 1960 test of a new Beetle sedan. "The increase in engine power is slight, but is noticeable—especially when slogging along at low speeds in top gear...." The magazine's Bug had a list price of $1,565 and a test weight of 2,035 pounds, which was distributed 43-percent front/57 rear. It reached 60 mph in 27.7 seconds and had a top speed of 71 mph. The editors were impressed.

"Overall, the new VW is so good that it leaves us a bit short of anything to say; the handling, while not of real sports car quality, is as good as the other sedans in the same class. The ride is much better than the price allows one to expect and, indeed, on very rough roads is almost unequaled. Shifting, always an easy task in the VW, is even better with the new transmission, and the synchronized 1st gear is a real boon in stop-and-go traffic."

VW built its five-millionth Beetle during 1961. In the same year, more than one million VWs were produced in a 12-month period for the first time. And with the opening of an assembly plant in Emden, on Germany's North Sea coast, VWs destined for the U.S. could roll straight off the production line, be driven a short distance to the dock, and loaded on a freighter for direct shipment across the Atlantic. So simple, so efficient and—so it seemed at the time—so VW.

A gas gauge replaced the reserve fuel tap for 1962, and the windshield washer now used the spare tire for air pressure. Changes over the next two years ran mostly to trim refinements, though a crank-operated sliding steel sunroof supplanted the fabric sunroof for '64.

So deliberate was the pace of evolution that Motor Trend admitted in its August '64 report that "there have been so few significant changes in the car that last year's road test is just as valid as it was then." The magazine's gray '64 Sunroof sedan stickered for $1,970, ran 0-60 mph in 29.5 seconds, topped out at 71 mph, and averaged 24.7 mpg in 4000 miles of what the editors admitted was hard driving. Braking, ride, and quality finish were praised. Tepid passing power was a shortfall Motor Trend was willing to rationalize, though the car's continued propensity to be blown into the next lane by gusty crosswinds was harder to accept.

VW by now was completing one car every 14 seconds for worldwide consumption, with Beetle production dwarfing that of other models. Stamping out all those Bugs took its toll on body-panel tooling. By '65, the tooling was worn out. The replacements were engineered to provide the car with larger windows and slimmer door and windshield pillars. Outward visibility increased by 15 percent, with the backlight alone growing by 19.5 percent, said Volkswagen.

Then, for 1966, came the biggest Beetle shake-up in more than a decade. The long-established 1200 engine was joined by a 1300 version (1,285cc, 78.5 cubic inches). Technically the change was simple enough—the cylinder stroke was increased 0.2 inches (5mm) by using the crankshaft from the Type 3 1500 model, compression rose from 7.0:1 to 7.3:1, and the size of the intake valves and the carburetor venturi were enlarged slightly. Horsepower went from 40 at 3900 rpm to 50 at 4600, and the engine seemed to rev more freely. There also was improvement in the suspension, with a switch to ball joints in front, new spring rates and shock-absorber valving, and most significantly, the addition of a front anti-roll bar.

"Driving the 1300 for the first time, the owner, or ex-owner of an older Volkswagen will notice immediately the smoother, quieter operation, the greater airiness of the interior, and a good deal

(continued)

Its design may have dated to Germany in the 1930s, but its attitude was right for America in the 1960s. The Beetle had become a cultural phenomenon, cutting across class lines and appealing to rebellious youth, iconoclastic intellectuals, and anyone on a budget. These were VW's salad days in the United States. By the mid 1960s, on the strength of the Beetle, it held 67 percent of the nation's import market and accounted for nearly seven percent of all the cars sold in the country.

Opposite page, clockwise from top left: *The five-millionth Volkswagen built since the end of World War II rolled off the line on December 4, 1961, VW chief Heinz Nordhoff presiding. By now, VW's giant Wolfsburg works was Europe's largest and most-modern auto assembly facility. Each of the company's 60 charter ships carried 1,750 Volkswagens per voyage to the U.S., then hauled grain and ore back to Germany. Above: With this cutaway of a '61, VW suggested that mom, dad, brother, sis, Fido, and their luggage could fit comfortably in a Beetle. Others clearly believed it could hold more (left). At least 23 heads are visible in this particular go at a popular '60s stunt. The 1960 model Bug (below) added a dished steering wheel, pushbutton door handles, and a padded sunvisor. It listed for $1,565, and VW sold 112,027 sedans and 5,841 of the $2,055 convertibles that year.*

Advertising for People Who Think

New York advertising man George Lois was in his office wrestling with the central problem of his new assignment when he spotted his boss, William Bernbach.

"Bill, I've got it!" Lois said. "You have the advertising?" Bernbach responded. "Well, no, we don't have the advertising," Lois admitted, "but I figured out the marketing problem: We have to sell a Nazi car in a Jewish town."

The exchange took place in the New York headquarters of Doyle Dane Bernbach shortly after the advertising agency had acquired the Volkswagen account. Lois, an art director, had pinpointed a conflict shared by many at the firm. It was 1959, and some World War II wounds were still very fresh.

"The German origins of the car were obviously going to inhibit some sales," said Julian Koenig, the campaign's original copywriter. "One of the wise things that the Volkswagen people did was that they did not want to 'Germanize' this car."

Taking VW's cue—and setting aside personal reservations—the Bernbach professionals played off the Beetle's small size, low cost, and odd appearance to give it an appealing persona. Their simple graphics and witty copy made for advertisements of uncommon intelligence. Indeed, a panel of judges assembled by *Advertising Age* magazine in 1984 called it nothing less than the best American ad campaign since World War II.

"The car, in response to advertising, became an affectionate as well as an economic possession," Koenig said. "A reverse chic is established. It became chic to have the economic, ugly little Beetle."

Koenig said that the famous 1962 "Think Small" spot initially set the tone for the campaign. In an America of bigger-is-better, it seemed to legitimize the Beetle buyer's anti-establishment sensibility. And when another spot drolly suggested, "Live Below Your Means," the Volkswagen owner could feel subversive and superior at the same time.

Think small.

Our little car isn't so much of a novelty any more.
A couple of dozen college kids don't try to squeeze inside it.
The guy at the gas station doesn't ask where the gas goes.
Nobody even stares at our shape.
In fact, some people who drive our little flivver don't even think 32 miles to the gallon is going any great guns.
Or using five pints of oil instead of five quarts.
Or never needing anti-freeze.
Or racking up 40,000 miles on a set of tires.
That's because once you get used to some of our economies, you don't even think about them any more.
Except when you squeeze into a small parking spot. Or renew your small insurance. Or pay a small repair bill. Or trade in your old VW for a new one.
Think it over.

"You could take an inverse delight in not having to keep up with the Joneses, in not responding to Detroit's planned obsolescence, in not being part of that competitive culture," Koenig explained.

Unlike conventional auto advertising, VW couldn't glorify annual appearance updates. "Of course that negative, was a big, fat positive," Koenig said. The focus instead became engineering refinements, while the unchanging looks were cast an advantage thanks to such lines as, "Since we never change the style, a VW never goes out of style."

Some VW ads came right out and called the car ugly. Some had shock value. A

Lemon.

This Volkswagen missed the boat.

The chrome strip on the glove compartment is blemished and must be replaced. Chances are you wouldn't have noticed it; Inspector Kurt Kroner did.

There are 3,389 men at our Wolfsburg factory with only one job: to inspect Volkswagens at each stage of production. (3000 Volkswagens are produced daily; there are more inspectors than cars.)

Every shock absorber is tested (spot checking won't do), every windshield is scanned. VWs have been rejected for surface scratches barely visible to the eye.

Final inspection is really something! VW inspectors run each car off the line onto the Funktionsprüfstand (car test stand), tote up 189 check points, gun ahead to the automatic brake stand, and say "no" to one VW out of fifty.

This preoccupation with detail means the VW lasts longer and requires less maintenance, by and large, than other cars. (It also means a used VW depreciates less than any other car.)

We pluck the lemons; you get the plums.

No point showing the '62 Volkswagen. It still looks the same.

Dealer Name

notable example showed a Beetle above the word "Lemon." It went on to explain that the chrome strip on its glove compartment door was blemished.

The ads were graphically daring, too. One didn't even show a picture of the car, just an expanse of white over the headline, "No point in showing the '62 Volkswagen. It still looks the same." And they broke ground thematically. "I did a lot of things to that car," Koenig recalled. "I showed it very dirty. I showed damaged Volkswagens when we were talking about the availability of parts... Nobody had ever seen a dent in a car ad."

The Doyle Dane Bernbach ads ran from 1959 to 1972, and not coincidentally, their end came as Volkswagen's sales declined. Subsequent campaigns by other agencies never matched Doyle Dane Bernbach's success: The cars were ordinary and so was the advertising.

A mid-1980s effort put German lyrics to the exuberant 1960s muscle-car anthem "GTO" and showed a speeding Rabbit GTI getting airborne as it crested hills. The ad had spirit, and came as VW was registering its best sales years since the early 1970s. But "Fahrvergnuegen," the 1989 try by DDB Needham Worldwide to convey VW's German flavor, didn't translate into new-car orders.

In 1995, Volkswagen changed agencies again, to Arnold Fortuna Lawner & Cabot, a Boston firm that came up with the "Drivers Wanted" campaign. It was another attempt to portray Volkswagens as fun-to-drive alternatives to mundane Japanese rivals. Ron Lawner, vice chairman and chief creative officer of the agency, said the ads were intended to educate shoppers about the character of the modern Volkswagen. "Far too many people have a positive feeling about the brand but are back on the Bug," Lawner said.

If VW is still in the shadow of the Beetle, it appears that thanks to the work of George Lois, Julian Koenig, and their colleagues, so is its advertising.

The '63 sedan (both pages) was changed only slightly from the previous year's Beetle, gaining a leatherette headliner, while losing the Wolfsburg hood crest. It enjoyed improvements introduced for '62, when the taillamps were enlarged, a gas gauge replaced the reserve fuel tap, and the pump-type windshield washer was supplanted by one that used air pressure from the spare tire. The engine still displaced 1,192cc, but horsepower had increased from 36 to 40 for '61. The front passenger position gained a sunvisor and grab handle that year, as well. The '63 sedan retailed for $1,595, and Beetle sales in the U.S. exceeded 200,000 for the first time: 209,747 sedans and 7,377 convertibles.

more liveliness," *Car Life* magazine said in its test of a '66 model. "Where the old models once trundled along, not unlike giant mechanical beetles, these newer ones seem to bounce about with a certain resiliency."

The *Car Life* editors were laudatory, but also realistic. "Though the parent company is fond of advertising its proclivity toward frequent refinement, but little outward change, the VW is still much the same car it was 10 years ago when many Americans first became acquainted with the waterless wonder of Wolfsburg," they said. "It still is relatively underpowered, it still does not utilize well the potential interior space it has available and it still is acutely subject to the whims of the wind; however, its fun factor has been increased."

For 1967, the company that had made an institution of slow change surprised everyone. "Wonder of wonders," declared *Road & Track* in its February 1967 issue. "Those Volkswagen people, after all the years of clever advertising about planned obsolescence and all that, are getting hooked into the annual model change themselves. Here they are, for the second year in a row, with a bigger engine; and on top of that, improved suspension and styling changes."

The new engine was the 1.5-liter that had debuted in the Type 3. This 1500 replaced the 1300 as standard in all U.S. Beetles, while the 1200 and 1300 engines remained available in other markets. It was rated at 53 horsepower at 4200 rpm and 78 pounds/feet of torque at 2600. This represented a 16-percent increase in displacement over the 1300, a 14-percent gain in torque, and a 6-percent rise in horsepower. The added torque was the most important engine improvement. The boxer was not only more flexible through the gears, but cut 0-60 mph times to 22.5 seconds, almost two seconds quicker than the 1300. Passing ability benefitted even more; Beetle drivers could now stay in third gear up to 58 mph. Top speed increased by only about three mph, to around 78 mph.

In a way, the revised suspension was more significant than the new engine because it was a tacit admission by VW that the Beetle had some handling problems. The revisions gave the rear suspension softer springs and a transverse torsion bar. This improved resistance to crosswinds, and reduced the propensity to oversteer. It was a safer Beetle, made more so by the addition of a more-efficient headlamp design, recessed interior door handles, soft dashboard knobs, and retractors for the lap safety belts. European models also gained front disc brakes, a feature that unfortunately never would make it onto U.S.-market Beetles.

U.S. sales of the Beetle sedan breached 300,000 for 1967 (6,349 convertibles also were sold). Annual price increases, though, had not been in lockstep with annual sales increases. Base price of a Beetle sedan was $1,565 in 1960 and had stabilized at $1,595 through 1964. It then *dipped* to under $1,575 through '66. However, with the addition of the larger engine and suspension improvements, base price of the '67 jumped to $1,639.

For '68, U.S. Beetles got a feature introduced to Europe the previous year: Automatic Stick Shift. This option cost $135 and basically was a standard VW manual transmission that, through the wonder of technology, had lost its clutch pedal. It had three forward speeds. First, or "Lo," was for getting away from a stop with a heavy load or for climbing steep grades. In normal driving, the driver would start out in second gear, then shift into third at about 40 mph. During gear changes, a pressure-sensitive switch at the base of the shift lever activated a vacuum cylinder that engaged the clutch.

Automatic Stick Shift Beetles got a 4.38:1 final-drive ratio compared to the manual-gearbox cars' 4.12:1, so acceleration was affected only slightly; *Car and Driver* timed a '68 Automatic Stick Shift at 16.8 seconds 0-60 mph. The option opened the Beetle to a new audience and by the end of the year, 40 percent of U.S. models had it.

A bonus on cars equipped with the automatic was a new rear suspension that was yet another step toward exorcising the Beetle of its handling demons. The swing-axle design was modified to incorporate "double-jointed" axle half-shafts: At the end of each axle was a constant velocity universal joint. In addition, VW added diagonal trailing arms to further stabalize the rear suspension in turns. The result made the Bug more predictable in changes of direction by minimizing unwanted movement of the rear wheels. In particular, the system helped maintain negative rear wheel camber—the "bottom" of the tires remained outboard of the "top" of the tires—regardless of body lean. Bolstering safety were new front-seat head restraints and a collapsible steering column.

In 1968, Beetle sales reached an all-time high in the U.S. at 390,079 sedans and 9,595 convertibles. The Beetle alone accounted for five percent of all cars sold in the U.S. that year, despite suffering by comparison to more-modern rivals.

European critics had realized the car's limitations for years. However, Americans, entranced by

(continued)

Beetle advertising was refreshingly devoid of the hard-sell. How wonderful. The car, meanwhile, marched on, acquiring a "1300" badge for '66 to mark its new 1,285cc engine. Horsepower increased from 40 to 50. Opposite: This '66 shows off the semi-circular horn ring and the center defroster outlet that were added that year. Ventilating wheel slots and flat hubcabs also were new. A crank-open steel sunroof had replaced the fabric sunroof for 1964, and new body-stamping equipment put into use for '65 gave all Beetles an airier cabin with slimmer roof pillars and more glass area.

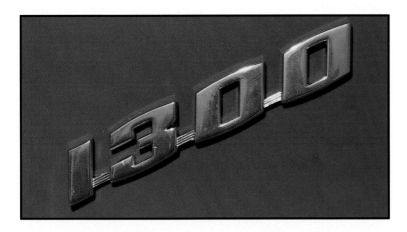

The wide world of the wildly adaptable Bug included production cars modified for international rallying (opposite top left and below). It also encompassed all-out racing machines. In 1963, VW launched the Formula V series for open-wheel single-seaters similar to this one (opposite top right). They were powered by the air-cooled flat four. The Beetle's engine and suspension were popular foundations for off-road racers, such as this competitor in the long-distance run down Mexico's Baja peninsula (opposite bottom). Beetles were frequently used as police cars, though seldom in the U.S. An exception was this patrol Bug in small-town New York state (above). Americans also preferred larger cars for taxis, a luxury not enjoyed in other lands, such as Brazil (left). Finally, a fellow named Malc Buchanan rigged a Beetle with a propeller and set out across the Irish Sea from the Isle of Man to England (below left). He ran out of gas 400 yards from land, but a favorable breeze blew the intrepid sailor ashore.

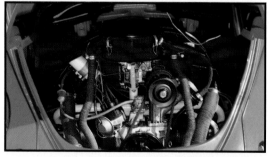

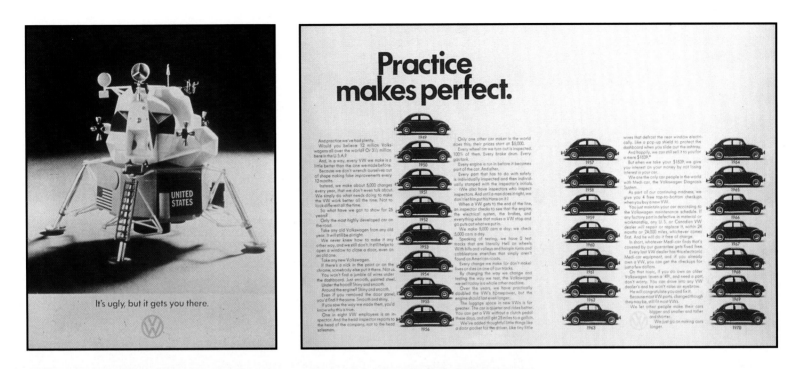

It's ugly, but it gets you there.

Practice makes perfect.

VW uncharacteristically altered the Bug for the second year in a row, bumping displacement to 1,493cc and making the 1967 Beetle (opposite page) a "1500." The change prompted replacement of the "1300" engine-lid badge with "Volkswagen" script. Horsepower increased from 50 to 53. Of 320,692 Beetles sold in the U.S. that year, 6,349 were convertibles. For '68, buyers could order Automatic Stick Shift, which eliminated the clutch pedal. VW seemed by now a part of the American landscape. In '69, it infiltrated Hollywood. Herbie, a Beetle with a mind of its own, starred in The Love Bug and launched a series of Walt Disney comedies (left). The same year, VW played off the first moon landing with this clever advertisement featuring the lunar module (top left). The Beetle was entering its sunset years, however, and by 1970, Volkswagen seemed increasingly conscious of the car's age, as this ad demonstrates (top).

the Beetle's social connotations, seemed blind to its technological shortcomings. But now there was a new threat that would begin to erode not only VW's market, but that of Detroit, as well.

Imports, which accounted for just 1.7 percent of U.S. car sales in 1956, grew to 7.3 percent in '66, and to 10.5 percent in '68. Volkswagen was by far the leader of this invasion, its share of the import market peaking at 67 percent in 1965. By 1968, VW's share of the import market had declined to 57 percent, but it still was the most-popular and recognizable foreign make in the U.S.: of 5.4 million imported cars on U.S. roads that year, 3.1 million were Volkswagens.

But the Japanese were coming. In 1966, the Europeans still controlled the lion's share of the U.S. import market. VW was first, selling 420,000 cars in the U.S. (Beetles, vans, 1500s, and Karmann-Ghias), Opel was second, at 31,000, and Volvo was third. The top Japanese brand was Datsun, in fourth place with sales of 22,000. Toyota ranked a distant eighth, with sales of just 16,000.

Over the next three years, VW increased sales a healthy 28 percent, to more than 500,000 annually, maintaining its top import ranking. But at the same time, its share of the import market melted to 51 percent, and the Europeans in general began to watch Japan's taillights. Toyota over that same period increased sales seven-fold, rocketing into second place at 117,000. Datsun held down third place, at 59,000. The portion of the American import market occupied by VW and by all European makes had begun a slide from which it would never recover. The reason was simple: The Japanese were offering small-car buyers high-quality American-flavored automobiles that beat VW and the other Europeans in overall performance, features, utility, and price.

When *Road Test* magazine pitted a 1968 Beetle against a '68 Toyota Corolla, the Japanese brand embarrassed the VW in every category measured. It was faster and more powerful despite having a smaller engine. It had more passenger space despite a 4.5-inch shorter wheelbase and smaller body. It held more luggage. It was quieter. It stopped shorter and handled better. It offered four doors. It had better outward visibility. It had cupholders. It didn't require the owner to remove the rear seat to reach the battery like the VW did; its battery was under the hood. The editors said the Corolla was built every bit as well as the Beetle and had sturdier bumpers. And at $1,575, the Corolla's base price was $124 less than the Beetle's.

All Beetles got the "double-jointed" rear suspen-

sion for 1969, along with such amenities as a rear-window defroster for sedans. But total VW sales in the U.S. fell by about 26,000, the first decline since the company began importing cars to America.

For '70, VW bored the 1500 to 1,584cc, enough to qualify it as the 1600. It had 57 horsepower at 4400 rpm, and 82 pounds/feet of torque at 3000—both figures up by four points over the 1500 engine. *Car and Driver* said it didn't notice the extra power, and in fact, the '70 Automatic Stick Shift Beetle it tested was slightly slower 0-60 mph than the '68 1500 it ran, despite no increase in curb weight. With the optional radio ($71), and the semi-automatic gearbox ($139), the price-as-tested was $2,084.

Sales recovered for 1970, as VW registered its all-time U.S.-market peak, delivering 569,182 Beetles, Karmann-Ghias, 1600 Fastbacks and Squarebacks, and station-wagon buses. Imports now accounted for 14.7 percent of U.S. car sales and while VW still dominated, its share of the import market had dwindled to 46 percent.

Volkswagen scrambled to respond for 1971, bringing over the 411 series to bolster the 1600 Fastback and Squareback. But 411 sales never took off, and there was no sign that Wolfsburg was willing to import the VW-badged front-drive NSU K70 sedan it had begun to market in Europe (see Chapter 9). American dealers continued to rely on the aging Beetle, which now was under attack not only from the Japanese, but from the constantly appreciating German deutsche mark.

Volkswagen fought back by stripping the most-basic '71 Beetle model to below the equipment level of the standard 1970 model, but its starting price nonetheless rose to $1,845. That was within a few hundred dollars of larger six-cylinder American compacts such as the AMC Hornet and Ford Maverick. There was less room to maneuver on the technological front, though VW tried with the '71 introduction of the 1302S, or, as it was known in America, the Super Beetle.

The Super Beetle cost $140 more than the new price-leader Bug, and for that the buyer got a Beetle with the MacPherson-strut front suspension first seen on the 411. To accommodate the new suspension, wheelbase was stretched by 0.8 inches over the base Beetle, and 3.2 inches was added to the nose sheetmetal. The new front suspension configuration resulted in a useful reduction in the turning circle, from 36 feet to 31.5, and allowed VW to fit a larger gas tank, increasing fuel capacity from 10.6 to 11.1 gallons. The Super also enjoyed a

(continued)

All Bugs were protected by bigger bumpers for '68. They handled more safely thanks to double-jointed rear axles for '69, and got more power from a 1.6-liter engine for '70. Horsepower increased from 57 to 60 for '71, the most ever in a Bug. VW also introduced the Super Beetle model in 1971 (middle and top). Its front sheetmetal was altered to accommodate a MacPherson strut front suspension, a change that nearly doubled trunk space over the regular Bug. The gas tank was larger, too. Super Beetles listed for $1,985, $140 more than a base '71 sedan. For '73, Super Beetles gained a curved windshield (bottom) and along with all Bugs got large circular taillamps, a padded dashboard, and even beefier bumpers.

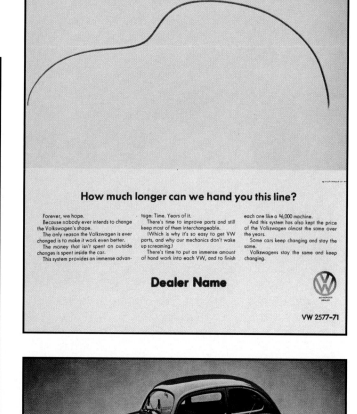

How much longer can we hand you this line?

Forever, we hope.
Because nobody ever intends to change the Volkswagen's shape.
The only reason the Volkswagen is ever changed is to make it work even better.
The money that isn't spent on outside changes is spent inside the car.
This system provides an immense advan-

tage: Time. Years of it.
There's time to improve parts and still keep most of them interchangeable. (Which is why it's so easy to get VW parts, and why our mechanics don't wake up screaming.)
There's time to put an immense amount of hand work into each VW, and to finish

each one like a $6,000 machine.
And this system has also kept the price of the Volkswagen almost the same over the years.
Some cars keep changing and stay the same.
Volkswagens stay the same and keep changing.

Dealer Name

VW 2577-71

Two ridiculous gimmicks of the 1940's.

Everyone laughed when they came out with the television.
A box that could show pictures from 3,000 miles away? Absurd.
But everyone really cracked up when we came out with the Volkswagen.
A car with its engine in the back? Its trunk in the front? And its radiator in neither the front nor the back?

It even looked like a joke.
But time marched on.
The television clicked.
The Volkswagen accelerated.
People liked the idea of a car that didn't drink gas like water. Or oil like water. Or, for that matter, didn't even drink water.
Some strange people even liked the idea that it was strange looking.

In fact, Detroit car makers now like the idea of the VW so much that they have decided to make their own.
But even with all those new small cars around, the fate of the bug is still secure.
This is the first year for all of the others.
We've had twenty-three years of re-runs.

The Beetle's best sales years in the U.S. were 1967 through 1973, when VW sold more than 300,000 annually. By February 1972, worldwide production had topped 15 million, and total Bug volume "overtook" that of the Ford Model T, as symbolized in a Volkswagen publicity shot (above). Despite the Beetle's popularity, objective observers realized the Japanese were building more-modern—and better—small cars. Indeed, this 1971 ad begged an important question (top right) while a '72 spot (right) archly defended the Bug's design.

An automaker traditionally introduces specially trimmed sub models to prop up interest in an aging design, and so it was with the beloved Beetle. Starting in 1972, VW offered a variety of dressed-up derivations, including the Baja Beetle, the Sports Bug, and the Sun Bug. None seemed more desperate than the La Grande Beetle of 1975 (this page). It had leather-grained seats with corduroy insets, a leather-grained steering wheel, rosewood dashboard appliques, color-coordinated carpeting, and blue or green metallic paint. Touted in a brochure that featured a jeweled badge and a chauffeur, the overdressed La Grande seemed incongruous, not ironic. Tellingly, Toyota overtook Volkswagen as America's top-selling import brand during 1975.

welcome three-cubic-foot jump in front luggage space, to nearly twice that of the base Bug.

In other markets, Wolfsburg still offered Beetles with the 34-horsepower 1200 engine, as well as the 44-horsepower 1300. In the U.S., all Beetles now used the 1600 engine, which increased from 57 to 60 horsepower for '71 (it continued at 50 horsepower in Europe). Also new were a flow-through ventilation system and larger taillamps.

Despite the changes, the '71 Bug continued to lose ground to more-modern rivals. "The best Beetle yet, but still not as good as the competition," was *Road & Track*'s assessment. Its four-speed Super Beetle test car stickered for $2,349, did 0-60 mph in 18.4 seconds, and topped out at 79 mph. Fuel mileage was a laudable 28.7 mpg. Complaints were familiar: engine noise, poor resistance to crosswinds, bouncy ride, cramped interior. "The Beetle, whether in standard or Super form, has three main points to recommend it: fuel economy, workmanship and its reputation for long life and good service," concluded *Road & Track*. "If you value those three virtues above all others, then the Beetle is for you. Otherwise it is hopelessly outdated and outdone by both Japanese and American economy cars."

VW sales continued to sink in the U.S., dropping nearly 10 percent, to 509,000 for '71, while Beetle deliveries declined 12 percent. Toyota continued to close on VW, with U.S. sales of nearly 271,000. In Germany, Wolfsburg celebrated the production of the 20-millionth VW vehicle.

For '72, it was a similar tune, with prices increasing and sales decreasing. Playing off the success of VW-powered racers in the grueling Baja, Mexico, off-road competition, Volkswagen added the "Baja Beetle" package for Super Beetles. The $130 dealer-installed option included Baja side stripes, a Superior Speed shifter, bumper-mounted Bosche fog lamps, a leatherette steering wheel cover, mag-type wheel covers, a walnut dash appliqué, and tapered exhaust tips. On the public-relations front, VW announced that with assembly of Beetle number 15,007,034 in February, the car had passed the Ford Model T production total. Historians pointed out that this figure reflected only Model Ts built in North America and that Ford had actually produced about 16 million worldwide. VW's spin doctors might as well have smiled sweetly and replied: "OK, we'll beat that figure by the end of the year." They did.

Super Beetles got a curved windshield for '73, and along with the base Bug, gained large circular taillamps and wider wheels and tires. Increasingly

stringent federal safety regulations resulted in a redesigned and padded dashboard and in stronger bumpers that added about one inch to overall length. Federal regulations registered underhood, as well, where emissions controls paired horsepower by 12, to 48 at 4000 rpm; torque fell by 10 pounds/feet, to 72 at 2800. All these changes were also carried out for the Cabriolet models, as well.

Finally, what the Baja Bug started, the Sports Bug continued. Offered only for 1973, this model featured specially contoured bucket seats, a three-spoke padded steering wheel, short throw shifter, optional tape stripes, and bright paint colors, such as "Pulsating Saturn Yellow."

It was another sign that VW was preparing to abandon the Beetle to its fate. Special-trim models are a telltale that the marketing department is anxious to prop up a declining car. And it wasn't confined to the U.S. Over the next few years, Europe got the Sports Bug-like Yellow and Black edition; the Jeans Beetle, a 34-horsepower 1200 in Tunisian yellow with denim seat covers; the City Beetle, a 44-horsepower Super Beetle with striped body-color upholstery; and the Big Beetle, a 50-horse-power Super with fat sports wheels and upholstery in thick cord. America was blessed with the Love Bug and Sun Bug for '74, and then things moved into the realm of the ridiculous with the '75 La Grande Bug. "You don't drive it, you arrive in it," huffed the La Grande brochure. This one had leather seats with corduroy inserts, a leather grained steering wheel, rosewood dashboard appliqué, thick carpeting, and special metallic paint. The Beetle convertible didn't escape this gilding, getting Champagne Edition models for '78 and '79. It was difficult to tell whether VW had its tongue in cheek, or had just grown desperate.

Technically, the Beetle was at the peak of its development in 1974, and there would be no additional changes to the basic layout or style. The market seemed to sense it. Pushed by the first energy crisis, worldwide Beetle production, which had been cruising along at more than one million since 1961, fell to 791,000 in '74. The decline would continue steadily until levelling off at around 100,000 in the early 1990s.

March 2, 1974, was an important date in the Beetle saga. On that day, the first front-engine, front-drive Golf was assembled at Wolfsburg (see Chapter 10). Golf production built so rapidly that by July 1, Wolfsburg had stopped building Beetles. (VW proudly recorded the exact time the last Beetle's wheels rolled off the assembly line: 11:19 a.m.) Production continued at Emden, where

VW ended U.S. sales of the Beetle sedan with the 1977 model, and the last one built in Germany rolled out of the Emden factory in January 1978 (above). Karmann continued to assembly the cabriolet, however, and VW continued to sell it into 1980. The final ragtops were positioned as chic classics. The 1978 Champaign Edition II, for example, cost around $7,000 and included an interior with ermine-colored upholstery and rosewood trim (opposite). These final U.S. Bugs were solidly built, and having gained the Super Beetle's MacPherson strut front suspension in '76, were competent handlers. Their 1.6-liter flat-four carried a net rating of just 48 horsepower. But with a top speed of 80 mph, the cabrios were suited to America's new 55-mph national speed limit.

Beetle number 18 million was built in October. Of more significance, 1974 was the last year Volkswagen would be America's top-selling import brand. Toyota overtook it during 1975.

Beetles gained electronic fuel injection for '75, but horsepower stayed at 48. Models sold in California were fitted with a catalytic converter and now required lead-free gasoline. VW's rear-engine era was nearly over. The front-drive Dasher, Rabbit, and Scirocco were all on sale in the U.S. and Beetle sales nose-dived from 226,000 sedans and convertibles in 1974 to just 82,000 in '75.

VW recast the mainstream Beetle as a sort of chic specialty car for '76. It killed the Super sedan and the Automatic Stick Shift option, but gave the surviving sedans and convertibles standard metallic paint, full carpeting, sports wheels, fancier front seats, and a two-speed heater fan. It also chromed all exterior trim. Base price for the sedan had reached $3,449. The ragtop, which carried on with the Super Beetle's MacPhearson strut suspension, listed for $4,545.

With the 1977 model, the curtain came down on the Beetle sedan in America. The last of the breed got adjustable headrests and plush velour upholstery, but was otherwise as familiar as a childhood chum. In fact, it was so familiar, that the word "Volkswagen" appeared no where on the car; the only identification was chrome "Fuel Injection" script on the engine cover and small VW logos stamped into the wheel covers.

"Take our word for it—in a lot of ways, the Beetle is like an old friend," confirmed *Road Test* magazine in its test of a '77 four-speed. "It's a car nearly anybody can feel comfortable in right away, because by our best reckoning, nearly everybody has driven a Beetle at one time or another. The latest version feels pretty much the same as the older versions, and it pretty much sounds the same." The magazine's test car listed for $3,959, including the optional AM/FM radio ($150), sunroof ($115), leatherette upholstery ($50), and California emissions equipment ($45). It weighed 1,890 pounds and took 17.2 seconds to get to 60 mph.

Sales in the U.S. during that final year were 12,000; the last time VW sold so few Bugs in America was 1954. The last Beetle sedan built in Germany came off the line at Emden January 19, 1978. But that didn't end the story.

Beetle Cabriolet production continued at the Karmann factory until January 1980. The only Beetles sold in the U.S. as 1978 and '79 models were these Cabriolets. List price was $6,170 for the final editions, but sales remained relatively strong; VW sold 9,932 of the '78s, 10,681 of the '79s, and an additional 4,572 stragglers during 1980. The company's advertising didn't have to talk up the last of the Cabriolets as chic. They were.

"[A]t $7000 out the door," said *Motor Trend* in its test of a '78, "the once diffident bug has taken on a new aristocratic mein; it is the status car of the rank-conscious; the new-wave image of the born again profligate; the adorable ornament of the Highway Culture." But it also was a pretty good car. Assembly was tight, handling had finally been rendered neutral, and the 80 mph top speed—which was still the cruising speed—was suddenly more than enough, given the new 55-mph federal speed limit.

Although the U.S. saw its last new Beetles during 1980, the car continued as a mainstay in developing countries around the world. As the 1980s opened, plants in Brazil and Mexico were turning out 250,000 Beetles annually for their own markets and for export. VW was shipping Beetles in crates to plants in Nigeria and Peru for assembly. For a time, Mexico even supplied cars for the German market, and it was from the factory in Puebla, Mexico, that the 20-millionth Beetle was produced in May 1981. In a fitting finale, the final consignment from Mexico to Germany came in August 1985, almost exactly 40 years to the month that Major Ivan Hirst's ramshackle little colony started to produce Beetles in the bombed-out chaos of Wolfsburg.

Brazil dropped the Beetle in 1986, then brought it back in 1993 to meet newfound demand. Production never faltered in Mexico where nearly 100,000 are still built annually. Even in the Third World, the Beetle is an antiquated car. But its simplicity and high-volume production allow it to undercut more-modern competitors on price. In effect, buyers can have a brand-new Beetle for the cost of a used rival.

The Beetle had put its homeland back on wheels after World War II. It had introduced Americans to the concept of high-quality small cars, and more important, to the habit of buying imports. It had been raced up mountains and customized for the beach. It had been personified in movies and politicized in print. And finally, with a design more than 60 years old and total production headed for 22 million, the Beetle had returned to its roots as basic transportation for the people.

Conceived as a car for the people, then elevated to middle-class acceptance, and eventually dismissed as a lifestyle ornament, the Beetle returned to its roots during the 1980s and '90s. VW's little sedan still provides ultra-low-cost transportation in developing nations, and continues to be assembled in Brazil (opposite top left) and in Mexico. In fact, it was VW's plant in Puebla, Mexico, that produced the 20-millionth Beetle in 1981, here shown with an original KdF-Wagen (opposite bottom). The dashboard has been updated (opposite top right), but inside or out, the Beetle is still among the most-recognized shapes on the planet.

A Van for the Uncommon Man

The Beetle was an automobile unlike any other, but Volkswagen didn't invent the economical subcompact car. Volkswagen did invent the minivan.

Variously called the Transporter, Station Wagon, Kombi, and Micro Bus, later the Vanagon and EuroVan, VW's boxy conveyance came to symbolize liberty and unconventionality for a whole generation of Americans. So strong was the original 1950 design that it survived until 1967, and by the time Chrysler launched its Dodge Caravan and Plymouth Voyager in 1984, the VW "bus" was already into its third generation.

The Transporter was born of Heinz Nordhoff's growing confidence in the still-young Volkswagen enterprise. Introduction of the Beetle Cabriolet in 1949 showed he was amenable to carefully considered variations on VW's one-note theme. By 1950, Nordhoff had determined that the Volkswagen was healthy enough to support a second model range.

The second model was the Transporter, or Type 2—the Beetle being the Type 1. Nordhoff took particular pride in the Type 2, noting that it was developed without input from the Porsche Bureau. Its genesis in fact was a 1947 pencil sketch by Ben Pon, the Dutchman who introduced the Beetle to the U.S. in 1949.

Numerous commercial versions of the Beetle had already been built, typically by entrepreneurs who cut, chopped, and added to the little Bug to produce a variety of open-bed and station wagon-type delivery vans. The Type 2, however, was a purpose-built factory design and there was nothing like it on the automotive landscape. Other manufacturers offered various commercial vans, mostly tall bread-truck-like delivery vehicles, but no other maker thought to scale down the design to suit passenger duty.

The Transporter debuted in March 1950. It used the Beetle floorpan and 94.5-inch wheelbase, but at 53.5 inches, its track was wider than the sedan's by 2.7 inches in front and a significant 4.3 inches in back. It retained the Beetle's standard, rear-mounted air-cooled boxer engine and four-speed transaxle, though a steep 5.13:1 final-drive ratio gave it impressive low-gear grunt. Using Kubelwagen-type reduction gears in the rear wheel hubs provided a full 9.5 inches of ground clearance, which, along with the traction advantages of having the engine over the drive wheels, was an important plus in back-road duty.

At 168.5 inches, its brick-shaped body was 8.5 inches longer than the Beetle's, and it had vastly more interior room than any conventional station wagon. Because the engine was so low and was set so far back, and because the driver sat well forward in a bus-like position, the new Transporter was a very space-efficient machine. Passenger versions could carry up to nine occupants on three rows of bench seats; there also were enclosed cargo vans, flat-bed haulers, double cab pick-ups, mattress-equipped campers, ambulances, and even a dump-truck variant.

Debuting in Europe with a 25-horsepower 1,131cc Beetle engine, the Transporter weighed 2,300 pounds (53 percent over the rear wheels) and had a maximum payload capacity of 1,650 pounds. It was not a fast machine. It never would be, despite increases in engine displacement and horsepower. But it was maneuverable, roomy, reliable, and like all VWs, it was cheap to buy, fuel, and maintain. It was the "people's van."

The Transporter was available in the U.S. shortly after its introduction, but few were imported before 1954. VW offered these early U.S. versions with an engine rated at 30 horsepower at 3400 rpm. Three models were available: the base Kombi, which was painted blue and retailed for about $2,200; the slightly better-outfitted Micro Bus, which was painted green and started at about $2,365; and the deluxe Micro Bus, which came in red-and-black two-tone and listed for about $2,500. The deluxe model's body was one inch longer overall than the other models. From the start, VW also offered the camper version with fold-out bedding for four, a built-in table and cupboard, window curtains, and an opening roof-panel "transom."

All Transporters had two front doors, a pair of swing-open side doors, and a small tailgate. Intrusive front wheel arches hampered ingress through the front doors, and the tall engine box floor made it difficult to load cargo through the

Volkswagen gave the world a new kind of vehicle in 1950 when it introduced its Transporter, the first minivan. This rendering from an early brochure captures the essence of the vehicle. It was more than an efficient carrier of people. Tasteful two-tone colors and a roomy cabin brightened by a huge sunroof bespoke a sense of unhurried leisure. And with just 25 horsepower pulling 2,300 pounds of curb weight, unhurried it was.

small rear hatch. But by taking a couple of minutes to remove the middle and rear bench seats, the owner of a passenger model could have 170 cubic feet of cargo room at his or her disposal.

Tom McCahill, dean of american automotive journalists, tested a Kombi for the January 1955 issue of *Mechanix Illustrated*. "Uncle Tom" was astonished at its spaciousness. "It is as versatile as a steamship con man and twice as useful," he wrote. McCahill rationalized the Kombi's slothlike acceleration by explaining that it was a vehicle born and bred in Europe, where drivers presumably were accustomed to taking most of a day to drive up a mountain road. "It will climb anything but not fast," he said. "When the grade gets real grim the Kombi speed is not much better than a fast walk but it will get there."

Indeed, *Road & Track* clocked its '56 Micro Bus at a sleep-inducing 75 seconds 0-60 mph. That in fact was the test vehicle's top speed, and it actually took less time, 27 seconds, to cover a standing-start quarter-mile. Curiously, VW placed a sticker on the dashboard that read, "The allowable top speed of this vehicle is 50 miles per hour," though *R&T* noted that with a tailwind, a Micro Bus was perfectly capable of cruising at 70 mph on a level highway. The '56 model was rated at 36 horsepower at 3700 rpm and 56 pounds/feet of torque at 2000. The one tested by *R&T* weighed 2,300 pounds.

"The Micro Bus is very easy to drive, has wonderful visibility and easy steering requiring only 3.5 turns lock to lock for a 39-foot turning circle," *R&T* said. A tall center of gravity kept cornering speeds to a minimum, so "handling" wasn't much of an issue. The buslike driving position was deemed comfortable. Ride quality was firm for occupants of the front seat, which was directly above the front axle, but better in the other seats. From the start, Transporter campers were recognized as the unique vehicles they were. No other manufacturer offered such a versatile package as part of its regular lineup. Germany's Westfalia Werke did the majority of the factory conversions, with such companies as Dormobile, Devon, and Danbury performing aftermarket work as well. *Motor Trend* recognized these special properties as early as October 1956, when it tested a "Volkswagen Kamper." It wrote: "More a way of life than just another car, the VW bus, when completely equipped with the ingenious German-made Kamper kit, can open up new vistas of freedom (or escape) from a humdrum life."

So popular was the Transporter—demand was outstripping production two to one—that in 1956, VW opened a new factory in Hanover to built it. In 1960, the bus got real split front seats to create a narrow aisle that allowed movement though the interior, and front-seat riders began to enter and exit through the side door rather than climbing over those high wheel arches. By 1961, the 1200 engine had 40 horsepower and VW had some competition. Ford introduced the Econoline, a compact van based on the Falcon platform, and Chevrolet used its air-cooled rear-engine Corvair as the basis for the Greenbrier Sports Wagon.

Car Life magazine compared the VW to these newcomers in its September 1961 issue. It said the VW Station Wagon had far superior build quality than the others inside and out. The VW had better overall handling, too, though it and the Greenbrier, which used a similar swing-axle rear suspension, suffered directional instability in crosswinds. No rival had more-efficient fresh-air ventilation, but the editors noted that the VW's heating system was "virtually ineffectual... Hot air from the engine cooling fan must travel through long, uninsulated ducts before reaching the driver." The Transporter averaged 20 mpg, about three mpg more than the others and nearly double the average of full-size automobile station wagons of the day.

The VW weighed 2310 pounds, yet its 25.6-second time in the quarter-mile was only about a half-second slower than the Chevy's, which had 80 horsepower but weighed 3560 pounds. The 85-horsepower, 3230-pound Ford turned a 23.3-second quarter-mile. The editors did not list a 0-60 mph time for the VW because it would go no faster than 59 mph for them.

Volkswagen built the one-millionth Type 2 during 1962. Changes in specification were slow, but for '63, VW installed the 1500-series engine, which at its most-powerful, made 53 horsepower at 4200 rpm in the bus. And for '67, a dual-circuit braking system was introduced in which front and rear brakes were independently pressurized in case either hydraulic circuit failed. As production approached two million in 1967, VW had a redesigned station wagon ready. The new 1968 model was obviously a lineal descendent of the original, but also was clearly a more-modern design.

The second-generation bus was larger, sleeker, and more powerful, though it remained Beetle-based and even retained the 94.5-inch wheelbase. The body grew in length by nearly five inches, to 174 inches overall, and height was up by about one inch, but width, turning circle, and front track

VW called its van the Type 2 (the Beetle being the Type 1), but most knew it first as the Transporter. It was immediately popular with European tradespeople and commercial users, providing generous cargo space in a vehicle that was inexpensive to purchase and maintain. As this 1951 delivery van demonstrates, the driving position was decidedly buslike and devoid of frills. The flat-four air-cooled engine was taken directly from the Beetle. Mounting it in the tail put enough weight on the rear wheels to provide great all-weather traction, and with low gear ratios and 9.5-inches of ground clearance, the Transporter was more capable than most other vehicles over back roads and on hills. One drawback to the engine position was a rear door that was too small for loading large objects.

hardly changed; nearly three inches was added to the rear track, however.

Gone was the eight-window design, taking with it the charming available skylights. In its place was a body with three long windows on either side and a one-piece windshield that was 27-percent larger than the two-pane unit it replaced. Passenger versions dumped the double side doors in favor of an industry first: a single right-side sliding door. Exterior door hinges were gone, so there was less to catch wind and dirt. Sacrificed also was the widow's-peak nose of the first-generation; the new bus had a flatter brow with less character but stronger bumpers and better headlamps.

Interior volume with the rear seats removed expanded by about six cubic feet, fuel capacity was 15.8 gallons, up from 10.6, and curb weight increased by about 400 pounds, to 2723. Two passenger models were offered. The Kombi was now the base model and started at $2,211. The base Station Wagon cost $2,495 with seven seats, and $2,517 for the nine-seater.

The basic '68 Campmobile listed for just $2,110, but for an additional $655, buyers could purchase purpose-designed camping equipment that included bedding and curtains, plus an icebox, stove, and sink with a 4.5-gallon water supply. Adding a pop-up roof cost another $280. The pop-up roof section was much larger than before and was hinged at the front. For $1,075, buyers could get the camping gear, the pop top, and a custom tent that mated to the sliding-door opening. Commercial models included panel vans and pick-up trucks with base prices ranging from $2,295 to $2,455.

All second-generation Type 2 models used the 1600 engine (1,584cc, 96.6 cubic inches), here rated at 57 horsepower at 4400 rpm and 82 pounds/feet of torque at 3000. Horsepower was up over the first-generation, but so was curb weight, so the '68 models really weren't much faster than the last of the '67s. Zero-60 mph still took about 37 seconds and top speed remained 65 mph. VW calculated fuel consumption with the vehicle traveling at 75 percent of top speed, which worked out to 23 mpg at 53 mph. At 65 mph, where most real-world buses cruised—weather and road conditions permitting—owners saw about 19 mpg.

A four-speed manual with a 5.37:1 final drive ratio remained the sole transmission. Eliminating the wheel-hub reduction gears shed some unsprung weight and along with the new double-jointed rear axle, ball-joint front suspension, and wider track, improved both ride and handling. Some reviewers went so far as to call it carlike.

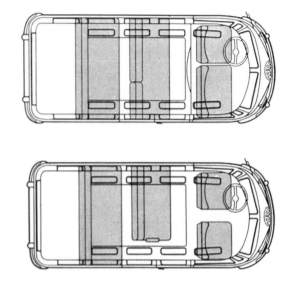

Safety features included a deep dish steering wheel—now mounted at a less buslike angle—a new padded dashboard, nonreflecting interior surfaces, safety belts for each seat, plus shoulder belts for all outboard positions.

Sales continued strong. The two-millionth Type 2 left Hanover in 1968. The bus had gained acceptance among suburban families, car poolers, and of course, counterculture types. VW Station Wagons had long been favorites of the young and young-at-heart, and "hippy vans" painted up in psychedelic designs were a fixture of the '60s. As *Road Test* magazine explained in its review of a 1970 VW Station Wagon, "[E]scape via a bus is far less expensive and more promising in terms of birds and bees than being encumbered with a bucket-seated, thirsty-engine GTO or Scat-Pack Dodge. Admittedly, however, flower symbols and curtained windows seem to attract the police as readily as racing stripes."

Braking got a boost for '71 with the introduction of front discs and a 20-percent increase in the lining thickness of the rear drums. VW also installed a regulator in the rear brake circuit that functioned like an early anti-lock system to help prevent premature wheel locking in hard stops. Wheel width also increased by half-an-inch, to 5.5 inches.

By 1971, Detroit had responded to the VW bus with a new crop of competitors. Unlike the com-

(continued)

The Transporter used the Beetle's 94.5-inch wheelbase, chassis, and basic running gear, though it had a wider track and a body that was longer by 8.5 inches. VW's 1959 U.S. model lineup included the base $1,955 Kombi, the $2,120 Microbus, and the $2,576 Deluxe Microbus (opposite top). Costing $2,737, the Deluxe Camper (opposite bottom) was VW's most-expensive vehicle, but no other manufacturer offered anything like it. It could sleep four, had plenty of cupboards, two folding tables, and a sink with a 23-gallon water supply. A two-burner propane stove and the colorful awning "porch" were optional accessories. All Transporters came with two swing-open side doors. This page: Passenger versions could carry up to nine on three rows of bench seats. Starting in 1960, buyers could order split front seating that provided a narrow passageway to the rear.

The Volkswagen Camper
with Westfalia De Luxe equipment

is a kitchen, bedroom and living-room with skylight, curtains, wall-lights and paneled walls. Comforts include: two upholstered benches that convert into a double-bed, beds for 2 children on driver's seat, wardrobe with full-length mirror, plenty of cupboard space, luggage net and outside roof rack. Convenient kitchen washroom cabinet connected to water supply in 23 gal, polyethylene tank under seat. Two folding tables. Cupboard with ice-box, portable chemical toilet and two-ring cooker are extras. Striped awning when stretched along one side of the car forms a porch.

Ask your dealer for catalog, giving full details and measurements.

Adopting engine improvements given the Beetle, Transporters climbed to 30 horsepower for '52, to 36 for '54, and to 40 for '61. This page and opposite top row: By the time this alluring blue and white 1963 Microbus was built, an optional 1.5-liter rated at 50 horsepower was available. With 0-60 mph times of more than 20 seconds, however, its forte was not performance. Instead, it harbored a host of other charms, foremost among them skylight windows and a roll-back sunroof that created the airiest cabin in motoring. Rear passengers had it best; front-seat occupants had to climb over the wheelhousings to get in or out, and sat above the front axle, where the ride was harshest. This Deluxe Station Wagon model started at $2,665 and displays the flat directional signal lamps that replaced the "rams horn" fixtures for '63.

Above and left: *The '67 bus gained the 1.5-liter engine as standard; it made 53 horsepower. This is the Kombi, the base passenger model, which retailed for $2,150. New for all models was a dual-circuit braking system in which front and rear brakes were independently pressurized in case either hydraulic circuit failed. Compared to American competitors that had cropped up, the Transporter had superior fuel economy, handling, and build quality. But it was slower and still relied on ineffectual convection heating. As production approached two million during 1967, VW prepared to draw the curtain on its first-generation Transporters.*

pact-car based vans that Ford and Chevy offered in the early 1960s, these were true trucks with front-mounted engines and optional V-8s that allowed them to pull heavy trailers. They dwarfed the VW in size and in price. The new Chevrolet Beauville Sportvan, for example, was nearly 17 feet long, had a 250-horsepower 350-cubic-inch V-8, weighed 4,600 pounds, and cost $4,775. A '71 VW Station Wagon with the optional radio and sliding steel sunroof listed for $3,164 and weighed 2,900 pounds.

In its April 1971 issue, *Motor Trend* compared a VW bus against just such a Sportvan, plus a Dodge Royal Sportsman B300, and a Ford Chateau Club Wagon. "The Volkswagen Station Wagon came out best in terms of size, finish, quality and ease of handling," the magazine said. "But, for sheer load space, the VW couldn't hope to match the Ford, Dodge or Chevy Vans. VW was also at a distinct power disadvantage, with an engine less than one-third the size of the optional V-8s available in the Detroit-made vans. For everyday driving, though, our staff still preferred the VW van over the rest of the group." So did many buyers, enabling Type 2 production to hit the three-million mark during 1971.

VW then began a four-year advance on the powertrain front. The 1972 bus gained the 1700-series engine from the 411 passenger car. It had 72 horsepower and cut 0-60 mph times to a more-acceptable 22 seconds. Quarter-mile times fell to 23 seconds, and official top speed increased to 75 mph.

For '73, VW offered the bus's first optional automatic transmission, a three-speed unit that cost $235. It was thoughtfully matched to the 1700 engine, maintaining each gear until well up in the rev range and downshifting promptly for good passing response. At about 23.6 seconds 0-60 mph, overall acceleration was little different from that of the stick shift. The automatic did not have an overdrive fourth gear, but its 4.45:1 final-drive ratio allowed the engine to turn at about the same rpm on the highway as the 5.37:1 ratio of the manual transmission. Fuel economy was not as good with the automatic, however, and could dip to around 16-17 mph.

The automatic arrived the same year VW stopped listing gross horsepower ratings and, like many manufacturers, switched to net ratings. Gross ratings were taken under optimum laboratory conditions. Net ratings were designed to reflect output with the engine installed in the vehicle and with power-sapping accessories and drive belts in place. Thus the 1700 was rerated at 63 horsepower

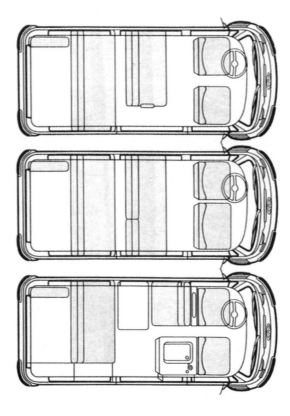

at 4800 rpm with manual transmission and at 59 at 4200 with automatic. Automatic-transmission models showed more torque, though, 83 pounds/feet to 81, at the same 3200 rpm, which helped account for their similar acceleration.

The bus regained some of the lost power for 1974. It borrowed the 1.8-liter boxer from the 412 passenger car range and also added electronic fuel injection. Horsepower was now 67, and a manual-transmission van could run 0-60 mph in 20 seconds flat. The 20-second barrier fell in 1976, when the bus borrowed yet another engine, this time the 2.0-liter flat-four from the Porsche 914 sports car. Horsepower remained 67 at 4200 rpm, but torque climbed to a relatively robust 101 pounds/feet at 3000. Even with automatic, VW buses could now run 0-60 mph in 19.9 seconds.

Evolution of the second-generation bus slowed dramatically after this. About the only major change was in price, which by 1979, had climbed to $7,595 for the seven-seat model. Driven by the escalation of the German currency, price increases were helping accelerate a sales decline that had been in progress for several years. VW sold 23,322 buses in the U.S. in 1978, but only 15,990 in 1979.

VW launched the second-generation station wagon for 1968. It retained the Beetle-based wheelbase and chassis, but its body was five inches longer than the original Type 2 and had more interior volume. Curb weights were up by about 400 pounds. Gone was the distinctive widow's peak nose and two-piece windshield, sacrificed in the name of improved frontal crash protection and better visibility. Side windows were fewer and larger, and there was an industry-first sliding side door. The steering wheel was mounted as a less buslike angle, but the driver's station was still businesslike. Power came from VW's air-cooled 1600 flat-four, still mounted in the tail and here rated at 57 horsepower. A four-speed manual was the only transmission. Drawings on this page show the standard seven-passenger seating (top), optional eight-passenger seating (middle), and the layout of the Campmobile, which seated five and slept four. The Titian Red/Cloud White Station Wagon pictured is a 1970 nine-passenger model, which retailed for $2,772.

Worldwide, however, the VW bus was still outselling all competitors and the company knew it had to update the design to protect its market share. Wolfsburg began to study the next-generation bus, considering a dozen proposed configurations, from front-engine/front-wheel drive to front-engine/rear-drive to mid-engine/rear-drive. In the end, it decided the original rear-engine/rear-drive layout would provide the most-efficient packaging and the best traction. Thus was the layout of the third-generation bus decided. It debuted for 1980, called the Transporter in Europe and the Vanagon in the U.S.

Other than the powertrain arrangement, the Vanagon was a clean-sheet design. It had a new platform, fresh sheetmetal, and a redesigned interior. Wheelbase was stretched 2.4 inches, to 96.8, and the body shell was widened by 3.3 inches. The platform's floor was lowered by 2.4 inches, the spare tire moved to beneath the nose on a drop-down cradle, and the fuel tank—now 16 gallons—was relocated to under the front seats. (Oil could be checked and filled from behind the hinged rear license plate cover.)

The suspension was completely new and qualified as a truly all-independent design. In front, trailing arms and torsion bars were discarded in favor of unequal-length A-arms, variable-rate coil springs, tube shocks, and an anti-roll bar. In back, the torsion bars were banished and replaced by a semi-trailing-arm design with progressive-rate coil springs and tube shocks. The track was wider by 6.9 inches in front and 4.5 inches in the rear.

As before, overseas markets were offered a variety of body styles, including commercial vans and pickup trucks, but Americans got only seven- and nine-seat passenger models, a stripper Kombi with just two front seats, and the Westfalia Camper.

About half of all VW vans were purchased for personal use, so designers concentrated on making the Vanagon user-friendly inside and out. Overall, there was a 15-percent increase in interior volume. The center aisle between the front seats was wider by 15 percent. The rear floor over the engine box was lowered 7.9 inches, increasing luggage space in the rearmost compartment by 40 percent, to 36.6 cubic feet. The sliding side door was bigger, the rear hatch increased in size by a full 75 percent, and the rear window was enlarged by 50 percent. Total glass area was up by 22 percent.

The interior featured upscale trim, full carpeting, and door map pockets. The angle of the steering wheel was a little less buslike than before, and the dashboard was as up to date as in most passenger cars. Heating and fresh-air ventilation were as good as ever with the Vanagon underway, but VW still didn't furnish a fan as standard; buyers had to pay extra for a three-speed blower. A another wise option was the gasoline-fired auxiliary heater, which cost $370.

The body contours were actually less rounded than before, though the windshield had more rake. On the safety front, three inches of sheetmetal had been added ahead of the front wheels to serve as a crush zone. Side-door beams and structural reinforcements satisfied all U.S. safety standards for cars, even though the Vanagon didn't have to meet them because it was classified a truck.

Though the new nose had what looked like a black plastic grille, the Vanagon was the only German-built VW product to retain an air-cooled engine. In the U.S., the only engine was again the all-alloy 2.0-liter horizontally opposed four with electronic fuel injection. It remained at 67 horsepower and 101 pounds/feet of torque. The standard four-speed manual transmission had a final-drive ratio of 4.57:1, but for the first time it had an 0.88:1 overdrive top gear. A three-speed automatic was optional at about $350 and had a 4.09:1 final drive. With curb weights up by about 250 pounds, to around 3,300 pounds for the basic Vanagon, acceleration was still not a strong suit.

Road & Track tried a four-speed seven seater, which had a test weight of 3,510 pounds, and clocked it at 21.2 seconds 0-60 mph and at 21.5 seconds at 60.5 mph in the quarter-mile. Top speed was 88 mph. "Clearly, this is not acceleration that will elicit gasps of glee," *R&T* admitted, "but it does permit the Vanagon to keep up with everyday, around-town traffic." *Car and Driver* wrung out a 17.9-second 0-60 mph time, turning 20.7 seconds at 63 mph in the quarter, but its top speed was only 75 mph. Fuel economy averaged about 17 mpg in most tests.

Nobody ever purchased a VW van for its power and that wasn't going to change with the Vanagon. But sensitive drivers would be rewarded by the Vanagon's road manners. Unladened weight distribution was now 50/50 and though the breadbox-on-wheels was still top heavy, the new suspension and wider track allowed it to circle the skidpad at a carlike 0.79 lateral g forces, compared to the previous bus's 0.63 g's. Resistance to crosswinds was better than ever, but much attention was again required of the driver in gusty conditions. The Vanagon's ride was firm, but overall control was

(continued)

Though cargo versions were available (opposite bottom right), Americans ordered few of them. By far, the most-popular alternative to the standard passenger Station Wagon was the Campmobile (other photos). Modified by German outfitter Westfalia and available as a regular-production model, it was a unique blend of compact van and mobile home. It used the standard Station Wagon chassis and mechanicals, but added a pop-top double-bed sleeper and a rear bench that folded down to form a smaller mattress. There was a zippered screen in the fiberglass and canvass pop top. An ice box and sink, water tank and pump, dinette table, linen closet, louvered side windows, and wood panelled ceiling and walls were standard. Pictured is a 1979 model, which listed for nearly $8,000. Powertrain additions during the second-generation model's 12-year lifespan included an optional three-speed automatic transmission in 1973 and several engine advances culminating in 1976 with adoption of the 2.0-liter flat-four from the Porsche 914 sports car.

Debuting for 1980, the third-generation bus was renamed the Vanagon (top left). It retained an air-cooled rear-engine layout, but had a larger platform not shared with any other VW. Interior volume increased by 15 percent and the dashboard was slightly more carlike. For 1983, the 2.0-liter boxer got water cooling (left) and the addition of a radiator behind the new front grille (above) allowed VW to fit a real heater.

The Camper was again a desirable model (top left). For '86, all Vanagons got a 2.1-liter engine and horizontal headlamps, while a Syncro model with permanently engaged four-wheel drive was introduced. By 1989, when this plush $19,000 Wolfsburg Limited Edition was offered (above and top right), Vanagon sales were taking a beating at the hands of Chrysler's passenger-car based front-wheel-drive minivans. VW shelved the Vanagon after the 1991 model year.

far superior to that of domestic vans, which still used solid rear axles.

"Once you get used to being seated a couple of stories above the pavement, you can slice through twisty roads with abandon," *Car and Driver* said in its first test of the new Vanagon. "Its steering is amply quick, and even has plenty of road feel and a strong sense of center. Bumps, even in the middle of corners, don't have a prayer of deflecting the Vanagon off course. But like many a German car, it thrums its way across tar strips and surface imperfections."

All this goodness came at a price. Vanagons started at around $9,500 for 1980, and with options such as the $290 AM/FM cassette system and auxiliary heater, the cost of a VW bus could top $10,200. Most reviewers found it worth the money, however.

"All in all, the Vanagon is a major improvement over its predecessors and, in our opinion, maintains VW's position as the manufacturer of the world's leading van," said *Road & Track*.

Motor Trend liked the new Vanagon so much it named it 1980 Truck of the Year. "The Vanagon is one of the best utilitarian vehicles ever to take to the highway," the editors said. "Its efficient use of space, attention to ride comfort and sedan-like handling position it as the new high mark the industry must strive to equal."

"Some things, it's nice to see, just never change," concluded *Car and Driver*. "The VW bus stood apart from the crowd when the children of the Sixties were dropping out, and it's still a vehicle for the alternative-minded now that they've dropped back in. Of course, these days the VW bus's special attractiveness results from engineering refinement rather than counterculture appeal."

Many things were changing, however. Chrysler was already at work on its front-engine/front-drive minivans that as the Dodge Caravan and Plymouth Voyager would revolutionize the market Volkswagen pioneered. As those rivals were under development, Volkswagen bolstered the Vanagon with a quieter, quicker, and more-fuel efficient powerplant. Introduced during 1983 was the Wasserboxer, which was the German way of saying that the Vanagon's flat-four had gotten water cooling.

Added to engine were passages for cylinder heads and piston sleeves through which liquid now flowed. Below the false "grille" was a genuine one and behind it was a radiator. Coolant circulating from the radiator to the engine passed through a real heater beneath the dash and another option-

al unit under the rear seat, finally providing a VW van with bona fide cold-weather comfort.

The new water jackets further isolated engine noise, and while the engineers were at it, they refined the boxer's pistons, valves, camshaft, and fuel-injection system and gave it a higher compression ratio—8.6:1 to the year before's 7.3:1. Displacement actually decreased by 55ccs, but horsepower increased by 15, to 82 at 4800. Torque grew by five pounds/feet, to 106, and now peaked at 2600 rpm, 400 rpm sooner than before. Zero-60 mph times fell into the low-18-second range, and overall fuel economy climbed to around 19 mph. The downside was a price that kept escalating, with the average passenger Vanagon now listing for around $12,250. It was still worth paying, though, according to the professional testers.

"In our initial Vanagon road test...we said that the VW van 'is clearly the leader in technological development in its class,'" *Road & Track* asserted in its May 1983 report on the waterboxer. "That's still true, as we discovered driving the standard shift and automatic Wasserboxers. The new engine's power, flexibility, economy and quietness are delightful and give the VW van a level of performance that is commensurate with its design."

This would be the final time most Americans would agree that Volkswagen could claim a clear design advantage in the small-van field. Vanagon sales had enjoyed a modest increase in '83, climbing to 15,193 from 12,847 the previous year, and sales advanced again in '84, to an all-time high of 17,985. But the Chrysler minivans, which were built on the company's front-drive K-car platform and were much more carlike than the larger Vanagon, took the market by storm from their launch in early 1984. Ford and Chevy weighed in for 1985 with the more conventional truck-based front-engine/rear-drive Aerostar and Astro, respectively. And the Japanese were now aboard with odd little home-market transplants. But it was the Caravan and Voyager that dominated, with combined sales of more than 160,000 in 1985, their first full year. Vanagon sales for '85 fell to 16,803.

VW responded by fortifying its '86 model with a larger waterboxer and high-tech traction-enhancing all-wheel drive option. Engine displacement grew to 2.1 liters (2,109cc, 129 cubic inches), compression rose to 9.0:1, and horsepower increased by 16 percent, to 95 at 4800. Torque jumped to 117 pounds/feet at 3200 rpm. A new grille with rectangular headlamps dressed up the nose, and power windows, central locking, and heated power mirrors were new options.

VW exchanged the time honored rear-engine/rear-drive layout for a modern front-engine/front-wheel-drive arrangement with introduction of the 1993 EuroVan. Wheelbase of this fourth-generation bus was 115 inches, a full 18 inches longer than that of the Vanagon. Its body was 6.6 inches longer and had chiseled contours with a pronounced nose. It still had a sliding right-side door, but the front doors were now aft of the wheel housings for easier entry and exit and, with no engine to clear, the rear hatch opened onto a bumper-level floor. It had a revised suspension and front-disc brakes; anti-lock brakes—a $853 option—were offered for the first time. With base prices in the $16,000-$22,000 range, the EuroVan was priced competitively against American rivals, but it retained too strong a German flavor to be much of a sales threat.

The 1986 Vanagon Syncro was the first all-wheel-drive passenger van sold in the U.S. It was available as a passenger model or a Camper. Its all-wheel-drive system was less-complicated than the center-differential setup VW was offering in Europe on its Quattro passenger car. Under normal driving conditions, the Syncro sent 95 percent of the engine's power through the rear wheels. But power was fed to the front wheels whenever the speed differential between the front and rear wheels exceeded six percent—meaning rear-wheel traction was being lost. The speed differential acted upon a gooey silicon fluid trapped in a viscous coupling integrated into the front-axle differential. Interconnected plates within the case were engaged by the fluid action and in turn transferred power to the front axles.

The amount of power transferred depended on road conditions and was infinitely variable, continuous, and undetectable by the driver. For maximum traction, an optional locking rear differential could be engaged via a dashboard knob. Syncro models rode 1.2 inches higher than two-wheel-drive Vanagons, had about one additional inch of suspension travel, and rode on 205/70R14 tires, two sizes wider than on regular Vanagons. Syncro models were available only with manual transmission, but they got a "creeper" 6.0:1 low gear, for five forward speeds. VW fitted Syncro models with an 18.4-gallon fuel tank, but mounted it in back, nestled around the gearbox. The spare tire also moved to a new aft location.

The Syncro was marketed not as a off-road vehicle but an all-weather van. VW demonstrated the system's mechanical reliability by driving a Vanagon Syncro around the world, covering 27,000 miles in a record 131 days in conditions that ranged from minus 20 degrees Fahrenheit in Canada to a roasting 123 degrees in Australia.

Though Syncro hardware, which included a front skid plate, added 330 pounds to the 3,270-pound Vanagon or 3,670-pound Camper, it did not seriously affect acceleration. *Car and Driver* tested a Camper Syncro, which tipped the scales at 4000 pounds, and recorded a respectable 0-60 mph time of 18.3 seconds. The feature wasn't cheap, however. It cost $2,175. Vanagons now started at $13,140 and a Camper Syncro listed for $19,335. Popular options were air conditioning ($990) and an AM/FM cassette radio ($575).

Syncros accounted for only small fraction of Vanagon sales, which continued to shrink in the U.S. The Vanagon was doing well in other markets and each day, the Hanover factory turned out near-

ly 500 of all types to satisfy worldwide demand. In 1986, VW built its six-millionth van. In the U.S. that year, Vanagon sales sunk to 12,669. The country was entranced by the Chrysler brands, which sold over 220,000 units for '86 and would soon be averaging 500,000 or more annually. Vanagon sales slumped to 10,656 for '87, then to 5,416 for '88, and there they hovered for the balance of the decade.

As the Vanagon played out its string, VW gave it some minor exterior styling changes and introduced plush Wolfsburg and Carat editions. It even briefly offered an inline four-cylinder 1.6-liter diesel engine, but with only 48 horsepower, it wasn't popular. VW didn't even offer a Vanagon for the 1992 model year; dealers had enough left-over 1991 versions. Clearly something different was needed. It came in April 1992 as a fourth-generation design with yet another new name and an entirely new powertrain layout.

The 1993 EuroVan exchanged the time-honored rear-engine/rear-drive configuration for front-engine/front-wheel drive. VW pitched it not as a "minivan" rival to the Chrysler brands, but as a "midsize" van capable of taking on the Astro and Aerostar. Indeed, with a wheelbase of 115 inches and an overall length of 186.6, it was larger than the Vanagon. And it looked different. But the big news was the new powertrain.

The only engine offered in U.S.-market EuroVans was a 2.5-liter overhead-cam inline five-cylinder. It made 109 horsepower at 4500 rpm and 140 pounds/feet of torque at a low 2200 rpm. The new five-cylinder drove the front wheels through a standard five-speed manual transaxle or an optional four-speed automatic. Base curb weight was 3,806 pounds, about 340 more than the comparable Vanagon.

Acceleration was a little better than that of the last Vanagons, whose 2.1-liter boxer had ended its run at 90 horsepower. But a EuroVan still wouldn't zip in and out of traffic or pass on a two-lane road without a lot of advanced planning. And maintaining speed on a long uphill grade still required downshifting from fifth gear to third.

EuroVan's body was sleeker than the Vanagon's, with a longer nose and chiseled contours. It could not be called handsome, but then VW's vans had lost a big chunk of charm with each succeeding redesign. None was more spacious that the EuroVan, however. Few vans were.

VW's desire to maximize interior volume led to a new, more-compact suspension. In front was a double-wishbone design that reverted to torsion bars instead of coil springs. In back was a semi-

EuroVans offered commodious accommodations for up to seven and, with the rear seats removed, a full 201 cubic feet of cargo space. The plethora of headrests interfered with the view aft, however. The dashboard and driving position were the best yet of any VW van, but while rivals were getting driver- and passenger-side air bags, the EuroVan offered neither. The only engine in U.S.-market models was a 2.5-liter overhead-cam inline five cylinder (opposite lower right), which was mounted transversely. It had 109 horsepower, but couldn't move the 3,800-pound EuroVan with much verve. Sales languished, and VW of America didn't introduce a 1994 model. For 1995, it offered just a camper version (above). This one was based on a 130.7-inch wheelbase model available in Europe, but its camper conversion work was done in the U.S. by the American firm, Winnebago.

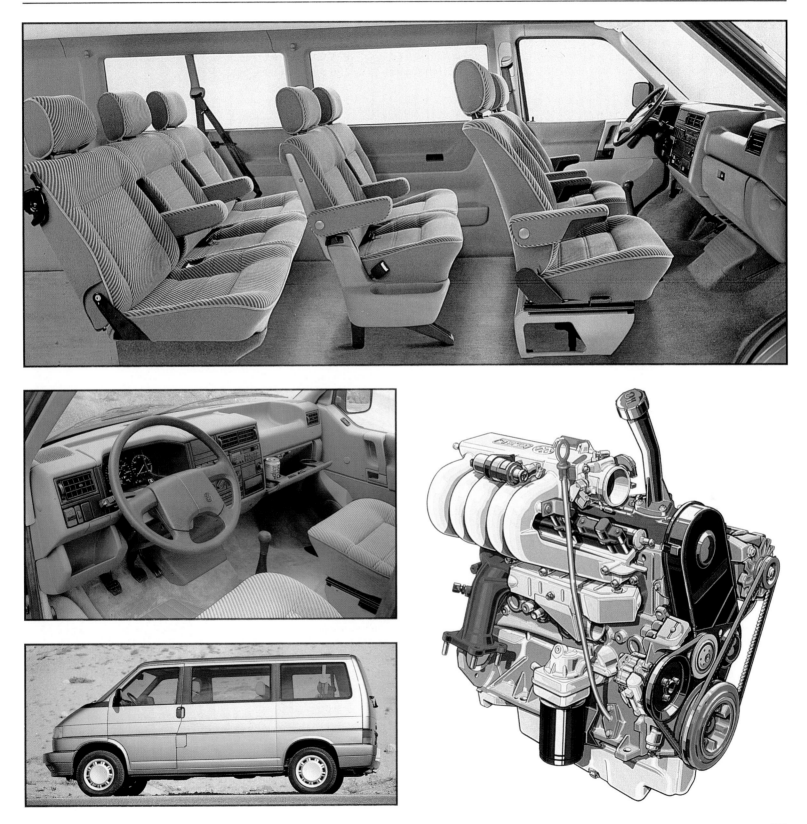

trailing arm and coil-spring setup. In width and height, the EuroVan was within fractions of an inch of the Vanagon, but managed to furnish a full 201 cubic feet of space with the rear seats removed. It could swallow a 4x8 sheet of plywood. Buyers had to go to a full-size domestic van to equal such capacity. The longer wheelbase took the front doors off the wheel arches, so it was easier to climb into the front buckets than before, but getting into or out of a EuroVan still was not as easy as in most rival minvians. Once aboard, the cabin was more luxurious than ever and the seats were more supportive, but the interior was still teutonically austere compared with that of competitors.

EuroVan's German character also came through in a suspension that noticed most every pavement flaw but provided a relatively flat ride and fine overall control. Noise from engine and road were quite evident, though wind rush at highway speeds was surprisingly low.

Gauges and controls were unobstructed, but the additional controls necessitated by the standard front and rear air conditioning on uplevel models made for a confusing array of climate buttons, levers, and dials. Compared to the carlike driving positions of rival minivans, EuroVan's steering wheel was still fixed at a buslike horizontal angle. Visibility was nearly panoramic, though as many as five headrests could be visible through the rearview mirror, confusing the view aft.

Braking was by ventilated front discs and rear drums, with an anti-lock system—unavailable on Vanagon—a new option. A driver-side air bag, which had become standard on most other minivans by 1993, was not available, however.

The only EuroVan model offered in the U.S. was the seven-seat passenger version. The Camper was superseded by an optional Weekender Package that included a pop-up roof with an integral double bed plus a refrigerated cooler and window curtains and screens. The usual assortment of commercial and utility models, as well as a 130.7-inch wheelbase camper, were offered in other markets.

Transporter and Vanagon loyalists could see that EuroVan was true to traditional VW-van virtues of lots of room and utility in a manageably sized package. But the world had changed. High style, carlike comfort, and sport-sedan acceleration were the fashion now. For once, EuroVan prices were in line with rivals, starting in the mid $16,000s to about $22,000, though options such as automatic transmission ($895) anti-lock brakes ($853), power windows and locks, and cruise control ($765) could push up the price. The Weekender Package was a hefty $2,530.

The American public was unenthusiastic. EuroVan sales in the U.S. totaled just 5,634 for 1993. VW didn't formally introduce a 1994 EuroVan, instead selling off some 4,675 leftover '93 models. And VW didn't even offer a EuroVan at all in the U.S. for 1995, though buyers could order a version of the 130.7-inch wheelbase camper. A small number of these campers were built with the help of the U.S. firm, Winnebago Industries Inc. of Forest City, Iowa. The $30,000 camper, which included sleeping accommodations for four, plus the usual cooking and storage equipment, was sold through an even smaller number of Volkswagen dealers who had signed up for this temporary venture.

Again, VW was at a crossroads. It had produced the Sharan, a sleek front-wheel-drive minivan for Europe in cooperation with Ford. Ford's version was called the Galaxy and the vehicle was built by Auto Europa, a jointly owned manufacturing company near Lisbon, Portugal. Even though the Sharan could be had with VW's fine VR6 engine, the five-to-seven-passenger people mover was designed expressly and exclusively for the European market.

When it pulled up stakes on the EuroVan in the U.S., VW said it would "relaunch" the vehicle as a 1996 model with the VR6 engine and standard dual air bags. Despite word that a redesign was indeed underway, no minivan was part of the U.S. lineup VW introduced for 1996.

The minivan market in America is the world's largest. Each year, 17 different nameplates slice up a lucrative 1.3-million-unit pie. But in a category of vehicle that it invented—one in which it had stood alone, inspiring imitators and generating a cult following—VW was without an entry.

The four generations of VW station wagons spanned a period in which the German company had a vehicle unique in the world of motoring, to a day in which the minivans it inspired were a fixture of American life. Ironically, for a time in the mid 1990s, Volkswagen did not offer a U.S. model in the very market segment it had created. Developed in conjunction with Ford of Europe and introduced in 1995, the Volkswagen Sharan (opposite lower right) was a sleek and modern front-drive compact van, but it was not for sale in America. Instead, VW planned to rework the EuroVan, fitting it with dual air bags and the capable VR6 six-cylinder engine for relaunch in the U.S. after 1996. It's shown here undergoing testing (opposite lower left).

Karmann-Ghia: The Volkswagen With Style

A sporty coupe from Volkswagen, the company that made only people's cars? An automobile in which appearance took precedence over function? From VW? In the 1950s? It couldn't happen...

But it did. Though it made little obvious marketing sense, VW sprung on the world a sinuously shaped coupe called the Karmann-Ghia, and between 1955 and 1974, when the last cars were delivered to the U.S., 387,975 had been built. They used the same platform as the Beetle, the same mechanicals, even made the same noises. But they had something no VW had ever had: style.

The car's name summarizes a very complicated pedigree. VW in the early '50s was a rapidly growing West German carmaker. Karmann was a long-established West German coachbuilder and already was building Beetle convertibles. Ghia was a top Italian styling house. Added to this alliance was an American connection—one that some Europeans are reluctant to admit even today—and the result was an unlikely recipe for success.

The story starts with Mario Boano and Luigi Segre of Carrozzeria Ghia. The Turin coachbuilders had done some confidential work for VW, suggesting (mostly ignored) refinements in Beetle styling. VW didn't seem to like any of the various Beetle proposals put forth in Germany by Dr. Wilhelm Karmann, either, and an increasingly discouraged Karmann approached Ghia for inspiration.

Gian Paolo Boano, Mario Boano's son, had recently bought a Beetle in Paris and driven it to Turin. The Ghia craftsmen removed the conventional two-door body, and within five months had fashioned a new coupe bodyshell.

The prototype was transported to Karmann's factory in Osnabruck where, on November 16, 1953, it was examined by VW executives, including top man Heinz Nordhoff. The VW people were intrigued, and wanted to know more, especially about the styling.

Ghia was happy to take credit for the shape, and while the true details of its origins are lost to history, it seems there was much of American designer Virgil Exner in it. Exner had established a distinguished track record as a stylist with Pontiac and at the Raymond Loewy Studio, where he headed the Studebaker account. In 1950, Exner came to Chrysler, first working in the advanced design studio, and then in 1953, taking over as the automaker's styling director.

Shortly after arriving at Chrysler, Exner had approached Ghia about producing prototypes, show cars, and design studies to spice up the image of Detroit's third-largest automaker. Ghia agreed, and went on to build several show cars and prototypes in Italy under Exner's direction. The first of these was the Chrysler K-310 of 1952 (K for Chrysler President Kaufmann T. Keller, the number for a theoretical 310-horsepower V-8). The K-310 begat the Chrysler/Ghia D'Elegance of 1953. Built on a 115-inch wheelbase, the sleek D'Elegance had a graceful rear-roof pillar treatment and a prominent lower-body line that swept into a rear-fender bulge. The Ghia De Soto Adventurer, which Exner himself used as a road car for three years, was a development on the same theme.

Although Chrysler commissioned a run of 40 D'Elegance coupes, the effects of the Korean War pared this back to 25 cars, which left Ghia with unused capacity and its designers with what they loved most—time to think. The result was the coupe prototype on the VW Beetle platform. It looked a lot like the D'Elegance scaled down to fit the Beetle's wheelbase and track. Whether it was a copy of Exner's D'Elegance concept is less certain. Some historians believe Ghia was simply applying similar themes to two different projects. Nonetheless, the cars had obvious similarities, particularly the general proportions of the greenhouse, the lower-body line and rear fender bulge, and the character of the C-pillars. Ghia added two front "nostril" grilles for effect.

Recognizing the pretty little Ghia coupe as a way to expand the VW line without much effort, Nordhoff gave the project thumbs-up and turned the job of production over to Karmann.

Complete Beetle platforms were shipped from Wolfsburg to Osnabruck, where Karmann made the bodies, and painted, trimmed, and completed the cars before feeding them into Volkswagen's normal distribution system.

(continued)

Volkswagen furnished the Beetle platform and powertrain, Italian design house Ghia provided the styling, and German coachbuilder Karmann did the assembly. The resulting Karmann-Ghia coupe and convertible blended show-car looks with reliable VW mechanicals. Volkswagen never suggested it was a fast automobile, or even one that handled particularly well. But the Karmann-Ghia did give its owners a dash of sports-car spirit at a VW price, and that was enough to sell nearly 400,000 of them from 1955 to 1974. This is a 1971 model.

Mystery blankets the origins of the Karmann-Ghia's styling. Ghia collaborated with Chrysler on the 1953 Chrysler/Ghia D'Elegance (right). Its visual similarity to the smaller VW-based coupe is obvious. Shown above and on the opposite page is a 1958 Karmann-Ghia. Like all Karmann-Ghias, it used the Beetle's 94.5-inch wheelbase chassis and air-cooled flat four. This year's 36-horsepower 1,131cc boxer gave a top speed of around 75 mph, slightly higher than the less-aerodynamic Bug. The dashboard was fancier than the Beetle's, befitting the $2,445 starting price—nearly $1,000 higher than that of a Bug.

Changes from the Beetle's underpinnings and powertrain were minimal. The chassis side rails were widened to accommodate the body, which at 64.2 inches, was four inches wider than the Bug's, and a front anti-sway bar was added to the suspension. The angle of the steering column was changed, there were different springs and dampers, and the gearshift lever was shortened.

Under the rear engine cover was the standard VW boxer, rated at the same 36 horsepower as in the Beetle, though minor relocation of components in the engine bay was necessary to get it to fit under the coupe's lower bodywork.

Suggestions for a name included San Remo, Corona, and Ascona. But VW finally called it the Karmann-Ghia, making a selling point of those responsible for the manufacture and styling.

Launched in 1955 in Europe and the following year in the U.S., this clearly was a different type of VW, and it soon generated its own clientele. The bodywork of course was the big draw. The coupe was three inches longer than the Beetle, but nearly seven inches lower. Design-house style touches included curved glass all around in a day when that was rare, frameless one-piece door glass, and tastefully applied chrome trim.

Was it a beautiful car? Was it even a pretty one? Some pundits damned it with faint praise, describing it as "ideal for the ladies." At the extreme, a few asked if it was the most attractive car in the world.

With a curb weight of around 1,750 pounds, the Karmann-Ghia coupe was about 150 pounds heavier than a Beetle sedan. Part of the additional weight came from the added width of the Karmann's body, which gave it nearly six more inches of front hip room than the Beetle. Despite the lower roofline, front head room was more than adequate for tall people. The front seats were wide and well padded, but being a true 2+2, the Karmann-Ghia had to make do with a nominal two-place rear seat—really not much more than a padded cushion just 41 inches across. It did fold down into a cargo platform and, combined with a seven-cubic-foot forward luggage bay, gave the coupe more carrying capacity than the contemporary Beetle sedan.

The dashboard used Beetle switchgear, but was more stylish and mounted a huge clock next to the speedometer (a fuel gauge wasn't added until 1958). A floor lever controlled the heater, which didn't warm the car on cold days any better than did its sister system in the Beetle. Fresh-air ventilation was inferior to that of the Bug because the coupe lacked vent windows.

Some Karmann-Ghia fans argued that build quality was even better than that of the Beetle because Karmann didn't have to churn out the cars as quickly as VW had to pump out Beetles. Suffice it to say that neither was matched by anything else in the price class, though Karmann-Ghias did rust more quickly than Beetles. This was because Karmann lacked the equipment to stamp out large body panels and instead fashioned certain areas of the body with lots of smaller panels and the resulting joints and seams were susceptible to corrosion.

As for the Karmann-Ghia's performance, VW insisted that it mirror that of the humble Beetle; some sources say the company didn't want to be goaded into comparisons with genuine sports cars. Indeed, one Karmann-Ghia ad pictured a coupe adorned with stripes and numbers on the doors, as if poised to race. "You'd lose." said the tag line. "The racy-looking car in the picture would have trouble beating a Volkswagen. Because it is a Volkswagen."

Nonetheless, the Karmann-Ghia had a much smaller frontal area than the Beetle, and the originals could hit a top speed of around 72 mph, maybe 10 mph higher than the sedan. Acceleration was no faster: Both cars could consume up to 36 seconds reaching 60 mph from a stop, and the transmission shifted with same rubberiness through the gears. But both had great straight-line traction in muddy or icy conditions.

Drivers with little exposure to genuine performance automobiles might have felt that the Karmann-Ghia's light steering and low-slung stance gave it sports-car moves. But despite the presence of the front anti-roll bar and a recommended rear-tire pressure three-pounds-per-square-inch above that of the Beetle, the Karmann really wasn't any faster on a twisty road than a well-driven Bug. And it could be just as perilous in wet weather or when cornered too hard—no surprise in a car that shared the Beetle's heavy rearward weight bias and swing-axle rear suspension.

The Karmann-Ghia always cost more than the equivalent Beetle. A 1956 Karmann-Ghia coupe, for example, listed for $2,395, $900 more than a Beetle sedan. And the little coupe was more expensive to repair if the bodywork was damaged in an accident. But the public liked what it saw, thought the value good, and made haste to place orders. Production took time to build up, but the 10,000th car was on the road by the autumn of 1956.

(continued)

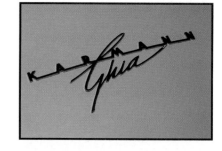

Badging the car in accord with its mixed parentage conveyed the Karmann-Ghia's high-toned pedigree. Coupes filtered into the U.S. for 1956, and the convertible arrived for '58. Karmann lavished the same attention on its insulated, double-layer folding top as on the Beetle cabriolet's. A '58 convertible like this listed for $2,725, $280 more than the Karmann-Ghia coupe, and with a curb weight of 1,786 pounds, it was 66 pounds heavier. Being rear-engine cars, the front "nostril" vents on all Karmann-Ghias were decorative. Sales of 1958 coupes and ragtops totaled 6,025.

Styling changes were very subtle and usually were made to stay abreast of safety regulations. A dished steering wheel was added in 1960, side marker lights arrived for '68, and by the time this '71 coupe was built, the car had wraparound signal lamps. Mechanical advances paced those of the Bug. The '71 shared the Beetle's 60-horsepower 1.6-liter engine, but Karmann-Ghias never adopted the Super Beetle's MacPherson strut front suspension. Front buckets were wide and comfortable, and both coupe and convertible had tiny +2 rear seating. The front luggage compartment was nicely finished, but small.

U.S. dealers were plagued by early supply problems, though VW didn't really promote the Karmann-Ghia in America until 1961. Those who wanted one in these years sometimes had to wait two years to take delivery. A two-seat convertible version was introduced in Europe in '57 and came to the U.S. for '58. It looked exactly the same as the coupe below waist level. The double-layer softtop was constructed with the same attention Karmann lavished on the Beetle cabriolets, and prices ran about $300-$400 more than contemporary Karmann-Ghia coupes.

For the next 20 years, there was virtually no alteration to the style, packaging, or marketing of the cars, though both models had their fender lines and headlamp height raised slightly in 1959. Most every successive change made to the Beetle was also made to the Karmann-Ghia. An exception was the Super Beetle's MacPherson-strut front suspension, which would not fit under the Karmann-Ghia's bodywork. However, the front anti-roll bar first seen on the Karmann-Ghia was adapted for 1960-model Beetles. That same year, Karmanns got a new steering wheel that was dished for safety, and a hydraulic steering damper to quell kickback. A vacuum-operated clutch was also introduced as an option, though sources differ as to whether availability was confined to European-market cars.

For 1961, horsepower jumped to 40 at 4900 rpm and the final-drive ratio changed from 4.43:1 to 4.37:1 to slow engine speed, through the ratios of first and fourth gears were tightened in an effort to preserve "acceleration."

Engine size increased to 1.3 liters for 1966 and horsepower rose to 50 at 4600 rpm. There was another bump to 1.5 liters and 53 horsepower for '67, and a step to 1.6 liters and 57 horsepower for 1970, and finally, to 60 horsepower in '71. The 1600s were the quickest Karmann-Ghias, capable of 0-60 mph in about 21 seconds and a top speed of around 82 mph. A switch in final drive for manual-transmission models in 1972 increased top speed to 90 mph. The 1600s also had better stopping power, thanks to their standard front disc brakes. When VW revamped its power ratings for 1973, switching from gross to net figures, the Karmann-Ghia was rerated to 46 horsepower.

Safety came to the fore in 1968 when, per new U.S. regulations, Karmann-Ghias adopted round side marker lights on the rear fenders, as well as an energy-absorbing steering wheel and steering column, and front seats with integral headrests. An external gas filler door appeared on the upper front bodywork.

VW's semi-automatic transmission was offered as an option starting in '68, and as on the Beetle, cars ordered with it got the new double-jointed rear suspension.

Demand was still relatively healthy into the early 1970s, but the Karmann-Ghia's days were numbered. Karmann needed all the space it could find to build the brand new Scirocco, and ceased production of the Beetle-based cars in 1974. It had built 283,501 coupes and 80,897 convertibles. An additional 23,577 coupes had been built at VW's plant in Brazil. Sales in the U.S. had peaked in 1970 at 38,825, of which 5,873 were convertibles.

Concurrent with its production of the Ghia-styled, Beetle-based cars, Karmann also built a four-passenger coupe based on the Type 3 1500-series sedan introduced in 1961. This coupe was called the Type 34 and shared the wheelbase and air-cooled, rear-engine running gear of the sedan upon which it was based.

The Type 34, however, lacked the visual charm of the Karmann-Ghia models and it sold slowly. Buyers were cool to the styling, which had nice proportions and an airy greenhouse, but was awkward around the front where two large outboard headlamps and two smaller driving lamps flanked a metal Roman nose. The Type 34 debuted in 1961 and was sold primarily in Europe. Ghia built a two-seat convertible version of the Type 34, but it did not go into production. With demand never very strong, production of the Type 34 coupe was halted in June 1969, after just under 42,500 had been built.

It is the original Karmann-Ghias that introduced the world to the idea of a sporty Volkswagen. If the Beetle was the people's car and the Type 2 VW bus was the people's van, then it might be acceptable to characterize the sensious-looking Karmann-Ghia as the "people's Porsche." Don't try to race a Porsche with one, however. You'd lose.

The 1972 Karmann-Ghia (yellow cars) got heftier bumpers and gained larger taillamps that eliminated separate rear marker lights. This was the final styling change before production ended in 1974. Far less successful than these classics was the Type 34, the VW-based coupe Karmann built from 1961 to 1969 (opposite, bottom row). It was a 2+2 that used the rear-engine platform and air-cooled running gear of VW's Type 3 sedan, which was a more advanced car than the Beetle. But the Type 34's styling lacked the visual charm of the Karmann-Ghia's. The four-headlamp nose was especially awkward. A Type 34 convertible was tested, but never put into production. Fewer than 42,500 Type 34s were sold, most of them in Europe.

The Porsche Connection

In 1939, when the VW Beetle was not yet in regular production and the Wolfsburg factory not yet complete, Adolf Hitler conceived the idea of a road race from Berlin to Rome. It was to be a graphic linkage of the Berlin-Rome Axis, a certification of the supposed bond between Germany and her junior partner, Italy. And it was assumed that German and Italian cars would demonstrate the technological superiority of the two Fascist regimes.

The race was scheduled for September 1939, over public roads closed for the occasion. As soon as he learned of the race, Ferdinand Porsche sought permission to build a sports-car variant of the still-evolving Volkswagen Beetle. The German government refused the request. It reasoned that Porsche's development of lightweight tractors, which would have war applications, was more important. But Ferdinand persisted, and ultimately was granted permission to build his sports car.

Porsche's engineers set about designing and building three streamlined coupes on the Beetle chassis. At first glance the project seemed terribly misguided, as the Beetle's engine had specifically been designed not to be a racing unit.

Dr. Porsche, a racing enthusiast, would not be deterred. If the engine could not be made significantly more powerful, he reasoned, then the motorcar would have to be shrunk around it. Porsche was already working from an assumption that the Beetle's engine and driveline were indestructible. But if there could not be a lot of surplus power for acceleration, it was up to Porsche's engineers to build a car with a high top speed.

Development continued quickly in Stuttgart during 1938-39, and focused on a body that was much lower and wider than the Beetle's. The designer, aerodynamicist Erwin Komenda, came up with a light, slippery shape wrapped around a small cabin. Competition rules mandated that each car be a two-seater, so the driver's seat was centrally located and a minuscule passenger space was offset to its rear. The car came to be known as the Type 64 or alternately the Type 60 K10 and four were eventually built.

Though based on the early Beetle, the racers' wheelbase was much longer than that of postwar

Porsches. Their unique light-alloy bodies were produced by Rupflin coachbuilders of Munich. The front and rear wheelarches were covered by removable, streamlined panels. The nose swept close to the ground between two rounded front fenders, with headlamps smoothly faired in. The Type 64 developed with design cues later picked up by production Porsches, notably the wide nose and bulged, integrated fenders, but the cars shared no body panels. The two-piece windscreen would later be used on the Type 356 Porsche, however, as would the general shape of the side windows, though the Berlin-Rome racer's rear-window profile was unique and would not been seen again.

Mechanically, the Type 64 cars were near-standard Beetle. Their air-cooled flat-four engine used two carburetors, and at 40 horsepower, output was a little higher than normal but not sensationally so; it was the superbly detailed bodywork that was responsible for their 90-mph-plus top speed. But they never raced.

Hitler invaded Poland on September 1, 1939, and the Berlin-Rome race was cancelled. Porsche's entries were ready and running, so he turned them over to the government for use by officials as rapid wartime transport. Dr. Porsche himself drove one throughout the war, and is said to have managed an average speed of 85 mph on the journey from Wolfsburg to Berlin over non-autobahn roads.

One of the prototypes was wrecked in a road accident. Another met a more-interesting end, as recalled after the war by Ferry Porsche: "[A]t the flying school at Zell am See the Americans had discovered one of the Berlin-Rome cars that was stored there, and were racing it on the airfield. It was such a beautiful hot summer that the soldiers eventually used metal cutters to remove the coupe's roof, turning it into a 'Roadster.' They had great fun with it, but they did not think of filling it up with oil and one day it ran dry, and the dream came to an end. The wreck ended up on a dungheap...."

The sole survivor was sold off and restored many years later. It surfaced ceremoniously at a number of postwar vintage events, providing a physical link between the 1939 ambitions of the Porsche Konstruktionsburo and the wondrous pro-

Ferdinand Anton Ernst Porsche poses with a European market Porsche 928 in 1978. His father's design work in the 1930s resulted in the original Volkswagens, and the subsequent Porsche family enterprise headed by Ferry remained an important, sometimes controversial, influence on VW. In turn, the engineering commonality between Beetles and the earliest sports cars from Gmünd and Stuttgart was fodder for Porsche critics. In reality, it was a mutually beneficial relationship in which each party went its own way none too soon.

duction cars to come.

The first of those cars was Porsche's 356. Its birth in 1948 was not an easy one. The Porsche Bureau was struggling to remain solvent in the immediate postwar years. If the engineers were not designing tractors they were helping with the repair and maintenance of vehicles for the occupying Allied forces. Some of these vehicles were Beetles, others were Kubelwagens and their derivatives. Then an Italian businessman named Piero Dusio commissioned Porsche to design a new rear-engined Grand Prix car. This, the Cisitalia (more properly known at Porsche as the Type 360), kept the company going until mid-1947. More importantly, the contract provided Ferry with the one-million franc bail he needed to free his father, whom the French had imprisoned—but never tried—for war crimes.

By the time ailing Ferdinand Porsche returned to his native Austria, work had already begun on the Type 356. Two things about the car's development were significant: It was being financed entirely by the Porsche organization, and it was a sports car.

To business-minded observers, the 356 must have seemed the height of frivolity. The war had ravaged nearly all of Europe, and for many people, simple survival was difficult. Something on the order of a sports car seemed absurd to many. Ferry Porsche, however, knew such a car was not only possible, but would have considerable appeal. "During the war I had an opportunity to drive a supercharged VW convertible with about 50 horsepower, which was a lot of power then," he later explained. "I decided that if you could make a machine which was lighter than that, and still had 50 horsepower, then it would be very sporty indeed."

The talented Porsche team began work on the 356 project in June 1947. The first designs, which had been sketched out at the Konstruktionsburo in mid July by Komenda and Ferdinand's old colleague, Karl Rabe, were completed at Gmünd, Austria. The resulting prototype was almost totally different from those that would eventually go on sale.

"The basis for our development work was the Porsche Type 60 K10, the sports car that had been built for the Berlin-Rome race," recalled Ferry. "The new car was known as the Type 356 and was to be a sports car. It had a tubular chassis which we had designed ourselves and welded together from steel tubes. The power unit was a 1131-cc Volkswagen engine fitted in *front* of the rear axle [italics added], while the gearbox was flange-mounted behind the axle. The front-wheel suspen-

sion, as well as the steering and gearbox, were also original Volkswagen components, as was the entire running gear...."

All the elements of the Beetle's torsion-bar rear suspension were employed on the 356. However, this was a true mid-engine car, with the engine and gearbox turned 180 degrees, so the suspension had to be reversed, too. Therefore, the transverse torsion bars were at the back and the "trailing" arms became the "leading" arms. This was a recipe for dangerous oversteer, so the engineers made front/rear weight distribution nearly even. Front suspension was stock VW, as were steering and the cable-actuated nine-inch-diameter drum brakes.

To circumvent the breathing restrictions deliberately designed into the Beetle engine, the 356 motor had higher compression, 7.0:1 versus 5.8:1. That boosted horsepower from the Beetle's 25 at 3300 rpm to 40 at 4000 rpm. Porsche-modified cylinder heads with larger intake valves and ports also contributed to the power gain.

The 356 was an open two-seater weighing a mere 1,314 pounds with a full fuel tank. It first ran as an unclothed chassis in March 1948, was completed in May, and got a roadworthiness certificate from the Austrian authorities in June 1948.

All along, Ferry Porsche had been doing research, asking his contacts what sort of car his company might be able to sell in small numbers and pondering how he could raise the money to build it. Almost everyone agreed that although "Porsche No. 1" was a fine car, it was not the sort that could be built in great quantities. The cost of fabricating the tube-frame chassis in small numbers was prohibitive. Further, such a frame took up a great deal of space, and market research showed that if the car were to have mass appeal, it would need a coupe top and a larger cabin with a better-trimmed cockpit and more luggage space.

During 1948, Porsche's team started again, developing a new version of Type 356 dubbed the 356/2. Four were built in 1948, all by hand. It was slow going. By the spring of 1951, just 51 had been assembled. But this was the variant that would ultimately achieve world fame, not only as a development of the VW Beetle itself, but as the definitive ancestor of every Porsche road car for the next three decades.

The original 356 had been purchased for 7,000 francs by a wealthy Swiss enthusiast named R. von Senger. He also committed to buying a batch of Porsche cars to sell in his homeland. Porsche was delighted with the deal because Senger was also able to arrange the supply of certain VW parts

The sporting origin of Porsche automobiles can be traced to the racer that Ferdinand Porsche's engineers built during 1938 and '39. Known as the Type 64, it put streamlined bodywork over a stretched Beetle platform. The rear-mounted air-cooled flat-four was a reworked Beetle engine with dual carburetion. It made 40 horsepower, enough to push the slippery coupe to 90 mph. The Type 64 was designed to compete in a Berlin-to-Rome road race scheduled for September 1939; the event was cancelled when Hitler's armies invaded Poland, igniting World War II. Three Type 64s were built, just one survives and makes occasional exhibition runs at vintage races.

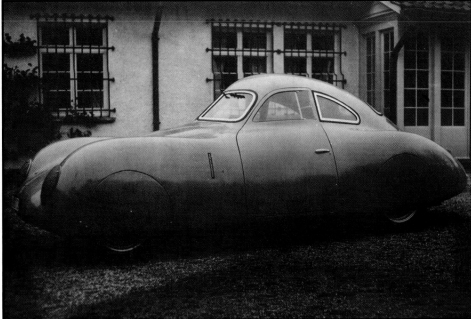

from Switzerland, and to supply the sheet aluminum needed by the Beutler coachbuilders to construct the bodywork.

Although Porsche might once have considered using the Beetle's platform chassis, as had the Berlin-Rome cars, the idea was eventually discarded because the chassis was thought to be too long and insufficiently rigid. For the Porsche production car, yet another new chassis was designed. It was a pressed-steel platform with integral bulkheads anchored at the cowl and behind the seats.

The engine was now in the tail, behind the rear axle, as on the VW. The only dimension shared with a period Beetle, however, was the track, at 50.8 inches front and 49.2 inches rear. The Porsche's wheelbase was a full 11.8 inches shorter, at a brief 82.7 inches, and its body was 8.1 inches shorter, at 151.6.

Most of the running gear of the first Porsches was lifted straight from the VW Beetle even though many components were not supplied directly by Wolfsburg, and instead were bought (via Herr Senger) from AMAG, VW's distributer in Switzerland.

Porsche's chassis was carefully detailed so the Beetle parts could be fixed directly to it without modification. At the front, the entire Beetle independent suspension, steering, and tubular cross-member structure, complete with trailing-arms, transverse torsion bars, brakes, hubs, and wheels, was bolted into place. At the rear, the Beetle engine (as modified by Porsche), transaxle, gearbox, transverse torsion bars, flexible trailing arms, swing axles, brakes, hubs, and wheels were all employed. And an inspection of the exterior showed that other items, such as headlamps and wheel covers, clearly came from the VW parts bin. If it had not cost Porsche so much to fabricate the frames, and to have the light alloy bodies beaten into shape on a wooden form, the bulk of the first Porsche's costs would have been in VW components.

Once automotive writers got their hands on the production Porsche, they quickly realized that the new sports car had not only inherited many of the Beetle's components, but its tail-heavy handling. Despite the almost 50/50 weight distribution, the car could be treacherous on slippery roads and in crosswinds.

The basic problem was twofold: slightly more weight at the car's tail than at the front, and the sizeable camber change of the rear wheels as they moved from bump to rebound. Porsche, like VW, spent years denying there even was a handling problem, followed by years of trying to deal with it

without actually admitting to anything. A completely satisfying solution, as owners of early Porsche 911s would have agreed, eluded them for years. With practice, though, good drivers learned to deal with the 356's oversteer, and motorsport successes mounted.

Flaws aside, the 356/2 amplified the good qualities that had distinguished the Beetle: surprising performance, astonishing reliability, credible fuel economy, excellent traction, and a reasonable expectation of a long life without breakdowns. There was something else too: character. Although the 356/2 was slower than some rivals, and certainly cost more than nearly all of them, it had solidity and an animal appeal that many enthusiasts found irresistible.

In September 1948, Ferry Porsche solidified his company's financial security by completing a multifaceted licensing and consulting deal with VW's Heinz Nordhoff. Porsche also became the import agency for Austria, gaining favored status on delivery of VW parts used in its own cars. Components and subassemblies could now be supplied directly from Wolfsburg, without having to be bought through AMAG of Switzerland. And, of

Ferry Porsche and his chief designer, Karl Rabe, supervised production of the Cisitalia Grand Prix car (this page, top). It never raced, but did furnish Ferry with the funds to free his father, who was held by the French for alleged war crimes. The first car to wear the Porsche name was the 356/1 (opposite). It was completed in June 1948 and was based on development work done for the Berlin-Rome racers. The open two-seater draped aluminum body panels over a tubular steel chassis. It had an 84-inch wheelbase, 9.5 inches briefer than a VW's, but it did use the Beetle's front suspension, steering hardware, brakes, and gearbox. The 356/1 was a mid-engine car, mounting a modified single-carb 1,131cc Volkswagen flat-four ahead of the rear axle. It weighed about 1,300 pounds and had a top speed of near 90 mph. This page, second from top: The Porsches, son and father, at the site of their fledgling firm's works in Gmünd, Austria, with the only 356/1 built.

vital importance, Porsche now enjoyed joint use of the worldwide VW sales organization.

By the end of 1948, small-scale production of Porsches had begun at Gmünd, though only a handful of cars left the converted sawmill each month. Growing demand had triggered another problem: It would not be possible to make more cars, even those using so many standard VW parts, until bodies could be built on a production-line basis. In mid 1949, Porsche struck a deal with Reutter Karosserie, a noted Stuttgart coachbuilder, to produce body shells—but now in steel, not aluminum. In return, Porsche would rent a 5,300-square-foot section of the Reutter factory in the city.

Porsche's first contract with Reutter was for 500 body shells and the first Stuttgart-built Porsches were completed in the spring of 1950. Now called simply the "356," they retailed for DM9,950, the approximate equivalent of $6,000.

Once Reutter began delivering new shells, production increased, though not very quickly. In the 1950 model year, a mere 410 cars were built; most days just one new Porsche rolled out of the small wooden-floored shop. If two made the trip, there was rejoicing. In the meantime, the Gmünd factory was closed after turning out just 46 cars in a little over two years.

For the next few years Porsche concentrated on building more of these VW-based sports cars, while gradually making them increasingly distinct and more Porsche-like until Porsche could claim that the last of the Type 356s, built in the mid 1960s, used virtually no standard Beetle parts.

Porsche's work on the flat-four, air-cooled engine is a case in point. The original Porsche powerplant kept the original cast-iron cylinder barrels from the 1,131cc Beetle engine, but used newly designed aluminum cylinder heads. For the 1950 model year, the first Reutter-bodied cars used a 1,086cc version of the engine, and modifications followed every few years. Subsequent 356 engines ranged from 1,286cc and 44 horsepower to 1,582cc and 75 horsepower. But none of the specially developed Porsche engines or even equivalent sizes were ever used in Beetles or in any other VW models; by the mid '50s, Porsche had persistently followed its own line of engine development. Chrome-plated cylinder barrels, roller-bearing crankshafts, and different carburetion were visible differences between the Porsche and VW engines, but there also were unseen departures, such as camshaft profiles. By the end of the decade, the Porsche engine was still similar to that of the

Beetle in that it was a flat-four with air cooling, but was different in almost every detail.

A slightly altered variant of the 356, the 356A, made its debut in the fall of 1955, and by the end of the '50s, physical links between Porsche production cars and the VW Beetle were few. With the launch of the Type 356B late in 1959, Porsche said the only VW parts were the two rear trailing arms and their bearings, the half-shafts, the crown-wheel-and-pinion assembly, and the differential housing.

Porsche built the 356 series from 1948 to September 1965, turning out more than 78,000 of the cars—peanuts by Beetle standards, but a great achievement for Porsche. And even as the 356 was in its prime, Porsche was developing a second model. Work on it began in 1956, under the code 695, and came to fruition in 1964 as the classic 911. With a rear-mounted air-cooled flat six-cylinder engine, the 911 surpassed the 356 in both performance and price. In 1965, Porsche introduced a less-costly 912 variant with the 356's four-cylinder engine.

By 1967, Ferry Porsche realized the 911 was headed invariably upmarket. He also saw that sales of the 912 were slowing (it would cease production in 1969). Unless the Porsche lineup was expanded to include a lower-priced entry, the marque would become too pricey to survive. But Porsche couldn't afford to develop a new model alone.

At VW, Nordhoff, influenced somewhat by Porsche's success and recognizing that his Karmann-Ghia was a paper tiger, was contemplating a genuinely sporty addition to his line. Ferry Porsche saw a way to bring his interests together with VW's, and Project 914 was born.

Ferry's planners had studied the market and conceived a car that would be smaller and consid-

The direct progenitor of the first regular-production Porsche was the 356/2, assembled in Gmünd beginning in 1948. Unlike the 356/1, which used a tubular frame and mounted its engine ahead of the rear axle, the 356/2 had a pressed-steel platform chassis (this page) and located its engine behind the rear axle. It, too, used a 1,131cc Beetle engine—but with dual carburetion—and had a European rating of 40 horsepower. Production of the 356/2 totaled just 42 coupes and eight cabriolets through the spring of 1951. They weren't cheap—the original coupes listed for $3,750 and the convertibles for $4,250. But virtues that characterized Beetles—careful construction and efficient design—made these Porsches most desirable. And if the 356s shared the VW's tail-happy swing-axle handling, it seemed less out of place in a sports car. (Note the familiar Beetle semaphore turn signal arms, here located in the front fenders.)

erably less expensive than the 911. This, it was thought, could effectively take over from the 912, and would redirect Porsche to the size, price, and performance of the much-loved but by now-obsolete Type 356.

With sketches and promising cost projections in hand, Ferry Porsche traveled to Wolfsburg, where Nordhoff listened enthusiastically. A deal was struck: Porsche would engineer a new sports car, and VW would build it. In addition, Porsche could use the car as a springboard to develop a more specialized Porsche. Right from the start, the project was an awkward one with too many masters. By mid 1968, with Nordhoff dead and new VW chief Kurt Lotz fast developing his own empire at Wolfsburg, friction developed between VW and Porsche.

According to the original deal, the new sports car would be badged as a VW, but Porsche could pick up the unit-construction bodyshell for its own use with a Porsche powertrain. An incidental benefit was to give the Wilhelm Karmann works something to build in lieu of the Type 3 Ghia, thus avoiding employee layoffs. Lotz, however, believed VW would never sell enough of the cars to make much money off the deal, and he proposed that Porsche's cost of each unit be increased.

An impasse was broken with a compromise deal. The new cars would be assembled in two places, and a new sales and marketing company would handle merchandising. VW-Porsche Vertriebsgesellschaft GmbH was the new organization established to sell the cars. It was owned 50/50 by Porsche and VW, and was headquartered on neutral ground, at Ludwigsburg, close to Stuttgart, in premises owned by Porsche.

Since the new company also assumed responsibility for the marketing of existing Porsche models, speculation arose that the arrangement was merely a prelude to a takeover of Porsche by Volkswagen. Ferry Porsche denied this, and was proved correct: Even in the cash-strapped 1990s, when Porsche began to sustain heavy losses, VW never came close to taking control.

In the meantime, it was decided to make not one, but two closely related cars. They would have a common structure and style, but two entirely different types of air-cooled engines. One car would be badged as a VW and would use VW Type 4 411 engines. The other would be a Porsche, an altogether faster car with a more-powerful air-cooled flat-six Porsche engine.

The choice of a mid-engine layout was the key to the project, for by the late '60s, the configuration

had become both fashionable and successful. Lotus had already put the mid-engined Europa on the market, and all modern racing cars were mid engine. Porsche, stung by criticism of the sometimes-squirrely handling of its rear-engined 911, was willing to break with precedent.

Because Porsche was small enough and aggressive enough in the late 1960s to move forward quickly, 914 development did not hesitate. It was agreed that the car had to be marketed at prices lower than the 911's, and that it should also look unique, neither like a VW nor a Porsche. But because the engine was to be located ahead of the rear axle, this placed severe limits on the size and shape of the passenger compartment. There would be no space for rear seats or even minuscule "+2" seating; the 914 could only be a two-seater.

Establishing design parameters for the new car's platform and finding space behind the seats for the engine was relatively easy. Settling on the styling took longer. VW had never built a two-seater, and except for the 356 Speedster of the 1950s, neither had Porsche. The seats had to be a long way ahead of the rear wheels, which would make it difficult to provide graceful lines. Beyond this, Nordhoff did not want the new sportster to look like a VW, and Ferry Porsche didn't want it to resemble a 911.

VW had never demonstrated a feel for striking style, and all Porsche's previous series-production road cars had been rear-engined machines, so perhaps the two teams were wise to entertain proposals from several outside consultants. An angular-looking study prepared by Gugelot Design GmbH got the nod. Gugelot had developed a prototype to demonstrate the properties of a foam core body material sandwiched between layers of bonded fiberglass. Tests suggested the material was unsuitable for mass production, but the prototype interested VW and Porsche. When design refinements executed by Ferry's son, Butzi, made the prototype look better and showed that it would work with the mid-engine layout, VW and Porsche gave the go-ahead.

Though it was no beauty—one cynic once described it as an oblong box with another oblong box on top of that—the 914 was certainly unique, with no obvious similarities to any VW or Porsche ever seen in public.

Wedging a motor between the cockpit and the transaxle meant the floorpan had to stretch, so after allowing space for various engine possibilities, the team settled on an all-steel monocoque structure with a wheelbase of 96.4 inches. A shallow cargo trunk was in the nose, ahead of the pas-

Porsche moved to Stuttgart in 1950 and began production of a line of successors to the 356/2. All had steel bodies, an air-cooled flat-four rear-mounted engine, a wheelbase of 82.7 inches, and open or closed two-door body styles. The first was called the 356 (opposite top left and top right). It started with a Beetle-derived 1,086cc engine of 40 horsepower (46 in the U.S.) and ended its run in 1955 with 1,488cc and up to 82 U.S. horsepower. It was followed by the 356A (this page), which lasted until 1959 and offered as much as 88 horsepower from 1,588cc. Closing out the series was the 356B of 1960-63 (opposite middle left and bottom), and the closely related 356C of '63-'65. Most roadgoing versions used the 1,588cc engine and had as much as 95 horsepower. All traced their design philosophy to that of the Beetle-related 356/2, but by the early 1960s, these Porsches had no components of significance in common with Volkswagens.

sengers' feet. Because the engine was so far forward, a second luggage locker was located in the tail, above the line of the rear axle.

Prominent features of the steel body included pop-up headlamps, carefully integrated bumpers (shortly reworked to meet American safety legislation), and a solid center roll-bar structure that served as the aft mounting for a Targa-type fiberglass roof panel. Engine access was via a hinged panel behind the seats, a poor arrangement that in the words of one observer, "allowed you to reach almost everything except the spark plugs."

The new car's front suspension and steering was lifted from the Porsche 911. So much for trying to reduce unit costs; this was a notoriously costly subassembly. There was, however, a novel semi-trailing arm independent rear suspension, with combined coil spring/telescopic shock absorber units mounted immediately behind the line of the rear drive shafts.

The VW variant used a fuel-injected version of the 411's 1,679cc air-cooled flat-four engine rated at 85 horsepower. Although this was the most-powerful VW engine yet put on sale, it was the least-powerful to be used in a Porsche sports car. This car was badged the 914. Some historians later referred to it as the 914/4, though such a name never appeared on the car.

The Porsche version used the 110-horsepower 2.0-liter air-cooled, carbureted flat-six from the entry-level 911. This iteration became the 914/6. The cars shared a Porsche five-speed gearbox, and although Porsche's own semi-automatic Sportomatic transmission was available, very few were ordered.

Lotz had decided the 914 would never sell in large enough numbers to justify being built at Wolfsburg. On the other hand, Porsche's plant at Stuttgart-Zuffenhausen could not cope with the numbers. So Lotz turned to Karmann of Osnabruck, which was VW's long-time associate in the production of the Karmann-Ghia and Beetle convertibles. Karmann got the job of tooling up the new shell for manufacture, and was also contracted to build the VW version of the car. For the 914/6, Karmann provided Porsche with slightly modified shells, painted and completely trimmed, so final assembly could take place at Stuttgart.

The four-cylinder 914 was launched in February 1970, and its styling was just one of several items of controversy. In Europe, the car wore a new "VW-Porsche" badge on the steering wheel and tail. In West Germany the name was soon colloquialized to Vo-Po. The problem was that "Vo-Po"

was also the diminutive for the much-feared East German police, the Volks-Polizei.

U.S. versions were visually and mechanically the same as the European cars, but wore only the Porsche name in block letters on the engine cover. Here, they were marketed through the new "Porsche+Audi" dealership network and there was no mention of Volkswagen.

The six-cylinder model appeared near the end of 1970. In all markets, it wore only Porsche insignia. It was further distinguished from the 914/4 by fatter tires, ventilated front brakes, full 911-style instrumentation, and a vinyl cover for the "basket handle" targa bar.

There was a clear difference in acceleration. The 914/4 had less-than-thrilling acceleration, running 0-60 mph in an average of 12.5 seconds with a top speed of 105-110 mph. The 914/6 was much quicker—under nine seconds 0-60 mph and about 123 mph in top speed. Handling was similar, and very different from that of other VWs and Porsches. Traction was as good as ever and the powertrain sounds were all familiar, but anyone expecting the usual tail-happy behavior would be disappointed. Like many other mid-engine cars, the 914 handled in a very precise manner, the only disadvantage being that rear-end breakaway, when it came, was sudden and particularly dangerous.

Once they got a look at the cars, Porsche fanatics were unhappy with the obvious VW sourcing of many visible pieces. American journalists in particular were critical of what was perceived as materials and workmanship below the Porsche standard, made worse because stiff spring rates brought out unseemly squeaks and rattles.

Most reviewers concluded that the 914/4 was too slow for the money and that although the 914/6 was fast, they'd rather pay a bit more to get the better-built 911. Indeed, far from heralding the return to much cheaper Porsches, the 914s turned out to be rather expensive. In the U.S., the 914/4 started at $3,500, where it was outclassed by the new, less-expensive Datsun 240Z. The 914/6 listed for $5,999, but for about $400 more, a buyer could get the tighter 911-T, which used the same 110-horsepower engine, but was a "genuine" Porsche. Neither version attracted a large following, and even within VW and Porsche there were many willing to write the 914 off because of its unorthodox layout and mixed-breed origins.

Only 3,107 of the 914/6 versions were built before Porsche killed it off in mid 1971. The 914/4 did better, selling at the rate of about 20,000 per year, some 15,000 of which went to North America.

Even before Porsche finished building the last of its 75,000 356-series cars in 1965, it unveiled a successor destined to become a classic: the 911. Compared to the 356, it had slipperier bodywork, a longer 87-inch wheelbase, more interior room, and features such as a MacPherson strut front suspension and four-wheel disc brakes. Power came from Porsche-exclusive horizontally opposed six-cylinder engines that made editions such as the 165-horsepower 911S of 1974 (lower right) among the world's most-exciting sports cars. When the market dictated, however, Porsche fell back on the flat-four as a way to provide lower-cost versions of this sports car. The 912 of 1966-69 (top and lower left) used the 356's 1,588cc engine, here tuned for 102 U.S. horsepower. The formula was resurrected for the 912E of 1976, which used an 86-horsepower 1,971cc flat-four drawn directly from that used in the Volkswagen 411 family car.

Karmann was quietly satisfied by this figure—it was, after all, producing the car on a contract basis—but by VW standards, these figures were disappointing.

The 914/4 soldiered on. In 1973, it gained an optional 91-horsepower 2.0-liter flat-four that brought performance closer to that of the defunct 914/6, but at a much lower cost. For '74, all American 914s got the 1.8-liter flat-four from VW's new 412 passenger car. It had 72 horsepower. After grafting bigger bumpers onto American-market '75s, VW and Porsche gave up on the 914. Production stopped at 118,947, including 914/6s—not a paltry total, but not what the partners had hoped for.

Long before the 914 was abandoned to its fate, VW and Porsche had embarked on a new joint project, initially given the code EA425. As with the 914, its birth, development, production, and history were to be swathed in controversy. The difference was that this car went on to be a huge success. It was the Porsche 924.

Kurt Lotz had been eased out of VW by the end of 1971, replaced as boss by Rudolf Leiding. Leiding had an aversion to complex mid-engine designs and it was he who froze further development of the 914. Leiding did not feel any obligation to ancient VW traditions, either, and he was ready to get rid of air-cooled motors and rear-engined layouts as soon as viable alternatives could be found. His first priority was the new Passat and Golf programs, but his next was to look again at the development of sporting VWs.

By early 1972, Porsche had started the design of its own water-cooled/front-engined car (to be launched in 1977 as the 928), so its planners had already worked through many of the problems that would have to be solved with Project EA425. Still, it would be a challenge to develop a new and strictly cost-controlled sports car that also would be Porsche's first front-engined design to make it to showrooms, the first to have front-engine/rear-drive running gear, and the first to have an inline four-cylinder engine.

EA425 (or Project 924, as it was always known at Porsche) took shape as a new Volkswagen, and one that would be an even more-extreme example of parts-bin engineering than the 914. Porsche believed that an all-new unibody coupe could be designed, but that the engineers must then use as many of the existing VW and Audi components as possible. This philosophy came to be known internally as Baukastenprinzip or "building blocks" and its roots lay with the accountants. Not only would the building-blocks edict reduce costly development time, it would also limit the investment that had to be made in expensive major items such as engines, transmissions, steering, and suspension.

VW and Porsche soon agreed that the new car would have to sell strongly in North America, where burgeoning emission and noise regulations made a water-cooled engine essential. It was this fundamental requirement that shaped the EA425 project.

From the start, the new car was identified as a front-engine/rear-drive 2+2 coupe. It had to have better performance than the best of the 914s, which meant the chosen engine would need at least 120 horsepower. VW's understanding was that although it was being developed by Porsche, the new car was to be a VW, not a Porsche. Porsche, on the other hand, quietly assumed it could persuade VW to allow a Porsche derivative to be developed.

During planning of the V-8 928, Porsche had looked at the layout of existing front-engined sports cars from Mercedes-Benz, British Leyland, Fiat, Alfa Romeo, Nissan, and others and became convinced that the 924 could improve on their traction and handling.

For the first time on a VW or a Porsche, the engine and transmission would be split, with the engine up front and the combined transmission/rear axle at the rear. The two units would be connected with a solid torque tube carrying a propeller shaft. Wheelbase would be an efficient 94.5 inches, suspension would be all independent, and overall weight distribution would be a very good 48 percent front/52 rear.

The parts-bin engineering now began in earnest. For the engine, Porsche chose a modified version of the 1,984cc (121 cubic inch) four-cylinder currently being used in the VW LT commercial vehicle. It was an evolution of an engine that had been used in Audi models for years. Audi applications included an overhead valve layout, but for the LT, an overhead-camshaft layout had been developed, and this was picked up for the 924. The final-drive assembly itself and the four-speed manual gearbox were direct swaps from the front-drive Audi 100. Porsche split the gearbox from the engine and moved it to the back of the car, turning a front-drive transaxle into a rear-drive transaxle. It was a neat solution to a potentially complex problem.

The styling of this 2+2 coupe with its large rear window/hatch, was originally drawn by Harm Lagaay, a Dutch designer in Porsche's styling department. Lagaay's work was modified over a

The Porsche-Volkswagen relationship entwined again with the 914 range of 1970 to '76. Engineered by Porsche, styled by an independent German design house, and built under a new Porsche-VW joint venture, the mid-engine 914 was really two cars. One used the flat-four from the VW 411 line and was commonly called the 914/4 (bottom and upper right). In Europe, it carried confusing "VW-Porsche" badging; in the U.S., it was sold only as a Porsche. Its companion was known as the 914/6 (upper left). It drew its flat-six cylinder engine from the Porsche 911 and was called a Porsche in all markets. Porsche customers dismissed the 914/4 for its Volkswagen heritage and shunned the pricey 914/6; just 3,107 of the 914/6s were built. VW had hoped the 914/4 would enable it to tap a sports-minded audience, but the two-seater's cost was too steep and its performance too average for it to be a high-volume hit. About 115,000 were assembled.

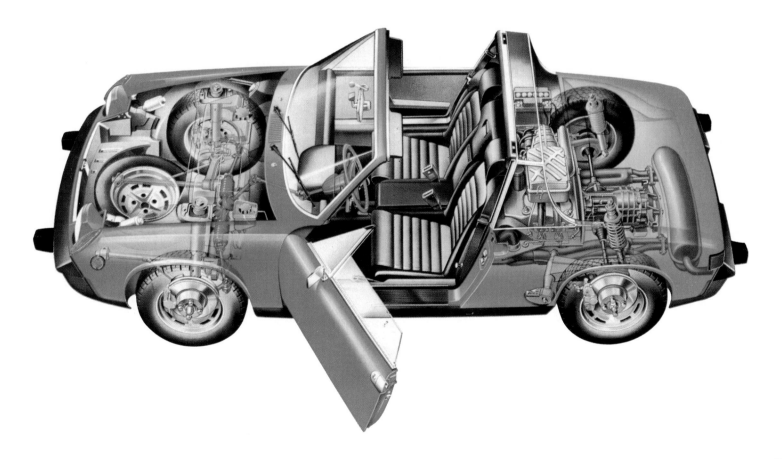

period of months following suggestions by VW's Leiding, who like many other top automotive executives, was a manager who loved to dabble in design.

Many expensive detail changes were made before the final shape was settled on. The finished car was less bulbous than the original, with larger wheel openings, more glass, and more detail in the flanks, which had started out totally smooth. Pop-up headlamps were fitted, not because VW and Porsche thought them trendy, but because this was the only way to provide a smooth front end and pass headlight height requirements in many countries, including the United States.

The cabin had considerably more space than the 914's; the 2+2 seating in fact was more spacious than that of the Porsche 911 family, although adults could never get comfortable in the tiny rear seat of either car.

The 924's MacPherson front suspension included Golf struts, Golf-related Scirocco lower locating arms, and Golf rack-and-pinion steering. The semi-trailing arm rear suspension, complete with torsion bars, came from the latest version of the VW Beetle, where it was still known as the "double-jointed" suspension. Added points of ingenuity included drive shafts taken from VW's Type 181 (The Thing), and front disc brakes and rear brake drums lifted from the VW K70. To their credit, Porsche engineers spent months poring over all these parts and more, making myriad detail changes to coordinate one subassembly with another.

The LT-derived engine was given fuel injection to bring its output to 95 horsepower in the U.S. and 125 in Europe, the difference being a compression ratio of 9.3:1 in Europe and 8.0:1 in the states. Because the engine was too large to fit under the hood of the shell that VW had in mind, Porsche tipped it to the right by 30 degrees. The propeller shaft was encased in a stout tube 3.3 inches in diameter. To ensure that the lengthy gear-change linkage would be as positive as possible, the shift lever and its bracketry were fixed firmly to that tube rather than to the body shell. To a VW/Audi expert, the transaxle looked very similar to the

Audi's, except for the aluminum-alloy casting that covered the front of the empty clutch housing and linked it all to the torque tube.

Once design and engineering were completed, development went rapidly, with the first complete body shell finished in June 1973. Production tooling was ordered and all looked promising—until the 1973 Yom Kippur War erupted in the Middle East and was followed at year's end by the Energy Crisis.

Within a matter of weeks, the decision-makers at Volkswagen lost much of their faith in the future of sports cars. With another front-engine, water-cooled sports coupe, the Scirocco, having hit VW showrooms in March 1974, the EA425 project was put on hold.

Porsche tried to buy rights to the car, but was refused by Leiding, who apparently entertained his own hopes of reviving it. But Leiding resigned in December 1974, and it was weeks before the new VW chief, Toni Schmucker, could review the project.

After studying forecasts that said EA425 sales would never exceed 20,000 per year, Schmucker decided VW really should not be in the sports car business after all. He seemed ready to kill the project altogether. Once again Porsche approached VW, and this time its proposition was accepted. Porsche would take over the project, the car would become a Porsche instead of a VW, and assembly would be in VW's ex-NSU Neckarsulm plant.

The arrangement made a lot of sense. VW needed something to fill assembly lines stilled by the faltering NSU Ro80 or the Neckarsulm factory would have to be closed. Porsche had no room at its own Stuttgart-Zuffenhausen plant to build a completely new model line, and Neckarsulm was a convenient 40 minutes from Porsche headquarters.

The Porsche 924 went on sale in 1976. It wasn't a road rocket—0-60 mph times were in the 11-12 second range, but handling and control were at the top of the class. The 924 begat the Porsche-engined 944 of the early 1980s and descendants, badged 968, were built until the mid 1990s. It had been a long journey and a worthwhile one, if not for Volkswagen, then certainly for Porsche.

The final VW-Porsche joint venture was a greater success than the 914. Development of the new 2+2 coupe began in the early 1970s. It was designed by Porsche for sale as a Volkswagen. Costs were controlled via parts-bin engineering. Mounted in front was a water-cooled inline 2.0-liter four-cylinder engine from a VW commercial van; the combination transmission/rear axle was located in back. Front suspension pieces were Golf parts, the rear underpinnings were adapted from the Beetle, and other components were borrowed from various VW and Audi models. After the fuel crisis of 1973, VW lost interest in the project and Porsche acquired rights to the car, putting it on sale in 1976 as the Porsche 924 (opposite top left and bottom). The design proved durable, evolving into the 2.5-liter Porsche 944, introduced in 1982 (opposite top right), and finally the 3.0-liter Porsche 968, which bowed in 1991 (opposite middle right).

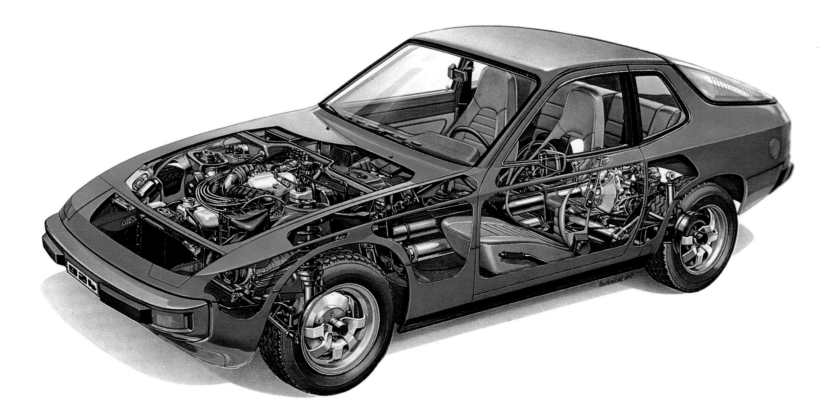

New Horizons: Front-Wheel Drive and Partners

Before the 1960s, Volkswagen was too busy securing its own future to start building an empire. With annual production leaping from 50,000 in 1950 to nearly 750,000 by 1960, Heinz Nordhoff and his team were otherwise occupied.

Then came the opportunity to absorb two other independent German companies, Auto-Union and NSU. The initial attraction was factory space that the growing Wolfsburg giant desperately needed. But both companies would soon be pressed into service in an historic expansion of VW's product line.

The first and most-important acquisition was Audi. It had emerged from World War II as a component of the state-run Auto-Union combine. Daimler-Benz AG took control of Auto-Union in 1958, inheriting a conglomerate that built front-wheel-drive cars with two-stroke engines. Technically, these machines had almost nothing in common with Volkswagen's Beetles, though the lower-priced versions competed in the same market segment. In fact, most of the world had long since abandoned the two-stroke engine. It was a simple design, having only seven moving parts—three pistons, three connecting rods and one crankshaft—and was inexpensive to build. But inefficiency, heavy exhaust pollution, and lubrication problems were drawbacks that had not been overcome.

As buyers gravitated to more-modern cars in the early 1960s, Auto-Union profits sagged. Daimler-Benz countered by exerting a stronger influence over the product and by casting about for a co-owner. VW was the obvious choice, though it was at first reluctant to join up. But Daimler had an exciting inducement.

Auto-Union's latest two-stroke car was set to go on sale in 1963 as the DKW F102. It was larger and faster than the Beetle or the VW 1500 and had been styled by the Mercedes-Benz studio. More importantly, it was slated to get a new Mercedes-designed overhead-valve four-stroke engine of 1.7-liters. Its tooling had cost Auto-Union dearly, increasing Mercedes' desire for someone to share expenses.

Daimler-Benz's pitch to VW's Nordhoff included the offer of factory space and the distinct possibility of turning a profit with the F102—particularly now that a four-stroke engine was on the way. VW warmed to the notion, especially after both sides agreed never to compete against each other with cars in the same market segment—a promise not always kept as the years rolled on.

In October 1964, VW and Daimler-Benz announced that Auto-Union was coming under their joint ownership. With 51 percent of the stock, VW would be the controlling partner. (VW added to its holdings over the years, though it never quite owned all the assets.)

The first modern-generation Audi—effectively the F102 with the new Mercedes four-stroke engine—went on sale in 1966. The name Audi was chosen because it was the only pre-war member of the Auto-Union family to market a front-wheel-drive car. The F102-based sedan debuted as the Audi 60 with a 55-horsepower version of the 1.7-liter engine, which Auto-Union was building under license from Daimler-Benz.

At the same time, Beetle assembly was added to the Auto-Union plant in Ingolstadt. The facility was under the direction of Rudolf Leiding, who would soon move upward in the VW hierarchy. Ingolstadt provided VW's product-hungry dealers with 61,800 extra Beetles before the close of the year. And by the end of 1966, VW had eliminated one of the Beetle's domestic competitors by stopping production of the last of the old two-stroke Auto-Union cars. In effect, Auto-Union had disappeared, replaced by the new Audi.

Audis were not sold through VW dealerships and the new model didn't directly compete with any Volkswagen. Yet, being a thoroughly modern front-engine, front-drive sedan, it made VW's best effort, the rear-engine 1600TL, look distinctly old-fashioned. Still, the Audi, now with variants labeled the 75 and Super 90, was being bought by people who might never have considered buying a VW, so Wolfsburg was reaping profits that might have gone elsewhere. Production of that first postwar Audi reached 63,500 in 1966, then 120,000 during 1969. It took just seven years for Ingolstadt to build the first one million modern-day Audis.

The original front-drive model was joined in

Volkswagen pushed itself into the modern age of front-engine, front-wheel-drive cars not by changing from within, but by acquiring outside products and sometimes by taking over whole companies. There were a number of false starts along the way, and a few less-than stimulating cars, including the 1978 Dasher line (opposite). But it was an essential process, and it inspired VW to generate some home-grown designs that did indeed shake the automotive world.

1968 by a bigger, fresher design badged the Audi 100, which benefitted from even more guidance by Mercedes-Benz, especially in the styling. The 100 was the car that spearheaded the entry of Audi into the U.S. market, where it began sales in 1970 under the newly established Porsche+Audi dealer network.

Audi's initial American line consisted of the older Audi 90 and the new Audi 100. The 90 came as a two- and four-door sedan and four-door wagon. As in Europe, the 90's wheelbase was 98.0 inches, overall length was 173.8, and curb weights averaged about 2,250 pounds. U.S. base prices ranged from $2,995 to $3,245 and it was sold here from 1970 through 1972.

The 100 was a two- and four-door sedan with a wheelbase of 105.3 inches, overall length of 182.6, and curb weight of about 2,350 pounds. It cost $3,695. Both models used the 1.7-liter engine, which had started life with advanced features such as high-swirl combustion chambers with 11.2:1 compression. U.S. versions were detuned slightly to 10.2:1 compression, but that still was higher than virtually all imports, including Ferrari and BMW. The engine was rated at 100 horsepower in the Audi 90 and at 115 in the Audi 100.

Meanwhile, VW was trying to pry itself from the rear-engine air-cooled rut. It began to look away from Porsche and toward Ingolstadt for direction in developing the next range of Volkswagens. Despite its shorter heritage, and its smaller technical and financial base, Audi was an extremely capable business, and it showed. Audi-developed engines, for example, would eventually be found in everything from VW buses to entry-level Porsches, and an Audi sedan already on the drawing boards would soon become a breakthrough car for Volkswagen. Indeed, buying into Auto-Union turned out to be a smart move, and compared to VW's next acquisition, it was painless. NSU was a far less-willing victim.

The prosperous ex-motorcycle maker had begun building air-cooled, rear-engine cars in 1957 and steadily increased sales during the early 1960s. Then it was seduced by Felix Wankel's technically exciting but commercially unproven rotary engine. Wankel had joined NSU in 1952 and his initial work was on conventional engines. He designed his first rotary unit in 1954, and persuaded NSU to fund all future development costs. The first Wankel engine was tested in 1957.

By the early 1960s, NSU had big ideas. It had set up a Wankel joint-development deal with Citroen of France, which resulted in Citroen taking 10 per-

cent of NSU's shareholder stock. NSU launched the Wankel Spider in 1963, a sports car with a mid-mounted single-rotor engine. And it sold Wankel development licenses to companies as diverse as Britain's Rolls-Royce and America's Curtiss-Wright. NSU was convinced the rotary had a big, profitable future and it invested heavily in Wankel-engine technology and production capability. But the real trouble began when it decided to build much larger cars than it knew anything about.

In 1966, NSU's biggest car was a rear-engine 1.0-liter family model. NSU was determined to be competing head-to-head with Opel, Ford, and Audi in the upscale-sedan market by 1970. That set NSU on a path it could ill afford. In 1962, NSU had built 56,000 cars, and in 1965 92,000 cars, but its share of the German market was still only 3.6 percent. To compete with the big boys, NSU would at least have to double its share.

Its hope rested with the Ro80, which debuted at the 1967 Frankfurt motor show as the world's first car designed for rotary power. It was a beautiful sedan, aerodynamic and space-efficient, and its sporty underpinnings included four-wheel disc brakes. Driving the front wheels was a 115-horse-power twin-rotor Wankel, which could propel the Ro80 to a top speed of 112 mph. A smitten European motoring press named it Car of the Year.

But by 1968, the dream was turning into a nightmare. The Ro80 was already being vilified for engine reliability problems and NSU, its resources stretched thin, was running out of money just as it prepared to bring to market its next model, the conventional-engine, front-drive K70.

Smelling blood, bigger companies closed in. Takeover rivals included Europe's two automotive giants, Fiat and Volkswagen. VW was now under the direction of Kurt Lotz, a man with expansionary ideas. Lotz was attracted to the Ro80. He thought its modern rotary engine might have a great future, and was confident that his engineers could solve the durability problems. And VW was again looking for extra plant capacity; Ingolstadt was filling with Audi production, elbowing aside Beetle assembly. At the same time, Lotz wanted to control any competition for the VW 411, which had bowed to a muted reception.

Keeping Fiat out of the German market was also a major consideration. Fiat initially bought Citroen's 10 percent share of NSU, and though it showed signs of wanting to acquire more, the Italian company was not ready to mount a full-

(continued)

In 1964, VW assumed majority control of Auto-Union, which was readying a new front-drive sedan called the F102. Volkswagen redressed the F102, created a new division under a name that had been part of the prewar Auto-Union combine, and went to market in 1966 with its first front-drive car, the Audi 60. The Audi marque came to the U.S. in 1970 with two front-drive models, the new Audi 100 (top), and the smaller Audi Super 90 (bottom). Both used a 1.7-liter four-cylinder engine developed by Mercedes-Benz. The 100 had actually been styled by Mercedes, while the 90 was a version of the original Audi 60. The Audi 90 lasted through 1972. Though it was attractive, roomy, and handled well, the 100 was mechanically trouble-prone. It hung on until 1978, when it was replaced by the Audi 5000.

Four Silver Rings.

Expanding the Empire

Rarely was there a time when Volkswagen was alone. The early years held links with Porsche, and starting in the mid 1960s, VW cast its corporate net around Audi, NSU, Seat, and Skoda. Here's a look at the background of VW's partners.

Audi

When VW acquired Audi in its 1964 take-over of Auto-Union, it joined forces with a marque much older than itself. Audi's roots go back to 1899, when August Horch, who had assembled cars for Carl Benz, opened his own firm to repair motor cars, then in 1901, to manufacture and race models of his own design. Horch left the company that bore his name in 1909 after a dispute with associates. The competitor he founded was legally prevented from using the Horch name, so in 1910 he adopted the Latin translation, "to listen," or Audi.

The first Audis were sporting machines that abounded with technical innovation, winning road races and rallys, sometimes with Horch at the wheel. By 1921, Audi offered a model with an aluminum cylinder block and four-wheel brakes.

Audi merged with DKW, with the car division of Wanderer, and ironically, with Horch, to form Auto-Union in 1932. The first Volkswagen connection came in the early 1930s through Ferdinand Porsche, who designed the original Auto-Union P-Wagen Grand Prix car, which was built at the Audi factory in Zwickau.

After World War II, the Zwickau plant found itself behind the Iron Curtain, where IFA, Zwickau, and later Trabant cars were built. When Auto-Union was nationalized by the West German government in 1945, the Audi marque disappeared, later to be resurrected under VW in 1966.

During the 1980s, Volkswagen gradually moved Audi further upmarket, and there was little engineering overlap between the makes. After the third-generation Audi 80 appeared in 1986, sharing of platforms ceased, and by the early 1990s, Audi had developed V-6 and V-8 engines not shared by any VW.

Audi has been fertile ground for VW management. Former Audi director Rudolf Leiding headed VW from 1971 to 1975, and Ferdinand Piech, grandson of Ferdinand Porsche, moved from the executive offices of Audi to assume control of Volkswagen in 1993.

NSU

By absorbing NSU in 1969, VW had brought the wheel full circle. One of Ferdinand Porsche's early-1930s projects that led to the KdF-Wagen was a rear-engine car with an air-cooled four-cylinder boxer that he built for NSU.

In 1873, Christian Schmidt and Heinrich Stoll bought a shop along the River Danube that made knitting machines. The concern moved to Neckarslum in the early 1880s and was renamed Neckarsulmer Strick-maschinenfabrik. By 1886, it was manufacturing bicycles and in 1888 entered motoring by supplying the chassis for the first Daimler automobile. In 1892, it changed its name to NSU and in 1901 was one of the early motorcycle manufacturers, producing bikes that set numerous world speed records.

The first NSU automobile was built in 1906 and was followed by a string of successful performance-oriented designs, including one that in 1925 beat Mercedes and Bugatti to take the checkered flag in Germany's first "sports car Grand Prix." The world economic crisis forced NSU to halt auto manufacturing in 1929 and its plant was purchased by Fiat, which for a time built and marketed cars under the NSU

this company was Spain's largest private automobile manufacturer. It was founded in 1953 and concentrated on making slightly modified Fiat designs, including a small, rear-engine model. Later placed under the control of the Spanish government, Seat languished as a money-losing concern with little technical capability of its own.

In the 1970s, Seat turned to ItalDesign for styling, Karmann coachbuilders for tooling expertise, and Porsche for work on engines and gearboxes. Its first major link to Volkswagen came in 1982, when it made a deal to sell VWs in Spain and to assemble Passat-based Santanas.

Wary of a partnership with a money-losing government-held company, Volkswagen in 1986 bought 75 percent of Seat's stock. The German company gained a foothold in Spain and gradually increased its holdings, restructuring Seat to begin wider production of VW-based models.

The first VW-based Seat appeared in 1991 as the Toledo and was drawn from the platform and running gear of the VW Jetta. It was followed by other Seats that used their own body designs but were always based on VW platforms.

Skoda

Skoda was already among the Austro-Hungarian empire's most important industrial giants when it entered automobile production in 1923. At first it put bodies of its own design on Hispano Suiza chassis and running gear, then began building cars under its own name in 1925.

As a designer for Austro-Daimler, Ferdinand Porsche had been assigned to the Skoda armament works during World War I, where he developed powerful hybrid electric tractors. After World War I, the restructuring of Europe put Skoda in the territory of the new Czechoslovak republic.

In the aftermath of World War II, Czechoslovakia was trapped behind the Iron Curtain and Skoda became a Communist-state run company reduced to building crude rear-engine cars based on pre-war designs. Some were exported to the West, where were usually retailed at price-dumping levels.

With the fall of European Communism in 1989, Western carmakers looked to former Eastern-bloc countries as both an untapped market and a source of low-cost labor. VW, which had already agreed to supply engines for Trabant to refit its old two-stroke cars, soon started talks with Skoda.

VW beat out Renault, which had also made overtures toward Skoda, and in December 1990, took a minority stake in Skoda. It assumed a majority control within a couple of years.

The first evidence of VW expertise at Skoda would come with the relaunch of the antiquated front-drive Favorit as the better-built Felicia. Skoda sales exceeded 200,000 in 1994, even before VW's investment in new facilities was completed.

Volkswagen's most-significant acquisition was the 1964 takeover of Auto-Union, a combine that once included Audi, DKW, Wanderer, and Horch. Only the Audi name survived, its four-rings logo symbolizing the former Auto-Union quartet. NSU, which built several successful prewar racing cars, was the final German company absorbed by Volkswagen. VW retired the name in 1977. Seat of Spain, in 1986, and Skoda of Czechoslovakia, in 1990, were important recent additions to the VW Group.

badge. In 1932, NSU regained its independence by severing its links with the Fiat group.

By 1938, NSU was building 40,000 motorcycles, 25,000 mopeds, and 122,000 bicycles per year, then stopped to assemble half-track motorcycles for the German army during World War II. It retuned to the manufacture of cars in 1958 with small, rear-engine, air-cooled models. In financial straights after committing to the Wankel rotary engine, NSU was taken over by VW in 1969. VW got much-needed factory space, but also was able to block Fiat, which also had designs on NSU, from getting a new foothold in Germany.

NSU's stillborn K70 became the first VW-badged front-engine, front-wheel-drive car, but when the last of the Wankel-powered Ro80s rolled out of Neckarsulm in 1977, the proud NSU name was retired.

Seat

Pronounced "See-ot" and standing for *Sociedad Espanola de Automobiles de Turismo,*

blown takeover bid. VW, on the other hand, came in with guns ablaze and made NSU a total takeover offer. NSU's bosses were convinced they could still go it alone, and discussions with VW took place in a chilly atmosphere. The rattled NSU brass made a hasty decision to postpone the public launch of the K70. They had already spent $20 million on the car, which was ready to bow at the Geneva Auto Show in March 1969.

VW agreed to negotiate an arm's-length takeover in which NSU would merge with Audi. Both were located in the south of Germany—NSU's headquarters in Neckarsulm was only 130 miles from Audi's in Ingolstadt, closer than either of them was to Wolfsburg. VW also suggested that a combined Audi-NSU could eventually assume third place in the German pecking order behind VW and Opel, and ahead of Ford. After much acrimonious debate, the deal was done. A new company, Audi NSU Auto Union AG, was established on August 21, 1969, with VW holding 59.5 percent of the shares. Later in the year, VW increased its holdings to about 75 percent.

NSU continued to build its range of small, rear-engine cars, which were popular and profitable. The Ro80 was neither. When NSU launched the car in 1967, it forecast enough demand to support the production of 70 per day, nearly 20,000 annually. But by the mid 1970s, further development of the Ro80 had ceased and production was down to five or six per day, which was ludicrously uneconomic. Ironically, the durability problems had been overcome, but the Energy Crisis brought to the fore questions about the Wankel's fuel efficiency and exhaust emissions. VW's bosses finally pulled the plug in mid 1977 after a grand total of 37,204 had been sold.

The Neckarsulm factory was a brighter picture. By the mid 1970s, it had become an important Audi assembly plant, and for a time was a source of tens of thousands of Porsche 924s and 944s. By the mid 1990s, it was devoted to Audi passenger-car assembly, making more—and more profitable—cars than NSU's bosses could have imagined possible.

Even as he grappled with the Ro80 question, Kurt Lotz realized the air-cooled NSUs had no future. His attention turned to the K70, which was still in limbo, labeled by one pundit, "The most publicized non-car in Europe." Lotz had the K70 whisked away from Neckarsulm and prepared for production as a VW. The plan was to recoup the capital NSU had already spent on the K70, while teaching Volkswagen's engineers and planners

about front-wheel drive and water cooling.

Concurrently, VW realized it would need a plant to build the K70. Newly inherited Neckarsulm was rapidly filling with Audis, and the Wolfsburg facility was running flat out building Beetles, Type 3s, and Type 4s. The choice for a new VW plant was the town of Salzgitter, only an hour's drive southwest of Wolfsburg. It was close to the Iron Curtain border between West and East Germany, where government development grants encouraged business to generate jobs in the politically sensitive zone. In addition to producing the K70, the new plant would be able to build up to 500 Beetles per day. And significantly, in a corporate culture that had known only rear-drive air-cooled cars, it would allow the K70 to take shape under a workforce that held no prejudices against front-wheel drive and water cooling. Salzgitter turned out to be the final new VW plant to be commissioned in West Germany.

To test the K70, VW had at its disposal the vast new top-secret proving ground at Ehra, north of Wolfsburg. Not only was this an ideal site—lots of space for ultra-long straights and special pavement surfaces—it was easy to keep secure. It was so close to the Iron Curtain, VW reasoned, that rivals would not dare to fly overhead to try to take pictures lest the Warsaw pact military shoot down the plane as a threatening intruder!

Security was important, because the VW-badged K70 was the car that would break the Beetle mold. It was to be a radically different Volkswagen in every way: the first with an engine mounted at the front; the first with water cooling; the first with front-wheel drive.

Although the NSU K70 had never officially been

VW's acquisition trail led up some interesting avenues. Among the most intriguing was NSU and its Ro80 (both pages). This car bowed in 1967 as the first automobile designed expressly for rotary power. Driving the front wheels was a 115-horsepower twin-rotor engine developed by Felix Wankel, an NSU engineer. Sporty, space-efficient, and a darling of the automotive media, the Ro80 was unfortunately costly to build and had engine-reliability problems. It was a drain on NSU's resources just as the company was attempting to launch a more-conventional front-drive sedan called the K70. Thus was NSU vunerable to the 1969 takeover by Volkswagen, which acquired the K70 in the bargain. Wolfsburg's technicians eventually cured the Ro80's engine problems and the car was kept on as a low-volume specialty model until 1977. The K70, meanwhile, became the foundation of the first VW-badged front-wheel-drive car.

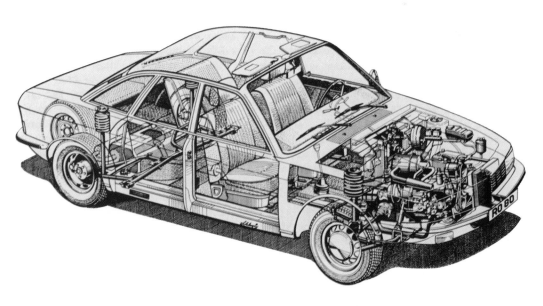

launched, its specification was already well known. A proud NSU had circulated information, pictures, and drawings well ahead of the '69 Geneva show.

NSU had intended the K70 as essentially a piston-engine derivative of the Ro80 chassis, but there were major differences between the platforms of the two cars. The K70 had a much shorter wheelbase, 105.0 inches to the Ro80's 112.5. And the K70's track was narrower than the Ro80's—by a full 4.5 inches in front. There were major changes between the suspensions of the Wankel-engine and piston-engine cars; at the front, for example, the K70's lower wishbone was made up of pressings, while that of the Ro80 used welded tubes.

The K70's engine was mounted ahead and above the line of the front wheels, with the final-drive components under the rear of the engine block and the four-speed transmission behind the line of the wheels. Power passed directly from the clutch to the transmission via an exposed quill shaft, turned through 180 degrees in the gearbox itself, and entered the final drive assembly from the rear.

For packaging reasons, the K70's engine was canted right by 32 degrees, and the front disc brakes were neatly tucked inboard at either side of the final-drive assembly. Although the K70's overhead-camshaft piston engine looked broadly similar to those of the smaller NSUs, it was water-cooled where the older NSU engines were air-cooled, and was generally larger. Originally, NSU had planned to produce the K70 as a 90-horsepower 1.6-liter car. VW decided to offer this engine, plus a less-powerful 75-horsepower version.

NSU's stylist Klaus Luthe had produced the shape, and although the cabin package was similar to that of the Ro80, there were virtually no common body panels. The Ro80 had a drag coefficient of 0.35, among the lowest of the day. Though the K70 had a more-upright grille, NSU claimed a respectable drag coefficient of 0.41 for the car, a figure VW was unable replicate in its own tests. The actual number was not disclosed, but was obviously higher, which may explain why the K70 was never as fast as its sponsors had hoped, and why fuel consumption was often disappointing.

Between the car's withdrawal from the March 1969 Geneva show and July 1970—a period of 16 months—the K70 not only inherited a new badge but was also subjected to a thorough workover. The car VW launched in the summer of 1970 looked almost identical to the stillborn NSU, but was in fact different in many important details. VW apparently spent twice the original NSU bud-

get to modify the car to its own standards. Because no journalist ever drove the NSU-badged K70, history is denied a verdict on whether it was money well spent.

Visually, the only alteration was to the grille, where the familiar VW badge now rested in the middle of a plain and rather angular snout. Under the skin, the major change was the available 75-horsepower version of the 1.7-liter four. VW also redesigned NSU's original aluminum cylinder block in cast iron, and substituted a one-piece aluminum cylinder head for the original two-piece casting. The VW-badged car had larger-diameter wheels—14 inches instead of 13. And the interior was revamped with a new dashboard and VW-grade materials.

Volkswagen launched its K70 a week after a particularly acrimonious annual general meeting of the Audi-NSU board that lasted 16 hours. Minority shareholders still thought VW had underpaid for the NSU business and argued that the K70 should already have been on sale, badged as an NSU.

Production finally started at the new Salzgitter factory in August, with the German market getting delivery first and export sales beginning in 1971. VW said the plant could produce 400 to 500 K70s per day—80,000 to 100,000 per year—though Wolfsburg officials stopped short of claiming they could actually sell the K70 in such numbers.

Volkswagen's problem was that the K70 was an expensive design, and even the company's own much-vaunted expertise couldn't do much to reduce it. Priced between the 411 models and the larger, more luxurious Audi 100, the K70 occupied a difficult middleground.

Sales were weaker than VW had hoped, but strong enough to keep the car alive. The K70 had a fine chassis, but it wasn't a very fast car; even the 90-horsepower version could only reach about 93 mph, and fuel consumption seldom climbed above the low-20 mpg range. Such mediocrity was hard to hide. As an important car for an important automaker, the media was scrutinizing every detail of the K70's performance. Looking to salvage the situation, VW considered using the K70's engine and transmission in other new models, but soon concluded that Audi components could do a better job at a cheaper price.

To liven up the K70, VW developed a new version of the engine for the 1974 model year. This was a 1,807-cc unit that had 100 horsepower. It gave the K70 a guaranteed top speed of more than 100 mph, but it was only a stay of execution. After a life of only five years, the K70 was quietly

Volkswagen performed an extensive underskin rework of the K70, which emerged in 1971 visually unchanged from the NSU version, except for VW insignia (top right). As the inaugural front-drive Volkswagen, the K70 attracted much attention, though it was lackluster in styling and performance. It set the scene for the Audi 80, which bowed in 1972 as the first front-wheel-drive car designed in-house by VW. Its inline four-cylinder was the first engine VW designed without outside help. Volkswagen gave its version of the Audi 80 a fastback roofline and launched it as the Passat in 1973. The Passat came to the U.S. later that year as the 1974 Dasher wagon and sedan (top left and bottom). The Dasher was an unremarkable car, but one that would prove influential.

phased out of production in the summer of 1975. A total of 211,100 had been produced—barely enough to pay off the tooling costs. The car was never imported to the U.S.

The K70 was of historical significance. But of far more lasting importance was VW's second front-wheel-drive model, the first truly modern car designed by the Volkswagen group.

Its story began at Audi in 1969, where Ludwig Kraus, a Bavarian, was director of development. Kraus had headed Daimler-Benz's race-car design, transferred to Auto-Union in 1963, and was the executive who launched the original F102-derived line and the new Audi 100. The success of those models had given him the clout to demand from Volkswagen funds to develop Audi's first true homegrown automobile.

Lotz agreed and now Kraus had to deliver. The tough VW boss gave him just three-and-a-half years to produce an all-new platform and a fresh family of engines. Adding to the pressure was Lotz's declaration that VW would probably pick up the same basic design for a new model of its own. Lotz's management considered the ex-NSU K70 a good stop-gap model, but they knew a new medium-sized VW would eventually be needed. If Kraus's efforts were as successful as they had been in the 1960s, maybe this was the fast way to get a brand-new model.

Having produced two successful front-drive designs, Kraus's team never considered building any other type of car. This time, though, there would be few compromises: If something new were needed, it would be developed, not borrowed.

From the start, Kraus made certain Porsche was not going to be involved in the new model. Privately, he blamed Porsche's thinking for many of Volkswagen's current problems. First there had been the dogged insistence on all cars having an air-cooled engine mounted in the tail, and then the lofty assumption that if mid-engine layouts worked well in race cars they should be ideal for road cars, too.

Kraus had been a key opponent of the stillborn EA266 mid-engine sedan—Porsche's proposed successor to the Beetle (see Chapter 10). By the time EA266 was cancelled, Kraus's work on the new Audi was well underway and his "Euro-standard" layout—front-wheel drive with a choice of front-mounted overhead-camshaft water-cooled engines—had been proven in the marketplace.

For this car, and for many successful VWs that followed, there was to be a brand-new engine, the

first that either VW or Audi had designed without outside help. Originally known as the 827 unit, it started life as a four-cylinder gas-powered design in 1.3- and 1.5-liter sizes. It would eventually grow in displacement to 2.0 liters and spawn five-cylinder gas and diesel variations. It was even the basis of a straight-six diesel sold to Volvo for its big sedans and wagons.

Like most of the world's successful powerplants, it was simple and rugged, undersquare (with a bore narrower than the stroke), and had a cast-iron cylinder block, an aluminum cylinder head, and a single overhead camshaft driven by an internally toothed belt.

The new unibody car was smaller than the Audi 100. It had a wheelbase of 97.2 inches and a track of 52.7 inches front, 52.5 rear. Front suspension consisted of independent MacPherson struts, coil springs, and an anti-roll bar. In back was a beam axle and coil springs. Two new longitudinally mounted overhead cam four-cylinder engines were offered in displacements of 1.3 and 1.5 liters with horsepower ranging from 55 to 85.

The concept, design, and initial development work was done by Audi at Ingolstadt. It was a crisply styled sedan with two or four doors, thin roof pillars, and a handsome nose. The interior was spacious and airy and the trunk was a generous 18.7 cubic feet. Overall length was 172 inches and curb weight a tidy 2,100 pounds.

The car was christened the Audi 80 and unveiled in the summer of 1972 to rave reviews and strong sales. European motoring journalists voted it Car of the Year. *Autocar*'s Technical Editor, Jeff Daniels, said the new 80 was "certainly very much the right sort of package size for Europe in the 1970s, remarkably similar in overall size to the VW Beetle, but with a great deal more room inside, much better motorway stability and a great deal of attention paid to ease of servicing."

Even before the launch of the Audi 80, VW had been working on its own version. Its variation bowed in May 1973 as the Volkswagen Passat. It was named after an ocean wind, beginning a VW tradition of naming cars after famous breezes. (Passat also was the name of a great German sailing ship.) Though they shared the same wheelbase, the Passat's body was nearly 10 inches longer than the Audi's. Mechanical specification was very similar, but the Passat's styling was harder-edged overall, with the big difference being that the Passat had a fastback roofline. To design the fastback roofline, VW had secured the services of the hottest stylist of the day, Italy's Giorgetto Giugiaro.

The Audi 80 arrived in the U.S. for 1974 as the Audi Fox (top left). Two- and four-door sedans were offered, both with a 75-horsepower 1,471cc inline four. A four-door station wagon was soon added. For 1977, the Fox got quad headlamps. It now used a fuel-injected 1,588cc four-cylinder rated at 78 horsepower (top right and bottom). American buyers were attracted by the upscale feel and sporty road manners of these cars, but the Fox was fraught with quality problems, and service at Porsche+Audi dealers was often unresponsive. Prices, which had started at a reasonable $4,000 when the car debuted, had climbed to well over $6,000 for 1979, the Fox's final model year.

But the Passat didn't look nearly as neat as the Audi design. The two- and four-door VW versions were joined later in 1973 by a station-wagon body style.

It was not merely for what the Passat was, but for what it suggested, that this was such an important car. It was not a Beetle replacement, which is what most everyone except VW bosses agreed that Volkswagen desperately needed. Larger, faster, more versatile, and costlier than any Beetle, it took VW into a new, unexpected direction, one it would have to stay with for years to come. Although many of the Passat's technical building blocks were shared with the Audi 80, so much investment had gone into them (particularly into the engine and the gearbox tooling) that it was clear these components would have to be used in other new VWs and Audis for many years.

The Audi 80 came to the U.S. for the 1974 model year as the Audi Fox. Offered as a two- or four-door sedan, it had the 1.5-liter engine in 75-horsepower tune. Prices ranged from $3,975 to $4,110. Later, a wagon was offered. The 80/Fox would stay in production for six years, with nearly one million built, but the car was always more successful in Europe than in the U.S.

Americans attracted to its looks and sporty road manners were soon turned off by reliability problems and often-arrogant treatment by dealers. The price escalated rapidly as well, from an introductory start of around $4,000 to well over $6,000 by 1979, its final U.S. model year. Slow sales were no indication of how influential the Fox was on American automakers, however. Its efficient use of space and well-thought-out platform was a virtual blueprint for Detroit as it developed America's first crop of front-drive automobiles.

The Passat went on sale in the U.S. in mid 1973 as the Dasher. Dashers were very similar mechanically to the Euro-market Passats, though their suspension was tuned for a softer ride. Both settled down for a solid run. By their retirement in 1980, 1,769,600 had been built, a total unimpressive next to Beetle numbers, but a fine achievement against the lackluster 411 and 412 range. As the design matured, additional body configurations were added, including three- and five-door hatchbacks, which simply added a liftgate to the fastback roofline. (Early Passats looked like hatchbacks, but actually had a conventional trunk.)

In 1976, the engine was enlarged to 1.6 liters and though there was no gain in advertised peak power, mid-range muscle increased and the car became easier to drive. That same year, U.S. versions dropped their two-barrel carburetor in favor of Bosch K-Jetronic fuel injection and were rated at 89 horsepower. In Europe, VW briefly offered a 110-horsepower version of the 1.6 engine.

American VW dealers, who had complained from the start about the Dasher's rather spartan interior trim, were rewarded in 1976 with upgraded cabin materials. The first and only major facelift came for 1978 with the addition of a four-headlamp nose, a change echoed by the Audi versions.

Road & Track tested a '78 two-door Dasher hatchback, a California-market car rated at 77 horsepower due to that state's emissions-control hardware. Still, a curb weight of just 2,130 pounds enabled it to run 0-60 mph in a respectable 13.2 seconds and average 26.5 mpg. The editors judged it "a very well done exercise in space and fuel efficiency." But the first fuel crisis had passed. Americans were buying gas guzzlers again, and an unexciting-looking four-cylinder German hatchback that started at $5,300 and could easily top $6,400 wasn't a hot item. "The Dasher is a good car caught outside its proper time frame," concluded *Road & Track*.

Like the Fox, the Dasher's reputation in the U.S. was damaged by poor workmanship. But the significance of these cars cannot be underestimated. They not only brought VW into the modern-car age, but by sharing components with one another and with other cars in the Volkswagen family, they taught Wolfsburg about the rationalization of resources that is essential in today's cutthroat automotive world. Links to the conservative VW of the 1960s had been cut, and from now on these German cars would be modified, mixed-and-matched, tricked-up, improved, restyled and generally re-jigged from season to season just as much as their rivals had ever been.

The Dasher acquired its own quad-headlamp nose for 1978, but was substantively unaltered from the first Euro-market Passats. These cars shared the Fox's powertrain. Dashers had the passenger and cargo room of a large car within the exterior dimensions of a compact. Curb weights of 2,300 pounds made them frugal at the gas pump, too. But fuel was in abundant supply by the late 1970s and American buyers wanted faster, flasher cars. Poor quality control and prices inflated by the rising value of the German mark hurt, also. But these cars showed VW how to mix and match components. And they influenced product planners within Detroit's Big 3, who copied elements of their design for America's first crop of front-drive automobiles.

The New VW: Scirocco, Golf, and Polo

The automobiles that saved Volkswagen in the 1970s—Scirocco, Polo, and Golf—were second thoughts, mid-course corrections after VW averted certain failure by killing a car that never got a name.

It did have a code, EA266, and a history filled with controversy. This was a Kurt Lotz project, monitored on his behalf by VW technical director Werner Holste, and speedily forgotten by Lotz's successors. It in fact became a non-car, never seen in public, and rarely mentioned.

Although it was never intended to replace the Beetle, whose future still looked bright in the late 1960s, EA266 would have aimed at the same market segment. Porsche was still the most important technical influence on VW, and EA266 originated in Stuttgart. In later years, Ferry Porsche was so embarrassed by this failure that he made no mention of it in his autobiography, *Cars Are My Life*. And yet, at the time, it was the largest and most costly project Porsche had ever tackled.

The root of the problem was that Heinz Nordhoff was never able to face up to replacing the Beetle. When he stepped down in 1968, handing the reins to Kurt Lotz, the legendary air-cooled car had not yet peaked technically or in the marketplace, and every time Porsche had suggested producing another model—invariably with an air-cooled engine—Nordhoff turned it down.

After Lotz arrived, there was a philosophical change at Wolfsburg. Before the end of his first year on the job, Lotz concluded a new car was needed, something more advanced than a car with its roots in the 1930s.

Given a free hand, Porsche chose a unibody two-door sedan with mid-engine layout, and a water-cooled one at that. Work on the mid-engine 914 sports car was nearly complete, and Porsche saw little reason to change its design philosophy for a new family car. Thus EA266 took shape with an engine located ahead of the line of the back wheels. To package it within a four- or five-seat cabin, Porsche positioned the engine literally underneath the rear seats. The powerplant would be a new inline four-cylinder, mounted on its side. It was to start at 1.3 liters and would have a single overhead camshaft and water-cooling.

Although cooling by circulated water was something quite alien to Porsche and VW, in the EA266 it was almost inevitable: With such an engine position, there was no alternative. Getting sufficient airflow underneath the car to keep finned cylinder barrels cool would have been near-impossible, even if a large cooling fan had been placed behind the cabin. But because Porsche planned to provide EA266 with luggage bays front and rear, there was no room for such a fan. (Later in the development cycle there would be a second version of this layout, where the engine was mounted upright, offset to the right side of the car.)

The first prototypes were ready in 1969 and by 1970, heavily disguised EA266s were being tested in extreme climatic conditions, including winter work in Lapland, the northern territories of Sweden and Finland. Technically, EA266 seemed to deliver everything claimed for it. Not only was traction and handling better than any previous VW, but it promised to be extremely reliable and to provide far more performance than Beetles of the same engine displacement.

Although EA266 was never seen in public, many design details are known. Engineers led by Dr. Ferdinand Piech had produced an engine with a chain-driven camshaft and hydraulic tappets. They placed it under the rear seat cushion and arranged for cooling air to enter the engine compartment through one rear wheel arch and exit through the other.

The chassis was conventional enough. Suspension was by MacPherson struts in front and semi-trailing arms at the rear. The packaging was slightly compromised by the rear seat cushion being higher than normal. This was to allow for larger engines, up to 1.8-liters at least. Engine access was a big problem. What was poor in the 914, became impossible on EA266. The 914's boxer could be reached only from above via a lid behind the cabin. The only access to the EA266's on-its-side flat-four was from below. Porsche's explanation that poor access was not an issue because EA266 was going to have the most reliable VW engine ever didn't placate the doubters.

By 1971, EA266 was well on the way toward launch, but there were still big questions: Could it

It took Volkswagen several years to create a front-wheel-drive automobile whose commercial acceptance approached that of the Beetle. The successful formula was a car small on the outside and large on the inside. It had hatchback versatility and smart styling by Italy's Giorgetto Guigiaro. The VW-designed transversely mounted four-cylinder engine and taut suspension made it fun to drive. Thoughtful construction made it light enough to return fine fuel mileage. And VW's enormous economies of scale held prices within reach of a broad audience. The car was the Golf, which debuted in Europe in 1974, and then came to the U.S. as the Rabbit (opposite).

sell at Beetle prices? Would it be as reliable? It sure was what Porsche wanted, but was it what VW customers wanted?

In the meantime, VW was staggering from crisis to crisis. The business had not been going well since Lotz had taken over. Lotz supporters asserted that he could not be blamed for the 411's poor reception; it was too late to stop it when he took over from Nordhoff. They argued that people would come to love the 914, which really was his baby. And they maintained that 1969's profit losses were linked to upheavals following the formation of Audi-NSU and were part of business life. Lotz critics, of course, blamed him for all of this.

Profession loyalties played a role here, for Lotz had eased several Nordhoff nominees off VW's board, one of whom was a well-liked and influential public relations manager, Frank Novotny, who had many powerful friends in the German industrial press.

But the fact is that when Lotz took over from Nordhoff, there were no new models coming to follow the 411 and the 914. True, the ill-fated EA266 was the first major project started under his regime. But Lotz also set in motion a massive new-model investment strategy that would help save VW. However, neither the German government (which still had a major stake in VW) nor the outspoken German media reflected such a realization in their attacks on Lotz. They decided he was a failure, an incompetent manager, a time waster, and that changes would have to be made. One of the most damaging magazine stories of the period was headlined succinctly: "Volkswagen—Lotz of Trouble." It did not help that Lotz was a Christian Democrat politician, at a time when the federal and Lower Saxony governments were opposition Social Democrats.

Over at Audi, meanwhile, Lotz's heir-apparent, Rudolf Leiding, could see a final management battle brewing. Leiding, a production specialist, had spent time at Volkswagen of North America, had built up VW's Kassel factory, and had been sent south to run the new Audi-NSU division. He served two years in South America, during which he made a success of VW's Brazilian subsidiary, then returned to Audi-NSU. Leiding cannily refused a promotion to be Lotz's vice-chairman, where he would have been tainted by the growing crisis. Lotz, with the end of his four-year contract approaching, resigned rather than be sacked, and Leiding moved smoothly into his place as VW's chairman.

In October 1971, only three weeks after Lotz walked away from Wolfsburg, Rudolf Leiding cancelled EA266—not delayed, not asked for a redesign, but cancelled it completely. Tens of millions of dollars had already been spent on research and development, and many contracts for production tooling, particularly for body panels, had already been placed.

No matter. Porsche was ordered to scrap every single prototype. Apparently, most of them were crushed during military tank-testing programs! Drawings were burned, photographs destroyed. One prototype was reputedly preserved (perhaps against Leiding's orders), though it has never been seen in public. All was not bad news for Porsche, however. Leiding realized his snap decision had cut away much of Porsche's existing workload, so he speedily replaced it with a development project for another new car—the sports coupe that eventually became the successful Porsche 924.

Even as EA266 work was underway at Porsche, VW technical director Holste and his staff were busy with their own in-house projects. They were inching toward the idea of building a front-engine car with front-wheel drive.

Their first effort, coded EA276, was conceived in 1969. It was a rather boxy affair with an air-cooled Beetle flat-four engine mounted ahead of the front wheels, which were driven through a new transaxle. The suspension was inspired by that of the Super Beetle, with MacPherson front struts and rear trailing arms with transverse torsion bars.

The EA276 was a one-off, as was the EA272 of 1970, in which Holste's team took the theme a stage further. This time, they used a water-cooled in-line four designed in-house by VW. (It's now clear that there was more rivalry than cooperation between VW and Audi during this late-1960s period, for it really made no sense for both companies to be developing their own new small four-cylinder engines.)

Holste would not be at VW to see his ideas blossom. New boss Lotz had revamped the technical staff, bringing in Director of Development Ludwig Kraus from Audi, and Holste left the company. Kraus, in turn, retired from VW in 1973, and Austrian-born Ernst Fiala became technical director in his place.

To replace the Beetle, the new VW management team decided it had to convert wholesale—and quickly—to building transverse-engine water-cooled front-wheel-drive cars. This would not move VW ahead of other European rivals already building such automobiles, but at least it would be on a par. Then came an even larger decision: The

VW probably averted a costly debacle by killing the EA266 (opposite). This was Porsche's idea of a Beetle companion, and development was underway as early as 1966. Its styling—a hatchback with a generous greenhouse and wheels pushed out to the edges of the platform—was quite advanced for the day. But its rear-wheel-drive powertrain layout promised huge problems. Porsche mounted a water-cooled 1.3-liter four-cylinder engine under the back seat. The location elevated the rear-seat cushion, reducing passenger space, and would have subjected the occupants to noise, heat, and odors. Complicated engine cooling and poor engine access were other drawbacks. Prototypes were undergoing tests in 1971 when Rudolf Leiding (above) took over from Kurt Lotz as VW chairman. Leiding promptly cancelled the EA266 project and ordered all prototypes destroyed. The cancellation embittered Porsche, but opened the way for development of the highly successful Golf.

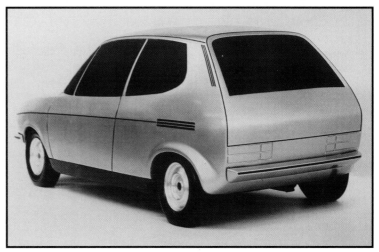

Beetle would be supplanted not by one new range, but bracketed by two—one smaller than the Bug, the other of a similar size, but much more powerful.

The new small VW would be named Polo. The more-direct replacement for the Beetle was to be the Golf—called the Rabbit for U.S. sales. Because the little Polo would take VW into a new market segment, whereas the Golf would take over directly from the aging Beetle, it was Golf development that took priority. Into this planning, VW tossed an extra complication: The days of the Beetle-based Karmann-Ghia sporty model were numbered, and VW wanted a successor developed as part of the wide-ranging Golf program. A new project, EA398, was begun as a sports coupe based on the new Golf platform. It would be built in its entirety by Karmann and eventually named the Scirocco.

Once the strategy was in place, VW moved remarkably quickly. Work on the Golf didn't begin until mid 1971, yet the Scirocco derivative went on sale less than three years later, and assembly of Golfs began just weeks later than that.

To do this, Leiding and his team cut many corners. VW normally would have produced up to 80 percent of the tooling required for a new model, but in this case it could only tackle 30 percent of the workload. The rest was farmed out to suppliers and consultants around the world. VW was learning the modern way of developing new models.

By autumn 1972, with work rushing ahead, but with nothing yet ready to show the world, Leiding was ready to talk to the press about his plans. In a lengthy interview with the doyen of the British motoring press, Gordon Wilkins, Leiding spelled out his strategy, which was "to broaden VW's market base with a new range of water-cooled cars from about 900 to 2,000cc."

Wrote Wilkins: "He has no time to lose. In Germany, GM Opel has nudged VW out of the top sales spot and in Europe as a whole Fiat has taken top position. In the USA which normally takes a third of all VW output, VW sales took a severe knock last year [1971] as a result of the revaluation of the Deutschmark, and the [President] Nixon measures to discourage imports."

This was the atmosphere in which work on the new Golf and Polo projects sped ahead. Although Audi's own stylists had made a neat job of the Audi 80, there was never any question of them being asked to shape the Golf, and VW's own stylists had little experience designing modern cars.

VW had consulted Pininfarina several times in the 1960s and the Italian concern had influenced

the 411, but Lotz was unimpressed by Pininfarina's work. He was still convinced the most-pleasing automotive shapes were born in Italy, however, so he visited the Turin Motor Show of 1969, where he found that the best-looking family cars had been shaped by Giorgetto Giugiaro of ItalDesign.

Not only was Giugiaro very talented, but his business could react quickly to pressure. First approached by VW in the spring of 1970, ItalDesign was soon contracted to style EA398 (Scirocco) and EA400 (Golf). By the summer of 1971, Giugiaro had produced acceptable packages. Thus, when Leiding took over from Lotz, the shape, if not the detail, of the next important Volkswagen range had been settled.

Although the sporty Scirocco two-door hatchback looked very different from the three- or five-door Golf hatchback, both cars were based on the same 94.5 inch wheelbase platform, and shared front-wheel-drive engine/transmission installations and suspension layouts.

The Scirocco and Golf names, incidentally, continued VW's new allegiance to Mediterranean breezes. Passat was a tradewind, and Scirocco was the German spelling of sirocco, a hot wind sweep-

Though the Scirocco was developed alongside the Golf and shared its front-drive platform and four-cylinder gas engines, it was introduced several months before its more-conservative companion. Scirocco—named for a desert wind—was another Giugiaro exercise and was assembled by Karmann coachworks. The sports coupe bowed during 1974, going first to Europe (this page), then coming to the U.S. later that year with fancier wheels (opposite top left). It combined hatchback utility with performance-car manners and was a hit with critics and buyers. Germans enjoyed a 110-horsepower GTI variant, but Americans got tamer versions. Among the best was the '79, (opposite middle right), which offered an optional five-speed manual. It had a fuel-injected 76 horsepower 1.6-liter four, weighed 2,000 pounds, and did 0-60 mph in under 12 seconds. Dashboard woodgrain, a wraparound bumper, and turn signals were added for '78. The 1981 (opposite bottom) was the last of the first-generation Sciroccos. This example listed for $8,860, including the $730 "S" package, which included blackout exterior trim, a front air dam, white-letter tires, body stripes, and Recaro-designed sports seats.

ing off the African desert. "Golf," VW insisted, had nothing to do with the sport of golf, but referred to the Gulf Stream air current. Many people nonetheless assumed that Golf referred to the game. VW eventually gave in gracefully—not by making an announcement, but naming the next VW after a sport: Polo. In fact, there would eventually be a limited-edition Polo called the Driver, and a pick-up-truck version called the Caddy...

Although Scirocco would be introduced before the Golf, it was the style of the mass-production Golf that had to be finalized first. Compromises could always be made in the layout of the sporty 2+2 Scirocco, but the Golf, meant to sell by the millions, had to be exactly right from the first day. In its general shape, the Golf was typical of ItalDesign thinking in the early 1970s, with a rather boxy cabin lightened by careful detailing around the wheelarches, headlamps, and body quarters.

There was no shortage of critics ready to suggest that nothing could take the place of the Beetle. But they obviously grasped neither the realities of efficient design nor the revolution sweeping VW. Perhaps it was no more than coincidence that the Scirocco/Golf wheelbase and wheel tracks mirrored those of the 40-year-old Beetle. But the packaging of the new cars was far more carefully worked out, and the squared styling helped produce much more capacious interiors.

Although the Golf was a full 14 inches shorter than the Beetle—short front and rear overhangs saw to that—it was three inches wider overall. That ensured that the cabin, though still for four passengers, was more spacious, particularly across the front seats (six inches wider) and rear seats (three inches wider), while there was more space for the driver, more headroom for rear-seat passengers, and significantly more luggage space.

Not only that, but the new unit-construction body shell was more rigid than that of the Beetle. Performance was in entirely a different league, as well, and fuel economy was much improved. Independent front suspension by coil springs and MacPherson struts was already familiar to Volkswagen customers and dealers. But Golf had a new type of twisting-beam rear suspension in which coil springs acted on trailing arms welded to a transverse torsion beam. This beam also acted as the structural cross-member. The assembly was pivot-mounted so there was extra suspension stiffness when the car was being cornered, but not when both wheels went up and down at the same time. The result was good control in turns, but a relatively soft ride in other conditions.

Beetle fanatics who had been mildly impressed by the 50-horsepower 1.6-liter engine of the latest Bugs were awed by the 70 horsepower of the original 1.5-liter Golf, and dumbstruck by the 110 horsepower produced by the fuel-injected 1.6-liter versions that followed.

Along with a new 50-horsepower 1.1-liter entry-level four, these overhead-cam engines were related to the 1.3- and 1.5-liter powerplants used in the Passat that went on sale in 1973. The Scirocco/Golf, however, used a brand-new all-synchromesh four-speed manual transaxle (automatic transmission was an optional extra, but not with the smaller engines). And there were major installation differences. In the Passat, the engine was mounted longitudinally, in a "north-south" alignment, and was canted right by 20 degrees. For Golf/Scirocco, both were mounted transversely, "east-west" across the car.

Internally, VW classified the 1.1-liter as the Type 801, and it was installed tipped forward by 15 degrees. The 1.5- and 1.6-liter engines were altogether larger Type 827s and were installed leaning back away from the grille by 20 degrees. VW didn't explain the mounting differences, but when the Audi 50/VW Polo was launched a few months later, it became obvious that the 1.1-liter's forward cant served to commonize its installation with that of the even-smaller new hatchback.

The VW twins of 1974, Scirocco and Golf, could not have arrived at a better time. The Beetle was already well past its prime. And the effects of the first Energy Crisis (which struck in October/November 1973) were reverberating around the world. Every carmaker needed smart, new, economical cars. VW could boast—and did—that the Golf was totally modern, faster, and more economical than the dear old Beetle. VW dealers, in the meantime, could point out that the Beetle was still available...

Scirocco was the first of the new generation to go on sale, hitting showrooms in February and March 1974. Karmann had been instructed to finish off the tooling and start production as rapidly as possible, shaking out the bugs before Wolfsburg began to churn out larger numbers of Golf types.

Giugiaro had provided slinky, though still hard-edged coupe lines set off by a rakish tail with a large liftgate. Early European versions had two large rectangular headlights, but Sciroccos for other markets used a neat four-headlamp nose later adopted for all models.

Although a handful of European Sciroccos were

VW replaced the Beetle with a new front-wheel-drive car launched in Europe in June 1974 as the Golf and in the U.S. in January 1975 as the Rabbit. At 94.5 inches, its wheelbase was identical to the Bug's. But the new car had a more-efficient design, with roomy two- and four-door hatchback body styles and a modern water-cooled engine driving the front wheels. Initial powerplants ranged from a 1.1-liter gas-sipper to a 1.5-liter; the latter, with 70 horsepower, was the only American-market engine. Prices for U.S. models (opposite) started at $2,999, just $104 higher than the cheapest Beetle. Despite poor gearshift quality, high noise levels, and early rust problems, the Rabbit was enthusiastically received. Part of the attraction was that unlike other subcompacts, it was downright fun to drive. By January 1976, U.S. dealers had sold 100,000 of them (above). No other imported model had sold more than 100,000 units in its first year.

fitted with the 1.1-liter economy engine, the lion's share got the 1.5 liter (1,477cc, 89.7 cubic inches). It was available in 70- or 85-horsepower tune in Europe. All U.S. versions used the 1.5 fitted with two Zenith carburetors. It had 70 horsepower at 5800 rpm and 81 pounds/feet of torque at 3500. Compression was 8.2:1. With a curb weight of 1,940 pounds, U.S. Siroccos could run 0-60 mph in 12.7 seconds. List price was $4,450, though some sources list alloy wheels as a "mandatory" $140 option. Regardless, it was a good price for a stylish coupe with up-to-the-minute engineering and road manners that set the standard for front-drive cars. A "truly remarkable small GT," was *Road & Track's* assessment.

In 1976, Europeans were treated to the 110-horsepower Sirocco GTI, while the 1.6-liter engine (1,588cc, 97 cubic inches) became standard on U.S. versions. The following year, U.S. models gained Bosch fuel injection and a boost to 78 horsepower at 5500 rpm and 83 pounds/feet at 3000. Zero-60-mph times fell into the low 12-second range.

For '78, VW reduced the engine's stroke, resulting in a displacement of 1,457cc (88.9 cubic inches). This new 1.5 was rated at 71 horsepower at 5800 and 73 pounds/feet at 3500. Base price rose to $5,695, but performance suffered little and *Road & Track* remained impressed, lauding the Sirocco's dual personality as a sports coupe and a utilitarian hatchback. "Few of the more prestigious and more expensive GT sedans can promise such versatility," it said.

The 1.6-liter was reinstated for '79, now listed at 1,590cc and rated at 76 horsepower. The addition of emissions and safety equipment and upgraded trim had added about 90 pounds to Sirocco's curb weight, but by ordering the newly optional five-speed manual gearbox, owners could recoup most of any lost performance. *Car and Driver* tested a 1980 five-speed that listed for $9,530, including S package trim ($730), air conditioning ($575), and a rear-window wiper ($95). It weighed 2,060 pounds and did 0-60 mph in 11.5 seconds. Top speed was 96 mph. The editors said the car felt slightly less energetic than earlier Siroccos, but was still a model of fuel-crisis fun.

The first-generation Sirocco was in production until 1981, with only minor changes. Despite some early problems with rust and cold starting, owners were happy, and VW sold 504,200 before the original gave way to a restyled second-generation Sirocco.

Golf assembly began at Wolfsburg on March 2, 1974. Beetle production had been moved out of

large parts of the complex to make way. The public launch came in June, with engine and transmission choice the same as for the Sirocco, including the 1.1-liter gas-sipper.

VW had confidence in the design of its new cars, but feared that escalating prices would depress sales. Inflation was driving up the German mark, boosting prices for the new models in every market. Plus, the Golf was a more complex car than the Beetle, so it inevitably cost more even without inflation. Within months, however, any fear that VW might have held that the Golf and Sirocco twins would flop was dispelled. Karmann was initially geared up to build 200 Siroccos per day—less than 50,000 per year—but demand soon outpaced production, so facilities had to be re-jigged. From the start, Wolfsburg's ability to produce 3,200 Golfs per day was taxed, and it took just 31 months to produce the first one million Golfs.

First deliveries of the Rabbit to North America took place in 1975. It was an immediate hit with buyers and autowriters alike. The Rabbit came only with the 70-horsepower 1.5 liter engine and was offered in two-door hatchback form starting at $2,999, or as the four-door hatch for $3,435. Base price of the two-door Rabbit was just $104 higher than the least-expensive Beetle, and VW finally had a car that looked capable of killing off the Bug. It not only was a lot faster, a lot quieter, and in every way more capable than VW's former mainstay, but it topped all competitors in terms of design and performance.

The Rabbit shared the Sirocco's wheelbase. Its body was just fractions of an inch shorter and narrower, though the roofline was 55.5 inches tall, a full four inches higher than the sports coupe's. Still, with the Sirocco powertrain and a curb weight nearly 100 pounds less, the Rabbit had fine acceleration and handled better and rode more comfortably than any of its rivals, including the Honda Civic. And it returned about 30 mpg.

That last was important, because the Rabbit arrived in North America just as gas prices were soaring and before the domestic automakers had a chance to downsize. Roomy, well-built, and fun to drive, the new VW was superior in every way to the Ford Pintos, Chevrolet Vegas, and AMC Gremlins populating the domestics' showrooms. All was not golden, however. Early Rabbits were noisy and suffered the same cold-start problems and poor shift quality as contemporary Siroccos. Still, the Rabbit outsold the Beetle in its very first year. Strong U.S. demand allowed VW to start building Rabbits at Emden, hard by the transport

VW defined a new breed of performance car, the hot hatchback, when it unveiled the 1976 Golf GTI (above). It got 110 horsepower from its 1.6-liter four, could run 0-60 mph in 9.6 seconds, and topped out at 110 mph. This version of the pocket rocket didn't come to the U.S., but Americans did get the new Cabriolet, introduced for 1980 (opposite top). Carefully built by Karmann from a two-door Rabbit, it was a little pricey but very pleasant. A second 1980 entry was the Jetta (opposite middle left). Basically a Rabbit with a trunk, its sedan proportions would prove particularly popular with Americans. The Jetta shared its interior with the Rabbit (opposite middle right). American cabins were somewhat plusher than their European counterparts, but still were refreshingly free of frills. In the Rabbit line, two-door hatchbacks accounted for about 70 percent of sales (opposite bottom). The 1.6-liter four had gained fuel injection for 1977 and made 78 horsepower. VW added a 48-horsepower 1.5-liter diesel four that same year.

ships that took the cars directly to North America.

Fuel injection and the 1.6-liter engine arrived for '77, and VW also began offering a Rabbit Diesel model. The 1.5-liter diesel four cylinder was a completely reworked version of the gas-powered Type 827 unit, naturally with a new overhead-cam cylinder head. It wasn't very powerful, rated at 48 horsepower at 5000 rpm and 56.5 pounds/feet of torque at 3000 in U.S. trim, but it was impressively smooth and refined compared with many 1960s-era diesels. It weighed a mere 11 pounds more than the equivalent gas engine, averaged about 45 mpg, and when mated to a Golf with more sound deadening and a lot of attention to mountings, was the smoothest small diesel in the world. It was a $195 option in the U.S. and proved surprisingly popular; sales of the Rabbit Diesel would reach as high as 100,000 per year in 1979-80.

As in the Scirocco, the gas engine's displacement shrunk to 1,457cc and horsepower dropped by seven, to 71, for 1978. But the engine ran smoother, and a switch from steel to polyurethane for the bumpers pared 23 pounds from the Rabbit's curb weight, so performance was undiminished.

"Volkswagen's bread and butter sedan, the Rabbit, is still the automobile against which other small cars of this type are measured," *Road & Track* said in its 1978 roundup of the American automotive market. Dress-up packages and other options could push the price of a Rabbit to nearly $6,000, acknowledged the editors, but buyers who were judicious with extra-cost goodies could still land an excellent value. "Spirited, roomy, economical, it outstrips most of its competition, even though its design has remained fundamentally unchanged since the car's introduction in 1975."

European buyers, meanwhile, had since 1976 enjoyed a version of the car that had spirit American enthusiasts could only dream about. It bowed at the 1975 Frankfurt Motor Show, and went on sale for '76 as the Golf GTI. This was VW's factory hot rod, a landmark machine that defined a new breed of low-cost, high-performance automobile. Wolfsburg imbued the 1.6-liter engine with Bosch fuel injection, a high-performance camshaft, and bigger inlet valves. It bumped compression from 8.2:1 to 9.5:1 and fitted an oil cooler. The result was a robust 110 horsepower at 6100 rpm. VW reduced the ride height by one inch and tuned the suspension for sporty handling, adding a rear anti-roll bar, different spring and damper rates, and wider, lower-profile tires. Ventilated rather than solid front disc brakes finished off the modifications.

Sporting drivers were ecstatic. VW's new pocket-rocket sprinted to 60 mph in just 9.6 seconds and topped out at 110 mph. It rode without harshness and furnished even better driveability than the standard-spec 1.6-liter Golf. Nothing on the market could match its combination of performance, manners, and price. Said Britain's *What Car?* magazine, "The Golf GTI is a truly remarkable car being quick yet frugal, sporty yet practical, and understated."

Then, in the spring of 1979, came one of the most appealing Golfs of all—a new Cabriolet. VW hoped long-time lovers of Beetle and Karmann-Ghia ragtops would take it to their hearts—and was not disappointed. Karmann built these convertibles using the platform, suspensions, running gear, and many front-end panels of the two-door Golf. As with the old Beetle, the heavily insulated soft top stood proud of the passenger area when folded down, but nobody seemed to mind.

The topless Rabbit came to the U.S. for 1980. Base price was a steep $8,895, but Karmann had produced a machine that combined Rabbit nimbleness with the high quality of a car costing even more. "The Rabbit convertible's over-the-road controls function with such well-oiled directness and consistency, you'd swear you have $20,000 worth of machinery at your beck and call," marveled *Car and Driver*. "The Rabbit convertible sparkles with a good humor not one car in a hundred has."

There was yet another body derivative for 1980, the Jetta. It basically was a two- or four-door sedan conversion of the Golf with a notchback roof grafted on. Behind the rear passenger doors was a conventional tail housing a 13.3-cubic foot trunk. The tail extended the rear sheetmetal, giving the Jetta an overall length of 167.8 inches, more than 12 inches longer than a Rabbit.

As the '70s drew to a close, the U.S. Golf/Jetta line stayed with the 1.6-liter gas and 1.5-liter diesel engines. In Europe, variety was the rule. The range of gas engines encompassed units of 1.1-liters/50 horsepower, 1.3-liters/60 horsepower, 1.5-liters/70 horsepower, 1.6-liters/85 horsepower, and the 1.6-liter/110-horsepower GTI screamer. The 1.5-liter diesel rounded out the lineup and was rated at 50 horsepower.

With demand for the Rabbit strong and anti-import rhetoric growing, Volkswagen was encouraged to study the possibility of locating an assembly plant in North America. In the early 1970s, study groups began looking at possibilities—from taking over existing buildings, to cooperative agreements with U.S. automakers for underused

Toni Shumücker (above) succeeded Rudolf Leiding as VW chairman in 1975 and oversaw establishment of Volkswagen's U.S. plant. With the April 1978 opening of its assembly facility in Westmoreland County, Pennsylvania (opposite), VW became the first foreign automaker in modern times to locate a factory in America. It took over an unfinished Chrysler plant and put it under the control of a management team stocked with former General Motors executives. Westmoreland's unionized workforce geared up to build 250,000 cars per year, starting with Rabbits. At its peak in 1980, the plant turned out 197,000 vehicles, but VW's focus on the American market had become blurred, and its new plant and workers would pay the price.

factory space, to building a brand-new facility of VW's own.

The first look-sees were made in 1973, but decisions were delayed while the Energy Crisis erupted, raged, and only gradually died away. It was not until there had been yet another change of VW's chief executive that the board made a definite decision. On January 10, 1975, Rudolf Leiding resigned from the chairmanship of VW AG's Board of Management. He was replaced the next day by Toni Shumücker. Shumücker already had a great deal of American car-company experience. He had started his career as a Ford-of-Germany trainee in 1940, became a buyer there after the war, and joined the board of directors when he was only 39.

By mid-1976 the need for a North American plant was urgent. Pressured by Japanese competition and by the growing strength of domestic rivals, VW sales in the U.S. were declining, from more than 500,000 annually before 1973, to 201,670 in 1976. Its share of the American market, a remarkable seven percent in 1970, had slumped to only 2.5 percent. Worse, the soaring value of the deutsche mark made it impossible to charge realistic prices for VWs in the U.S., so the company was losing $100 on every vehicle it sold.

The search committee surveyed every state except Hawaii and Alaska before preparing a short list of locations—two in Ohio, one in Pennsylvania. Authorities in the latter state offered attractive financial incentives, including new road and rail links, and on May 18, 1976, VW announced that it would locate its first North American assembly site in Westmoreland County, Pennsylvania, a 30-minute drive from Pittsburgh. VW would renovate the empty shell of an unfinished 1960s-era Chrysler plant. The German giant took a 30-year lease on the facility and backed its commitment to the market by buying from American Motors a body-panel stamping plant in Charleston, West Virginia, and setting up new executive offices in Warren, Michigan (VW's main U.S. headquarters remained in Englewood Cliffs, New Jersey).

At about this time, VW also replaced Stuart Perkins as president of Volkswagen of America. Perkins had been with VW's U.S. arm since 1955. His successor, James W. McLernon, was hired from General Motors, where he had spent 27 years, most recently as manufacturing manager for the Chevrolet Division. VW also installed several other former GM executives into its U.S. management team, including Duane Miller, who had been Pontiac's assistant chief engineer.

Westmoreland opened in April 1978, making VW the first foreign automaker to begin North American assembly since Rolls-Royce in the 1920s. VW said the facility could eventually build up to 250,000 cars per year. At first, just 50 percent of the components of each car came from North American sources, but VW said the figure would climb to 75 percent by 1980. The Westmoreland workforce, 40 percent of whom were previously unemployed, voted in the United Auto Workers union as its bargaining agent. VW accepted the vote on good terms, but was less happy with some of the early output from North American parts suppliers, many of whom were not delivering the quality VW demanded.

The first cars off the Westmoreland line were Rabbits, but plans were to eventually build Jettas and the Rabbit-based pickup truck there. Mechanically, Rabbits built in the U.S. were identical to those from overseas, including their 1,457-cc gas and 1.5-liter diesel engine. But American Rabbits had rectangular headlights, vertical side marker lights, and bright-trimmed door handles. Bigger differences were found inside, where American Rabbits were plusher than German ones. In fact, they looked like mini Oldsmobiles, with overdone color-coordinated trim in which the window winders matched the steering wheel, which matched the safety belts, which matched turn-signal stalks, etc. "At least you can't say VW isn't consistent," remarked *Car and Driver*, "even if you wind up feeling you're enveloped in some kind of institutional womb."

More importantly, the U.S. cars were screwed together just as well as the German ones, and performed similarly. A Rabbit tested by *Car and Driver* went 0-60 mph in 10.5 seconds, topped out at 99 mph, and averaged 29.5 mpg in the city and 35.5 on the highway. The two-door four-speed test car listed for $4,899 and had a curb weight of 1,880 pounds. "So a Rabbit is a Rabbit, be it German or American," concluded *Car and Driver*. "VWoA has done a remarkable job of producing, in a remarkably short period of time, a U.S.-built car that seems to be the equal of the German original in almost every respect."

Westmoreland built 42,000 cars in 1978, 173,000 in 1979, and 197,000 in 1980, by which time the majority were diesels. Overall VW sales in the U.S. were see-sawing, however, while imports as a whole set annual sales records. After an upturn from 202,000 in 1976, to 261,000 in '77, U.S. sales slipped to 217,000 in '78, then jumped to 292,000 in '79, and fell back to 268,000 in 1980.

While VWoA was coping with a fast-changing

Rectangular headlamps and vertical side marker lights identified the first Westmoreland-built Rabbits. The cars were assembled just as well as those made in Germany, and were lively performers, able to go 0-60 mph in as little as 10.5 seconds. Even their advertising had a touch of that traditional VW wit. But instead of teutonic purposefulness, Rabbit interiors were now gaudy. Suspensions would get progressively softer, as well. A chastened Volkswagen would later admit it was a mistake to water down the cars' German character. Sales of U.S.-built Rabbits peaked in 1980 at 177,000. A facelift for '81 (opposite bottom right) was accompanied by introduction of an S model with sporty trim but no mechanical alterations. These changes, plus a move to a 1.7-liter engine (still with 78 horsepower), couldn't stem the sales slide that began that year.

HOW DOES THE MAN WHO DRIVES THE SNOWPLOW DRIVE TO THE SNOWPLOW?

this one drives a Volkswagen Rabbit. Now, we would love to tell you what a brilliant choice he made. How many different cars he checked out. How smart he was to choose a Rabbit.

But the fact is, he didn't have much of a choice at all.

A snowplow driver has two crucial needs: 1) Easy starts in the middle of winter. 2) Very good maneuverability in very bad weather.

Which means he needs both fuel injection for those starts and front-wheel drive for that maneuverability. Guess what?

With the exception of our own cars, there is only one car in the Rabbit's class that can give you both fuel injection and front-wheel drive: the Rabbit itself. And with these features it's safe to say

that only one car combines the starting ease and maneuverability in snow like the Rabbit itself: the Rabbit itself.

Snowplow driver or not, we think you'll be impressed with the way the Rabbit is put together. With its performance. Its handling. Its carrying capacity.

Car and Driver was very impressed: "The Rabbit does more useful and rewarding things than any other small car in the world."

Now the question is:

Does the man who drives the snowplow own a Rabbit to help him do his job?

Or does he do his job to help him own a Rabbit?

VOLKSWAGEN DOES IT AGAIN

U.S. market, VW in Europe was expanding its product line yet again with the 1976 introduction of a new and very small car, the Polo. At this time, VW was still building five basically different product lines: Beetle, K70, Polo, Golf, and Passat, plus the Scirocco at Karmann, and the perennial van-bus, too. Only the Polo and K70 would fail to make it to the U.S. market.

Plans for EA337, the car that would become the Polo, were drawn during 1970 under Kurt Lotz. The Polo was conceived before the Golf, and was to have slotted under the size/price class of the K70. But the K70's lukewarm reception changed VW's priorities. To further muddy the timeline, Polo's kissing cousin, the Audi 50, hit the market in September 1974, six months ahead of the new VW. In reality, the Audi 50 was conceived as a Volkswagen, but was retrimmed and rebadged to give Audi retailers a low-priced model.

This was the smallest car ever to carry the VW name. The Audi 50 version had a more upmarket interior and plasticy wood dashboard appliqué. For the Polo, trim and equipment were only slightly simplified, though the quality of door panels and carpets was often criticized. But the Polo did sell for 12 percent less than the Audi.

Both versions were built at the VW factory in Wolfsburg. However, the Type 801 engines designed by the Audi team at Ingolstadt became the entry-level power units and the Polo/50 was also styled in-house by the Audi team, though VW-Audi admitted that Bertone of Italy had been consulted and had inspired the curled end to the waistline under the rear quarter window.

Although the little Polo was a four-seat hatchback, it was significantly smaller than the Golf: At 92 inches, the wheelbase was 2.5 inches shorter, and its overall length of 138 inches was 8.5 inches shorter. Track and body width were some two inches narrower and curb weight was about 150 pounds less. The differences seemed minimal, but were important. Knowing full well that Fiat was committed to making front-drive 127s and 128s, that Peugeot was building the 104 and the 204, and that Ford-Europe was about to produce a new Fiesta, VW knew that it had to produce exactly the right car for this hotly contested small-car class.

While it shared the same basic mechanical layout as the Golf—transversely mounted water-cooled engine, front-wheel drive, MacPherson strut front suspension, and torsion-beam rear suspension—the Polo/50 differed in almost every detail. The Type 801 engine was physically smaller than the Golf's Type 827. Detailed as a simple overhead-cam four, it had a cast-iron block and an aluminum head, and was canted forward by 15 degrees. Two displacements, 895cc and 1,093cc, were available. The smaller unit had 40 horsepower, the 1.1-liter produced 50 or 60, depending on the model. The need to minimize size was so important that cylinder bores were siamezed, meaning there was no cooling water circulating between the bores, only on their outer peripheries. Although a 1.2-liter version was planned, it would have to have a long-throw crankshaft, and no further stretching would then be possible.

Polo/50 was an economy car of modest performance; top speed of the 40-horsepower model was only 82 mph. The original intention was to use tiny 12-inch wheels and all-drum brakes, but all versions of the production cars had front disc brakes and 13-inch wheels.

The Audi 50 was discontinued in 1978, but Polo soldiered on, and even got a slightly larger notchback derivative in July 1977. As the Jetta was technically identical to the Golf, the Derby was similar to the Polo, and it, too, replaced the hatchback with a tail that held a conventional trunk. Overall length increased by 13 inches, while weight was up by a mere 35 pounds. The 895cc engine was never available in the Derby; most got the new 1,272-cc unit, which was added to the Polo range at about the same time. Derby outsold Polo for its first few months, but both cars were discontinued in 1981 after slightly more than one million had been produced.

Volkswagen in the 1970s had undergone tumultuous change. It had solidified important alliances and adapted to the realities of component sharing and badge engineering. Most importantly, VW had propelled itself not just into the age of modern automotive design, but was designing great cars that others were compelled to copy.

While Volkswagen of America was coping with a fast-changing U.S. market, VW in Europe was expanding its product line with the 1976 addition of the Polo (this page). The smallest car ever to wear the VW badge, it used a transverse front-engine, front-wheel-drive layout, and would become a permanent part of VW's overseas lineup. Westmoreland built mostly Rabbits, and eventually turned out some Jettas, but its most-unusual product was the Rabbit-based pickup truck (opposite top row). Built starting in 1980, it used the Rabbit's powertrains and platform, but its 103.3-inch wheelbase was nearly 10 inches longer. It was among the world's few front-drive trucks, but it did not prove popular. Sales peaked at 37,392 in 1981, and had dwindled to just 2,079 by 1983, when the plant produced the last of the 75,947 built. One Rabbit not assembled at Westmoreland was the convertible (opposite bottom). It retained the spirit that would have to invigorate all VWs if the company was to reassert itself in the 1980s.

Triumph and Turmoil— Volkswagen in the 1980s

As the 1980s dawned, obsolete Volkswagens such as the Beetle and other rear-engine models had been largely swept away. Audi had been given the chance to develop its own future. And VW was ready to update its model range. The company was a titan in Europe, and new products unveiled in the '80s would make it even stronger. In the U.S., the decade would be marked by poor decisions, a struggle for identity, even tragedy.

VW wasn't happy that so much of what had been achieved in the 1970s had been with outside help. The new engines had come from Audi, the Golf's styling had been inspired by ItalDesign, the flagship Passat owed its origins to the Audi 80, and the Scirocco was built by Karmann. In the next few years, most ties with consultants would be cast off, and in-house expertise would take their place. Although the company's major building blocks from the 1970s—engines and transmissions—would stay in production for years, new models would be developed totally at Wolfsburg.

The second Energy Crisis that erupted with so little warning in 1979 and the global recession that followed quelled car demand worldwide. VW suffered, but not as much as most competitors. Production in the German factories, 1.3 million in 1978, didn't dip below one million through 1982. And in 1982, the company also built 305,143 Audis in Germany, 271,068 VWs in Brazil, 125,663 VWs in Mexico, and 84,027 Rabbits in the U.S. In the whole of Europe, only Renault was bigger than VW.

Still, all four Volkswagen car lines had been launched between 1973 and 1975, and replacements were overdue. Because the Audi 80, which inspired the birth of the first Passat, had been replaced by a second-generation car in 1978, observers bet the next new VW would be a new Passat.

The observers were right. The first new VW for the 1980s was a redesigned Passat and it appeared in October 1980. The product planners had reasoned that if VW could sell 1.8 million first-generation Passats in seven years, they should provide more of the same for the 1980s. Thus, the new model was another mid-size, mid-priced, front-wheel-drive car. It was, however, larger, roomier,

faster, and potentially more economical than its predecessor.

Honing its badge-engineering skills, VW tried to distance the new Passat from the second-generation Audi 80, which was known as the Audi 4000 when it came to America. The two cars shared the same new platform/underframe, suspensions, doors, and some inner panels. They dipped into the same box for engines and transmissions. But they catered to different customers. In the same way Ford might separate a Mercury from a Ford, the Audi was a better-equipped, more expensive, and somehow a more exclusive proposition than the Passat. The Audi 80/4000 was a four-door sedan and, later, a coupe. Passats were two- and four-door hatchbacks and four-door wagons.

The look was evolutionary, rounded slightly, but still obviously a VW. The important difference was that it was the work of VW's own styling department, which shaped the car after studying what Audi and ItalDesign had done.

The new Passat was strategically larger than its predecessor. Wheelbase was 100.4 inches, 3.2 inches longer than the first-generation, and the track was 2.5 inches wider. The body was nearly six inches longer than before, and 3.5 inches wider. It all meant the cabin was that important bit more spacious. The new car retained the same type of independent suspension layouts: MacPherson strut front, trailing arm/torsion beam rear. Somehow, VW had held down the inevitable weight increase to a mere 46 pounds so the cars tipped the scales at around 2,300 pounds.

In Europe, four engines were available, ranging from the small 1,272cc/55 horsepower Type 801 unit, to a choice of gas or diesel 1,588cc four-cylinders, to a 1,921cc inline gasoline five-cylinder rated at 115 horsepower. The five had debuted in the latest range of Audi 100 models (Audi 5000 in the U. S.), marking the first use of such a configuration in a regular-production passenger car. It took considerable engineering skill to mount the five-cylinder so that its inherent vibration was kept to acceptable levels. VW believed the effort worth it, and touted the five as a step up in performance from a four, but not as expensive as a six-cylinder.

The new Passat came to the U.S. for the 1982

For decades, American car buyers had identified Volkswagen primarily with the unchanging and ubiquitous Beetle. But by the 1980s, the German automaker offered vehicles in an array of market segments, as evidenced by this view of the 1985 line. VW strategists no doubt believed this was necessary to compete with formidable rivals such as Toyota. But in the absence of an appealing core product, such as the Beetle, traditional VW owners had fled to other makes. And potential new customers were not being fed a clear message about what a VW was. Sales suffered, and VW learned some painful lessons.

model year, but eschewed the Dasher name for another new moniker, Quantum. In America, it qualified as a roomy automobile built to near premium-car levels, but one that was overpriced for its modest performance abilities. Initially, just the two-door hatchback and station wagon were offered, with the only engine being the familiar 1.7-liter four-cylinder. It was rated at 74 horsepower at 5000 rpm and 90 pounds/feet of torque at 3000. Transmission choices were a five-speed manual or optional three-speed automatic. Base price for the hatchback was $10,250 and popular options, such as air conditioning ($690), AM/FM cassette ($640), alloy wheels and wider tires ($375), and metallic paint ($125), could push the price to near $12,100.

That was a lot of money for a roomy car that handled competently, but rode rather stiffly, was short on midrange power, and when driven hard, could muster a best time of 14.1 seconds 0-60 mph and a 91 mph top speed. Fuel economy was good for the car's size, averaging in the mid 20-mpg range. But unlike the machines Americans had come to expect from the "new" Volkswagen, the Quantum broke no ground. Instead, it seemed to fade into the mainstream family-car mold that was available for less money in such models as the Chrysler K-cars, or with more performance and value in cars such as the Datsun Maxima.

"The Quantum...doesn't herald the beginning of a new era—or the end of an old one, for that matter," said *Car and Driver* in its test of an '82 hatchback. It concluded that "the only really unexpected thing about the Quantum [is that] this time around, Volkswagen is following everybody else."

Withholding a sedan body style from the second-generation lineup was part of VW's effort to differentiate the Passat/Quantum from the Audi 80/4000. But when the public asked for such a body style, it required no great work to provide one, since the platform was already accommodating the Audi sedan. When VW introduced the four-door notchback sedan to Europe in September 1981, however, it pitched it not as a derivative of the Passat range, but as a new flagship model called the Santana. No one was fooled. Every major dimension of the platform was the same, as were the wheelbase, wheel tracks, suspension assemblies, even engine choices. The Santana name was another meteorological reference and was meant to recall the Santa Ana, the hot wind that sweeps through Southern California.

The four-door kept the Quantum name for its 1983 unveiling in the U.S., and it introduced the five-cylinder engine to America. It was a 2.2-liter

version (2,144cc, 131 cubic inches), and was rated at 100 horsepower at 5100 rpm and 122 pounds/feet of torque at 3000. It was the largest, most-powerful VW engine offered to date in a U.S.-market car. It was available only with automatic transmission and only in the four-door sedan and station-wagon models.

Road testers liked the engine and the new four-door body style. "It brings a definite element of luxury and class to the Volkswagen camp," said *Road & Track*. The magazine's test car listed for a pricey $13,980, but that included the automatic transmission and amenities such as power windows and AM/FM cassette, which were standard. Air conditioning and metallic paint were options. Though the engine ran smoothly, provided decent midrange punch, and averaged 21 mpg, its 0-60 mph time of 12.6 seconds was not remarkable.

Equipped with the five-cylinder engine, the Quantum was known as the GL5. The 1.7-liter four-cylinder still was standard, but there was another new engine for '83 that brought with it the Quantum TD tag. TD stood for Turbo Diesel. This was a new 1.6-liter diesel four-cylinder boosted by a turbocharger to a respectable 68 horsepower at 4500 rpm and 98 pounds/feet of torque at a usefully low 2800 rpm. With the standard five-speed gearbox, it propelled a Quantum to 60 mph in 14.3 seconds, but more importantly, ran with little fuss or harshness and would return around 34 mpg.

When it was conceived, Santana was given its own name partly because it was intended to be something of a world car. In addition to being built in West Germany, it was also slated for assembly in China, Spain, and the United States. Chinese assembly, in association with Nissan, actually began in 1983, and assembly from kits at a Seat factory in Spain was significant as the first step toward much-closer cooperation with the Spanish concern. But the idea of building Quantums in the U.S. came to nothing. Although Volkswagen of America had signed a contract in 1980 to develop a second assembly plant in Sterling Heights, Michigan, the downturn of VW's fortunes at Westmoreland, Pennsylvania, and the recession in general, caused that to be abandoned.

The European Santana model, as such, had a life of less than four years. After 193,540 were built, the name was quietly dropped and the cars continued as Passat sedans. The second-generation Passat carried on with few changes, and after 1986, when the third-generation Audi 80 appeared, the Passat

(continued)

Volkswagen entered the decade of the 1980s with a lineup that didn't include a design under five years of age. Instead of updating the Golf/Rabbit, however, it released a new version of its largest car, the Passat. It bowed in Europe in 1980 (top left) and was larger than the first-generation Passat. Its front-drive platform and longitudinally mounted engines were again shared with an Audi. The new car came to the U.S. for 1982 and dumped the Dasher tag for a fresh name, Quantum. It was initially offered as a two-door hatchback (lower left) and station wagon, both with a fuel-injected 74-horsepower 1.7-liter four cylinder. For '83, a four door (middle right) came to America, along with a 100-horsepower 2.2-liter inline five-cylinder Audi engine. This was VW's flagship model and the company fiddled with pricing, packages, and powertrains to attract buyers. A new grille was added for 1987 (bottom right). Overall, the Quantum was roomy and sporty, but noisy and largely ignored. It was discontinued after 1988.

The second new VW of the 1980s was the revamped Scirocco. It debuted for the 1982 model year both in Europe (above) and in the United States (right and opposite top row). It retained its predecessor's wheelbase, front-drive platform, hatchback body style, and transverse four-cylinder engines. But instead of crisp Giugiaro lines, there was rounded styling from VW's own studios. It gave the car a larger cabin, but was less engaging to the eye. The second-generation Scirocco wasn't as nimble as the original, though it was still a genuine performance coupe. Euro versions with the 110-horsepower 1.6 liter did 0-60 mph in 8.9 seconds. During '83, U.S. cars traded their 74-horsepower 1.7 (0-60 in 11.5 seconds) for a 90-horse 1.8 (9.7 seconds). Performance blossomed for '86 when VW put a 16-valve twin-cam head on the 1.8, boosting horsepower to 139 in Europe and to 123 in America. Imbued with a revised suspension, wider tires, and aero addenda, 16V U.S. Sciroccos (opposite bottom) now did 0-60 mph in a quick 8.0 seconds. The car faded from the U.S. lineup after 1988, but hung on in Europe until 1992.

did not share its platform with any other car. In Europe, the 1,296cc engine ended its run in 1986, though both the naturally aspirated and turbocharged diesels lived on. And as the economy-conscious early 1980s gave way to the more-exuberant mid 1980s, VW tried to inject the aging Passat with some semblance of a sporting image by offering the 2.2-liter five tuned for 136 horsepower.

In an eight-year life, the Passat/Quantum rarely made headlines—good or bad—but sold pretty well. By the time it was displaced after 1988, 2,171,740 of all types had been produced in West Germany alone, and more were built in other countries, including Brazil where there were specially developed Santana/Quantums, including two-door sedans never sold elsewhere.

By this time, there had been yet another change of top management at Wolfsburg. The popular and effective Toni Shumücker had suffered a heart attack in June 1981. He recovered, but elected to retire and was replaced by Carl H. Hahn. Hahn had run VW's American sales and marketing operation in the 1950s and '60s, at the height of Beetlemania. He had returned to Wolfsburg to direct worldwide sales in the mid 1960s, but moved out of the limelight in the mid 1970s. Now he was back in the position that many had forecast for him as early as 1971, when Kurt Lotz was elbowed out.

The first new model to bow on Hahn's watch was the second-generation Scirocco. Early in its life, this Karmann-built coupe had comfortably outsold the Ford Capri and Opel Manta, but had since been eclipsed by newer models, such as the Toyota Celica.

This time around, VW put the styling of the new-generation Scirocco to open-market competition. ItalDesign made several competent suggestions, but it was VW's much-expanded styling studio at Wolfsburg, under Herbert Schafer, that finally got the job. Schafer later admitted he had never warmed to the angularities of the original Scirocco, so the new car was to have more rounded lines.

After much time with models and full-size mockups in the Wolfsburg wind tunnel, Schafer's team produced a softer-edged and significantly more-roomy new hatchback. It was still built by Karmann, and although the body was nearly 10 inches longer than before (mostly for added luggage space), the drag coefficient had been reduced from Cd 0.42 to 0.38. The new sheetmetal, incidentally, was mounted on the original 94.5-inch-wheelbase 1970s Golf platform, and not on the longer-

wheelbase/wider-track platform of the next-generation Golf, which was already under development.

Was the new car prettier than the old? Some preferred the original clean-cut ItalDesign work to the softer, bulkier second-generation machine. The car's real problem, however, was not that it lacked performance, but that its handling wasn't as sharp, nor its character as emphatic, as that of the original or of the Golf GTI. Some critics even went so far as to call it dull.

For 1982, European Scirocco IIs were available with a familiar mixed-bag of Type 801 and Type 827 engines, from the 60-horsepower 1.27-liter to the 110-horsepower fuel-injected 1.6-liter, which appeared in the new Scirocco GTI. The GTI could run 0-60 mph in 8.9 seconds, had a maximum speed of 116 mph, and would return about 23 mpg in daily driving. After his first drive, renowned automotive writer Paul Frere said the Scirocco GTI is "not only a delightful little car but also probably the quickest production 1.6-liter available anywhere in the world, and one that provides the best performance/economy and the best performance/price ratio."

U.S.-market Sciroccos all had the 74-horsepower 1.7-liter (1,717cc, 105 cubic inches) four that was also fitted to contemporary Rabbits. The new car

While Volkswagen's U.S. market share dwindled during the 1980s, the company remained a titan in Europe, where its broad model lineup was an asset. Representing VW in the important mini-car segment was the Polo. It was redesigned in 1981 and fielded an assortment of models and body styles (opposite bottom). They included (opposite, clockwise from top left) the hot 115-horsepower supercharged G40, the two-door Derby sedan, and the Polo Coupe. Known collectively as the Polo II, these cars sold in annual volumes of 150,000 to 200,000, but were not imported to the U.S. When heart problems forced Toni Shumücker to retire in 1981, Carl H. Hahn (this page) took over as chairman of the VW Group. Hahn had overseen U.S. sales and marketing in the 1950s and '60s, when the Beetle was king.

weighed about 100 pounds more than its predecessor, felt roomier, and was quieter. The suspension was still taut, but a bit more compliant over bumps. And while the steering was firmer, the new Scirocco felt noticeably less-crisp changes of direction.

"If the new car doesn't feel quite as racy as the old, it still drives better than almost any Honda, Toyota, or Mazda," said *Car and Driver*. "The Scirocco still exudes a special tingle that serious drivers will feel in their bones." The magazine's test car had a curb weight of 2,160 pounds and listed for $11,090, including air conditioning ($690), metallic paint ($125), and a rear-window wiper/washer ($125). Zero-60 mph took 11.5 seconds and top speed was 102 mph. An interesting illustration of the new car's aerodynamic advantage came through when *Car and Driver* drag-raced one against a 1981 Scirocco. "Off the line the lighter '81 pulled out a clear lead of half a car-length to about 60 mph...but by 85 mph, the new car was ahead and pulling slowing away."

VW tinkered a little with engine output over the next few years, dropping the 1.3 from its European line, and offering a fortified 1.8-liter four of 1,781cc (109 cubic inches). Along with a new close-ratio five-speed manual, the 1.8 was made standard on U.S. Sciroccos during 1983 and was rated at 90 horsepower at 5500 rpm and 100 pounds/feet of torque at 3000. It cut 0-60 mph times to a brisk 9.7 seconds and lifted top speed to 108 mph.

Then VW unleashed a blockbuster 16-valve four-cylinder. This engine was available in Europe for 1985, and came to the U.S. for 1986 in a new top-line model called the Scirocco 16V.

It reflected Volkswagen's determination to get the most out of its Type 827 engines, which had already been on sale for more than 10 years. Below the cylinder head, there were few changes. It still displaced 1,781cc, but wore a brand new cylinder head, with twin overhead camshafts and four valves per cylinder. The result was a powerful and torquey unit rated at 139 horsepower in European tune and capable of propelling a Scirocco to 130 mph.

American Scirocco 16Vs were rated at 123 horsepower at 5800 rpm and 120 pounds/feet of torque at 4250. Since the second-generation car had bowed, the U.S. market had been flooded with a new range of multi-valve, turbocharged rivals—mostly Japanese—that had cut the eight-valve VW sports coupe from a contender to a pretender. Now it was back.

"With one fell swoop, the wizards of Wolfsburg

have transformed the ho-hum VW Scirocco from an also-ran into a supercoupe to be reckoned with," asserted *Car and Driver*. "This VW—the fastest and most powerful machine ever to wear those initials in America—is ready for all comers."

Zero-60 mph now took just eight seconds flat, and top speed was 124 mph. Most of the power was concentrated above 4000 rpm, but testers said the engine was strong through most of the speed range. Scirocco 16Vs got wider 185/60HR14 tires on new teardrop-style alloy wheels, a recalibrated suspension, and monochrome fender flares, sill moldings, and spoilers. VW also relocated the radio antenna to the trailing edge of the roof to limit electrical interference from the new engine's ignition system. At 2,380 pounds, the 16V car was lighter than most any of its competitors, though it wasn't any less expensive, going out the door for almost $14,000 once air conditioning, power windows, and the cassette audio system were fitted.

The emissions equipment that took some of the starch out of U.S. versions was making its way to Europe by 1987, when homemarket Sciroccos got a catalyst version of the 16-valver with 129 horsepower.

Scirocco was always a niche seller for VW, but even at that, its popularity was dwindling. U.S. sales had declined from 13,500 in 1985 to just 6,970 for 1987 and then to 3,750 in '88. When VW announced its 1989 U.S. model lineup, the Scirocco was not aboard. The car hung on in Europe until 1992, offered as a lower-cost companion to the new Corrado. The second-generation's legacy was as the first VW-styled sports coupe and as the car that introduced the world to multi-valve VW power. In 11 years, it had sold to 340,700 customers worldwide.

Because Karmann had borne most of the work in tooling, testing, and building the second-genera-

Volkswagen's smallest U.S. model was the Fox (both pages). It was based on VW's Brazilian-market front-drive subcompact and was offered in America from 1987 through 1993. Two- and four-door sedans and two-door wagons were featured, all with a longitudinally mounted 81-horsepower 1.8-liter four cylinder engine. The Fox was relatively roomy, better built than most Third-World cars, and had good performance, running 0-60 mph in about 10.5 seconds. Lack of an available automatic transmission was a drawback, but VW's aim was to recapture the entry-level buyer that had been snared by the Beetle—a link made clear by this advertising-work-in-progress (opposite lower right). However, inflation in Brazil erased most any price advantage, and a car that started at a reasonable $5,990 in 1987 was listing for over $9,000 by 1993. Fox sales in the U.S. peaked in 1988 at just 57,000.

If you lose an old friend, you better find a new one twice as good.

The words you are now readinu are not the text That actual development of the message, so that th resemble a complete advertisement in every re purpose is for size and color only. This is importa particularly important, for test purposes, so tha physical aspects of the message will not be a pro The words you are now reading are not the text advertisement. The words you are now reading. This "dummy" copy is placed here in lieu of actu

development of the message, so that this adwilles is for size and color only. This is important. This is larly important, for test purposes, so that the phy aspectso will not be a problem. That you the text his adve

The new
Fox
$0,000.

tion Sciroccos, VW could afford to simultaneously develop another major new car. Most observers expected it would be a new Golf, but VW confounded them in September 1981 by announcing a new Polo range instead.

It was with this new-generation Polo that VW seemed to make one of its increasing, and expensive, mistakes. Stung by constant criticism, especially from German customers, that the original Polo was too small, with a cramped cabin, the designers set about rectifying this.

They were held back by two major constraints. First, the existing Polo was already uncomfortably close to the Golf in price and in size (its wheelbase was just 2.5 inches shorter). Second, the bean-counters decided the existing platform and mechanical layout would have to be used again.

With an unchanged wheelbase, only marginally widened wheel tracks, and an overall length increase of just two inches to play with, the designers could do little. They reshaped the cabin, giving more head room, and lengthened the body by two inches, but they were unable to move the rear seats backward for more rear leg room. The new styling was largely without charm, though VW claimed a much reduced drag coefficient, down to Cd 0.39. The new two-door hatchback had a roofline extended to nearly that of the wagon model. And a two-door sedan appeared early in 1982, called the Polo Classic in some markets, a Derby in others.

Tightening exhaust-emissions regulations meant the engine range had to be shuffled to keep up the power. The original 895cc unit was killed, and for Polo II there were 1,043cc, 1,093cc, and 1,272cc versions of the little forward-leaning Type 801. With 40, 50, and 60 horsepower, respectively, these were neither fast nor particularly fuel efficient cars. Automatic transmission was never available on any of them.

There was no badge-engineered Audi to boost sales, but the Polo II sold steadily, usually between 150,000 and 200,000 per year, which was neither spectacular nor financially disastrous. Yet VW could not do without it.

In 1982, a Polo Coupe bowed with a 75-horsepower version of the 1,272cc engine. And in 1986, Volkswagen launched the Polo G40 coupe, adding a supercharger for an output of 115 horsepower and a claimed top speed of 122 mph. All engines had Bosch fuel injection by the end of the 1980s. This was to meet emissions standards rather than boost the power. Peak power ratings, in fact, were usually unaltered. A new small diesel engine also had been added to the range.

VW never offered the Polo in the U.S., but in 1987, it did introduce a car that slotted below the Rabbit/Golf in size and price. It was called the Fox and it was a front-drive subcompact based on the Brazilian Volkswagen Voyage sedan and Parati station wagon, both substantially revised for the U.S. market. The Fox was offered as a two- and four-door notchback sedan and a two-door wagon. Prices started at a reasonable $5,990. All used an 81-horsepower version of the 1.8-liter four-cylinder, but it was mounted longitudinally instead of transversely, as in the contemporary Golf and Jetta. The only transmission at first was a four-speed manual.

VW's Brazilian import was a refreshing change from other Third World cars of the day, such as the Yugo or Hyundai Excel. It offered spunky performance along with good fuel economy. Zero-60-mph acceleration was 10.5 seconds, top speed was 95 mph, and combined city/highway mileage was about 25 mpg. It was enjoyable to drive and had far sturdier construction and a higher-grade interior than other entry-level cars.

The shift linkage was hard to wrestle into reverse, however, and the tall overdrive top gear put the engine well below its useful power range. The stiff manual steering required extra muscle at parking speeds, head room was at a premium for tall people, and the spare tire cut into the usefulness of the already small trunk.

The Fox was little changed during its U.S. run. A five-speed manual was made available during 1988, and for '91, the wagon was dropped while the remaining notchbacks got rectangular aero headlamps. VW hoped the Fox would recapture the sort of entry-level buyer that had been snared by the original Beetle. But sales were never strong. They started at 40,000 in 1987 and climbed to 57,000 in '88, then dwindled to 6,700 in 1993. VW didn't offer a 1994 Fox, and discontinued imports after the final 3,900 were cleared off dealer's lots. VW's plans to sell the car at bargain-basement prices were thwarted when inflation in Brazil pushed up its price, which had reached the $9,000-range. It was another try that went wide of the mark.

In fact, it seemed VW had been missing its U.S. target since the early 1980s. Lulled by ready fuel supplies, Americans had returned to large cars, though VW's problem seemed to be that its cars were too American. The former General Motors men running Westmoreland had drained U.S.-built

Plummeting sales prompted Volkswagen to reassess its U.S. marketing strategy. It concluded that the American operation needed to reassert VW's German heritage, which held that driving was serious fun. The first tangible evidence of this shift was the Rabbit GTI. It debuted for 1983 and was heralded in advertising that conveyed the car's exuberant nature (top). In place of the regular Rabbit's 74-horsepower 1.7-liter four was the Scirocco's 90-horsepower 1.8. The GTI also got a tauter suspension. It stormed through corners and zipped to 60 in 9.7 seconds. Reinforcing its message was black-out exterior trim, sports seats, and a dashboard mercifully devoid of fake woodgrain (bottom right). The Rabbit GTI listed for a reasonable $7,990 and signaled a change in philosophy that would continue with VW's next round of American-market products.

(continued)

Fly GTI.

Volkswagen unveiled the second-generation Golf in Europe during August 1983 (both pages) and followed with the next-series Jetta in January 1984. Numerous styling proposals were assessed before Wolfsburg settled on one from its own studios. The shape was an aerodynamic evolution of the one that had helped sell six million original Golfs and Jettas. The new car was larger and wider than the original. Wheelbase increased by 2.6 inches, to 97.3, and bodies were longer, by as much as six inches for the Euro Golf. There was now seating for five instead of four, and more luggage room under the Golf's hatch (opposite bottom left) and in the Jetta's trunk. Curb weight for the Golf increased by 256 pounds, to 2,150. Front-wheel drive and the transverse mounting of four-cylinder engines were preserved. Europeans could choose from among six gasoline engines, as well as turbocharged and naturally aspirated diesels. Sales were strong right from the start.

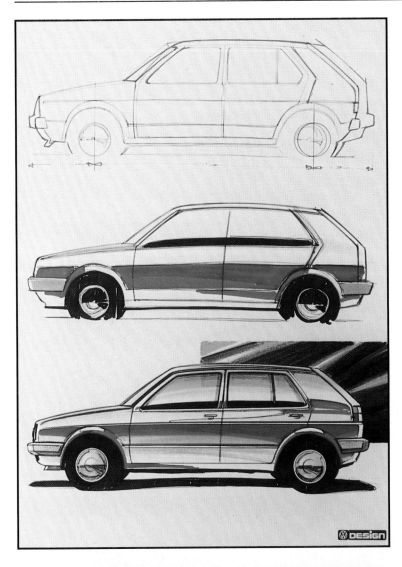

The Rabbit name died when VW brought its second-generation mainstays to America as the 1985 Jetta and Golf (above). U.S.-market Golfs were assembled in Pennsylvania with same conviction that went into the German-built Jettas, a point VW tried to convey in advertising (opposite bottom). Indeed, the baby-Buick feel had been replaced with a European bearing. Suspensions were stiffer, interiors less gaudy (right). An 85-horsepower 1.8-liter four was the standard engine; optional were a naturally aspirated 1.6-liter diesel with 52 horsepower or a Jetta-only turbodiesel with 68. The Golf GTI (opposite middle and top row) shared with the Jetta GLI beefier underpinnings, sports seats, four-wheel disc brakes, and a 102-horsepower version of the 1.8-liter four-cylinder.

Rabbits of their Teutonic edge, offering instead mushy suspensions, soft seats, and baby-blue interiors with woodgrain appliqués. Even VW Chairman Carl Hahn noticed. "When I drove the American Rabbit," he said, "it felt like a Chevrolet. If you want a Chevrolet, you should go to General Motors."

Sales of U.S.-built Rabbits peaked in 1980 at 177,000, then took a nosedive. Sales in the first half of 1982 were down 45 percent from a year earlier and a four-month inventory of unsold Rabbits languished on lots. VWoA laid off 10 percent of its white-collar workers and closed Westmoreland for six weeks. Into this mess stepped James R. Fuller.

Fuller had put in time at Ford, then at Renault U.S.A., before joining VW's Porsche+Audi division, where he had presided over a sales increase. VW created a new position, vice president, Volkswagen Division, and put Fuller in it. Fuller instituted a new campaign to reinvigorate American VWs with driver-pleasing German flavor and called it "Roots." The first evidence of the change came for the 1983 model year.

"The car we've all been waiting for," was the headline *Car and Driver* used to herald the arrival of the Rabbit GTI. Outside it had blacked-out trim set off by tasteful red moldings and red badges. Inside were firm sport seats, the padded four-spoke Scirocco steering wheel, and on the dashboard, simulated aluminum trim instead of the regular Rabbit's fake woodgrain. The suspension was beefed up to get the most out of 185/60HR14 Pirelli P6 tires on alloy wheels.

The big news was underhood. In place of the regular Rabbit's 74-horsepower 1.7 liter four was the 90-horsepower 1.8-liter four fresh from the Scirocco. It had 16 fewer horsepower than the hot 1.6-liter in the German GTI, but VW said U.S. versions had more around-town torque to suit American driving tastes. VW did use the German GTI's five-speed gearbox, plus its sway bars and ventilated front disc brakes.

The Rabbit GTI blended quickness and agility with refined manners, hatchback utility, and fuel economy of around 25 mpg, all for an introductory price of just $7,990. *Car and Driver* wrung a 0-60 mph time of 9.7 seconds out of its GTI and hit 104 mph. The testers at *Road & Track* loved the car, too. Their assessment: "Plain and simple, go-for-it fun, and we mean FUN!" *R&T* managed 10.6 seconds 0-60 mph, but that still was quicker than the 11.1 seconds it recorded with a $13,300 BMW 320i.

Though VW sales continued soft in the U.S., demand for the GTI was strong and the car served

notice that the German company hadn't forgotten its heritage. It was a theme carried through in the next-generation Golf and Jetta.

VW had built six million original Golfs and Jettas before revealing the successor in August 1983 as the 1984-model Golf. The Jetta followed in January 1984. Westmoreland would continue to build the old models for another season, but when the new cars went into production, the Rabbit name was dropped and, in keeping with the "Germanization" of the U.S. line, the Golf badge was adopted to go along with Jetta.

The only surprise about the new car was that there were no surprises. Developed around a totally new platform, at a huge cost for the day—VW admitted to spending around $1.4 billion on new tooling and facilities—the new-generation car nonetheless looked much like the old, though it was larger and heavier.

Work on the new generation had started in May 1979, when VW realized that its sharply detailed ItalDesign-styled Golf was being paced by European and Japanese opposition. The established Golf was still selling in huge numbers, but VW felt it should become larger, with better equipment, and be more refined. It should, in other words, grow up a little.

Wolfsburg assessed no fewer than ten different styling proposals. Some were from outside companies, including ItalDesign, which had lost its place as a favored consultant and had to pitch for business along with everyone else. The chosen design came from VW's own styling department, and one reason it looked so much like the old was that the play-it-safe marketing staff wanted it that way.

The second-issue Golf was bulkier than the original, for it was meant to be a full five-passenger car. In particular, VW wanted it to have more space in the rear seat and in the luggage compartment. At 97.3 inches, the wheelbase had grown by 2.6 inches. The track was wider by 1.6 inches in front and 2.6 in back. Overall length went up by 6.7 inches on European Golfs, while U.S. versions, with their different bumpers, were longer by 4.7 inches. Jetta bodies grew longer by 3.9 inches. Both cars were 2.1 inches wider. Luggage capacity was up by 30 percent; with the rear seat folded, Golfs now had 34.4 cubic feet of cargo space. Jettas didn't get a folding rear seatback, but did have a generously sized 16.6-cubic-foot trunk. Fuel capacity increased by four gallons, to 14.5 gallons. Curb weights were up significantly. The Golf weighed in

(continued)

While the second-generation Golf was quickly becoming one of Europe's most-popular cars, U.S. buyers gravitated to the Jetta. The American market tended to see hatchbacks as synonymous with low-cost economy cars. A notchback sedan was considered more upscale, and its trunk was recognized as more secure for valuables. Thus, the Jetta outsold the Golf by more than two-to-one in the U.S. It's represented here by a 1987 four-door (top) and an '85 two-door. Still, no Volkswagen was demonstrating much appeal to the millions of Americans who had grown accustomed to buying Japanese small cars. U.S. sales surged above 200,000 in '85 and '86, then fell to 169,000 in '88, beginning a nearly decade-long decline. Volkswagen was forced to close its Westmoreland factory in 1988, and to source most U.S. Golfs and some Jettas from its plant in Mexico.

Four-Wheel Drive and Supercharging

Once the the mid-1980s model lineup was set, Volkswagen's engineers turned their attention to new mechanical features. Europe's other automakers were already following two distinct trends, one toward all-wheel-drive systems, the other toward forced-induction engines. VW decided to follow both of them, and at the Frankfurt Motor Show in September 1985, it unveiled both four-wheel-drive layouts and supercharged engines.

Until the late 1970s the only successful four-wheel-drive vehicles had been Jeeps and similar off-road machines. Britain's Jensen company had produced a few hundred colossally expensive FF types in the 1960s, though a handful of other manufacturers, including Subaru in the 1970s, and AMC, with the Eagle in 1980, had limited success with lower-cost 4WD cars.

In Europe, though, the big breakthrough came in 1980, with the launch of the Audi Quattro. It combined four-wheel drive, a five-cylinder engine, and turbocharging. The result was a ferociously fast 200-horsepower supercar that changed the face of international rallying. VW, BMW, Ford, and Mercedes-Benz all followed up with similar competition-oriented cars.

Providing four-wheel drive, whether permanently engaged or as a part-time, on-demand system, was easy enough. But making it compact, refined, versatile, and suitable for passenger cars was much more difficult. Each engineering team had its own ideas, and at VW, a system called Syncro was developed. It debuted in the Transporter as a conversion built by Steyr in Austria, then in the second-generation European Golf from the autumn of 1985.

Syncro was as clever and unobtrusive a way of providing four-wheel drive as anyone had come up with. Nonetheless, it was still bulky and expensive. Because a new floor pan and new semi-trailing arm rear suspension were needed, not to mention a raised rear floor and the four-wheel-drive hardware itself, this was a complex piece of reengineering that added 214 pounds to the weight of a Golf.

On the chosen Golf production model—the 90-horsepower, 1.8-liter version at first—the transverse engine and five-speed manual transmission looked much as they did in the front-wheel-drive cars, and in fact, the front wheels always received power. What was different was the addition of a driveshaft extension from the front differential, a three-piece propeller shaft leading to the rear of the car, and a body-shell-mounted differential linked to exposed rear drive shafts.

Syncro was in effect an on-demand system, that is, it operated in 4WD only when conditions demanded. Its key was a Ferguson-type viscous coupling and freewheel mechanism, which were attached to the nose of the rear differential. Although the long propeller shaft to the rear was always turning when the car was in motion, the viscous coupling/freewheel arrangement meant that power and torque were only fed to the rear wheels when the speed of front and rear wheels differed, which told the system that the front wheels had lost traction. Due to assembly preloads in the system, there was always a small amount of torque being fed to the rear wheels.

The freewheel disengaged power to the rear when the brakes were applied to prevent locking the rear wheels—this being before VW's use of anti-lock breaking sys-

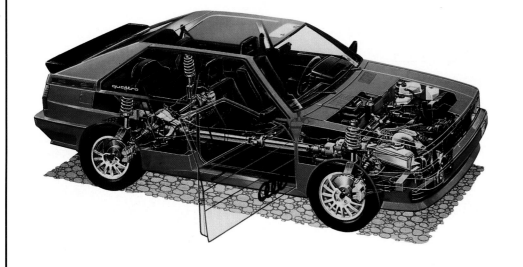

Syncro offerings in the U.S. were limited to the 1986–88 Quantum passenger car and the 1986–91 Vanagon (top left). The landmark Audi Quattro of 1980 (left) pioneered VW's use of four-wheel drive and turbocharging. VW preferred the supercharger, however, and chose one with G-shaped veins (opposite top left). It helped boost power in a variety of vehicles, including the Corrado, Polo G40, and Golf GTI G60 (opposite top right). The first VW to combine supercharging, Syncro, and anti-lock brakes was the Europe-only 160-horsepower Golf Rally G60 of 1988 (opposite bottom).

tems. VW made much of the fact that there were no locks, levers, buttons, or overrides the driver had to learn to use. The Syncro system would provide maximum traction, uphill or downhill, on good or poor traction surfaces.

By choosing supercharging instead of turbocharging to boost the performance of its four-cylinder engines, Volkswagen flew against European trends. Because turbochargers are driven by engine exhaust gases that would otherwise go to waste, their power was "free." VW, however, was not happy with a turbocharger's characteristics, in which there was little boosting of power output until the engine was revving well, while at the top end, the output had to be limited so the turbo did not overboost the engine itself.

Because VW wanted to produce more low- and medium-speed torque, its only choice was a mechanically driven supercharger. This would be belt-driven from the crankshaft, which meant that it would absorb more power than a turbo unit. But power delivery would be easier to control and less prone to lag. The first application was in the Polo G40, which was introduced

in 1986. The supercharged eight-valve Type 827 engine in the Golf was not ready for sale until 1989. VW never applied supercharging to the twin-cam 16-valve engine, though it was no doubt technically feasible.

For their supercharger design, Wolfsburg engineers resurrected a 1905 French patent that used several spiral-shaped internal veins and a spiral impeller to compress the air. It was known as the G-Lader system, after the G-shaped configuration of the veins. The supercharger was driven by a ribbed belt, drew in its air from the outside, compressed it, fed it through an air-to-air intercooler, then propelled it into the engine at a maximum boost of 9.5 pounds-per-square-inch/0.65 Bar. Peak power went up

to an impressive 160 horsepower at 5,600 rpm in standard tune, though a great deal more was available if boost pressure was further increased and the owner was willing to risk impaired reliability.

Anti-lock brake systems appeared on VWs in Europe starting in 1987, and were soon applied to the four-wheel-drive Synchro types—a rather difficult technical exercise.

The first car to combine all these fixtures was the Golf Rally G60 of 1988, a two-door hatchback homologation special that used the 160-horsepower supercharged engine, Synchro, and anti-lock brakes. It was joined in 1990 by the GTI G60, which was a sporting front-wheel-drive two- or four-door hatchback designed for street use. These cars were offered only in European markets.

In the United States, Volkswagen offered the Syncro system beginning in 1986 on the Vanagon, though it never extended its availability to the EuroVan successor. It was also offered on the Quantum sedan and wagon in a period from 1986 to 1988. A Syncro version of the second-generation Golf was discussed, but never imported. The G-Lader supercharger was offered in the U.S. only on the Corrado, where it debuted in 1990 making 158 horsepower. It was dropped during the 1992 model year in favor of the VR6 six-cylinder engine.

at 2,150 pounds, 256 pounds more than the last Rabbit, and at 2,330 pounds, the second-generation Jetta had gained 126 pounds.

When looked at side by side, the new car was obviously bulkier, but subtly smoother than the original, and VW claimed a dramatically lowered drag coefficient, Cd 0.34 instead of 0.42. A sloping nose and rounded front corners, the integration of rain gutters, and the nearly flush mounting of front quarter windows were new wind-cheating details.

Under the skin, there was development but no innovation. Suspension, steering, braking and engine installations were much as before. Europeans could choose from among six engines—four gas-powered, beginning with a 55-horsepower 1,272cc unit, and a choice of naturally aspirated or turbocharged diesels. Americans could choose an 85-horsepower version of the 1.8, a 52-horsepower 1.6-liter diesel, or for the Jetta only, the 68-horsepower turbodiesel. In mid 1985, VW specified a "high-output" version of the 1.8 for the Golf GTI and Jetta GLI. It was rated at 102 horsepower at 5250 rpm and 110 pounds/feet of torque at 3250. Within weeks of the European launch, VW unveiled the Golf GTI with the 139-horsepower twin-cam 1.8 from the Scirocco GTI; this engine was later extended to homemarket Jettas.

The new cars were indeed roomier and more refined than the first generation. True to VW's word, the U.S.-built versions differed little in character from their German counterparts, aside from emissions and safety changes (and the fact that only European models could be ordered with anti-lock brakes, which appeared in 1987). Prices were reasonable, too, at least at first. U.S. models started at just $6,990 for the base Golf and $7,775 for the two-door Jetta (diesel models were about $200 more). Compared to the ever-more-refined Japanese competition, the latest VWs rode stiffly and were rather noisy. But they were drivers' cars.

Their sporting nature was strongest in the GTI and GLI models. They added such features as tauter springs, wider tires, and rear disc brakes, while still starting at under $10,000. In a test of six hot hatchbacks by *Road & Track*, the GTI acquitted itself well. It had the quickest 0-60 mph time, 9.0 seconds, the highest slalom speed, 62.4 mph, and the second-shortest stopping distance from 60 mph, 147 feet. The editors picked the GTI second overall, however. It was beaten in a "fun-to-drive" tiebreaker by the only rear-wheel drive car in the bunch, the 112-horsepower Toyota Corolla GT-S.

On the strength of the new Golf and Jetta, Volkswagen's U.S. sales inched above the 200,000-unit mark for 1985 and '86. The cars were hits in other markets, too; the Golf became Europe's best-selling car. The success helped justify VW's huge financial investment, much of which was in a new two-level assembly facility at Wolfsburg, Hall 54, which had a usable floor area of more than 570,000 square feet. Heavily robotized, and conceived with a production limit of 2,400 vehicles per day, it was soon working to capacity. The six-millionth Golf was built in September 1983, and the 10 millionth would follow in June 1988, at which time VW said 64 percent of them had been exported or assembled in overseas plants, 2.56-million had been diesel powered, and 790,000 had been GTIs.

One version not included in these numbers was a Cabriolet. There never was a convertible version of the second-generation Golf. VW just kept on selling the original Karmann-built soft top, even renaming it the Volkswagen Cabriolet after the Rabbit badge was shelved in the U.S. Driven by the 90-horsepower 1.8-liter four, it lived happily on into the 1990s. More than 230,000 were built for worldwide sales, with 100,000 units delivered in the U.S. alone.

Rivaling the convertible for smiles-per-mile in the U.S. were the 1987 Golf GTI and Jetta GLI, which gained the twin-cam 16-valve version of the 1.8-liter four. For American consumption, the engine had 123 horsepower at 5800 rpm and 120 pounds/feet of torque at 4250. Pulling 2,444 pounds of curb weight, the 16-valve GTI could do 0-60 mph in 8.3 seconds.

Car and Driver pitted the new GTI against a field of nine other front-drive "econohunks." The group included four Japanese entries (Acura Integra LS, Isuzu I-Mark Turbo, Mitsubishi Mirage Turbo, and Toyota Corolla FX16) four domestics (Chevrolet Cavalier Z24, Dodge Shadow ES, Ford Escort GT, and Pontiac Sunbird GT), and one other European, the Renault GTS.

"The dynamics of the [GTI] are second to none," *Car and Driver* said. "It's capable of great moves with no white knuckles. It's sure-footed over the humps and bumps, it's nicely balanced in the turns, and it cuts cleanly through the twisties. The steering tells you what you need to know. You have the feeling that nothing will ever come up that the GTI can't handle."

Nonetheless, it judged the GTI a shade less-desirable than the Acura, which outpolled every other car in the categories of engine, transmission, ergonomics, comfort, ride, and value. The VW tied

(continued)

Volkswagen never built a convertible off the second-generation Golf platform. Instead, the friendly Rabbit-based ragtop carried on from 1980 through 1993. It got minor upgrades along the way, including a new grille and aero-body cladding for 1988. It was the first VW with a driver-side air bag, added for 1990 to meet federal passive-safety requirements. The only engine was the 1.8-liter four, which made 94 horsepower at the end. A variety of models were offered through the years, including the Boutique and another called the Etienne Aigner. In the top photo is a 1991 base model, which started at $16,540. The others are 1993 Classic Collector's Edition models, which listed for $19,930 and included leather upholstery and heated front seats. The best U.S. sales years for these cabrios were between 1985 and 1988, when VW sold more than 12,000 annually.

In 1987, the second-generation Golf GTI gained the 16-valve twin-cam 1.8-liter four, which made 123 horsepower in U.S. tune (left). Europeans could buy a four-door GTI (top), but Americans got only the two-door (above). The '87 started at $10,325, weighed 2,400 pounds, and did 0-60 mph in 8.3 seconds. In 1989, VW's ad agency conjured up "Fahrvergnügen" (opposite top left) in an effort to describe the cars' German driving feel. A better understanding came from behind the wheel of a 16-valve Jetta GLI. The '89 Special Edition model (opposite page) had unique upholstery and two-tone BBS alloy wheels. It cost about $17,000, including $995 for anti-lock brakes, which were a new option that year.

the Integra in utility and driving fun. Keeping the GTI from first place was what *Car and Driver* judged to be a harsh-running engine, vague shifter, and poor assembly quality. Price also was a factor, the editors said. "The GTI's base price, $11,825, tops the as tested prices of six of the other cars on the menu, and the $14,340 sticker of our heavily optioned test car was the highest of the group by a good margin, even though some of the others were also packed with options."

The poor quality, which included air leaks around the doors, was ominous, for the GTI, like all U.S. Golfs and some Jettas, was assembled at the Westmoreland plant. It was more evidence that VW's American strategy wasn't working and may have been one reason the Pennsylvania plant was again operating far below capacity.

Until the 1980 recession, VW had been delighted with its investment in Westmoreland. But as worldwide production of Volkswagens plummeted from 8.5 million in 1979 to a mere five million in 1982, production of U.S.-assembled Rabbits also slumped—from near 200,000 to a miserable 84,027.

Then, to VW's amazement, as the North American market recovered strongly, Rabbit sales lagged. In 1983, only 98,230 Rabbits rolled out of Westmoreland. VW could only grit its teeth and persevere. The upturn with the introduction of the second-generation Golf in 1985 raised hopes, but even with production hitting 97,128 in 1985—the high point of the car's run—more than 130,000 other types of VWs were being exported from Germany to the U.S., which was not the balance the company had forecast a decade earlier.

By 1986, VW privately was certain it could never make money in Pennsylvania at these volumes, but it also knew that it could never sell enough Golfs to reverse the situation. Hahn's public position to the European media was that, "We keep our plant in the U.S.A. as an insurance policy, in case protectionism should develop there, and force us to use our American plant more. With our level of automation in Germany, it is more profitable to export cars made here, even at the present level of the dollar."

When asked how much money was being lost in the U.S., Hahn answered, "Taking into account our exports, we have never lost one cent there since

1983 or 1984." That was no answer at all, though it did imply that Westmoreland was not a profitable operation.

Well before the end of 1987, the company had decided to take the brave pill, and admit that the Westmoreland operation no longer made economic sense. Production had slumped to 66,193 in '87. In '88, only 36,998 Golfs were produced at Westmoreland, the last American-assembled cars being completed in July of that year. The entire project was then closed down, and most Golfs and Jettas were sourced from VW's plant in Mexico, which was suffering its own quality-control problems.

With the company in disarray, U.S. dealers had come to rely on Jim Fuller's enthusiasm as a light in the darkness. On December 21, 1988, the popular Fuller was on Pan Am Flight 103 from Frankfurt to New York when, over Lockerbie, Scotland, a terrorist bomb exploded onboard. All 270 passengers were killed. VW's U.S. marketing director, Lou Marengo, also lost his life in the disaster.

By February 1989, Wolfsburg had appointed a new president of VWoA, former German export sales manager Hans-Jorg Hungerland, and a replacement for Fuller, former automotive consultant William Young. VW and its U.S. dealers now looked to the 1990s with an unfamiliar management team and a model lineup that didn't seem suited for a return to high-volume profitability. A redesigned Golf and Jetta weren't due for several years, and most of the new models VW had planned for the meantime were to be priced around $20,000. On top of that, Young told reporters that he intended to abandon Fuller's "German engineering" theme for one that pitched VWs as "honest value."

While U.S. sales languished, the company was still a profitable giant in Europe and elsewhere. Americans, however, no longer saw Volkswagens as delivering outstanding value, especially against Japanese cars, which were furnishing more creature comforts—and in some cases, more performance—for less money. The Audi division was suffering as well. The 1990s were going to be an interesting decade for one of the world's proudest automakers.

Battered by quality problems, rising prices, and Japanese competition, VW's U.S. sales slipped to 91,700 in 1991, the first sub 100,000-unit year since the 1950s. VW loyalists were rewarded with some tasty performance cars, however. Golf GTI models adopted the European headlight treatment (above) *and offered a $10,680 version with a 105-horsepower eight-valve 1.8 liter. The $13,370 GTI 16V* (opposite bottom) *and the $14,880 Jetta GLI 16V moved up to a twin-cam 2.0-liter with 134 horsepower. The base Jetta* (top) *remained the best-selling VW in the U.S. lineup and got subtle lower-body streamlining to close out its second-generation run. Volkswagen of America was entering the new decade in disarray. It paired costs, held the line on prices, and tried abandoning its "German-flavor" campaign for one promising "honest value." Things would get worse before they got better.*

Shaping the Future— The 1990s and Beyond

Volkswagen lovers in the United States had sensed it, tried to deny it. But it was true. "Somewhere along the way we lost our sense of direction and our pride and self-confidence," acknowledged Steven F. Wilhite, Volkswagen of America's senior executive for North American marketing. That frank assessment, made to reporters in 1995, summed up VW's transformation during the 1980s. Once a robust innovator, it had become a tentative fringe player.

The journey was a very different one in most other parts of the world, where Volkswagen was delivering the right cars at the right time. In Europe, VW Group's market share increased from 10 percent to 17 percent between 1982 and 1992. Its slice of the global car market in the period grew from four percent to seven percent.

Still, by late 1992, Daniel Goeudevert, deputy group chairman and VW's second in command, had declared that Europe's biggest automaker faced a "crisis situation" and was barely breaking even, despite worldwide sales of about 3.5 million vehicles. As a German company, VW's cost of building cars was 15 to 25 percent higher than that of competitors, especially the Japanese. Sales in the U.S. had sunk to their lowest levels since the 1950s. Equally troubling, Goeudevert said, was that the quality of German-built VWs was deteriorating. "I agree that we have lost some of our huge reputation for quality," he said. "We know there is a problem. VW has to build even better [cars than rivals] because we have a premium price."

As 1993 approached, Volkswagen embarked on an ambitious cost-cutting program. It trimmed hundreds of thousands of vehicles from its production schedule, shed 36,000 jobs worldwide, and addressed quality problems in the Mexico plant that supplied Golfs and Jettas to the U.S. But it was the product that would determine VW's future, and there was growing evidence that the people who shaped the character of VW's cars had regained their sense of direction, if for no other reason than they were willing to admit they had lost it.

In a sense, the first new Volkswagen of VW's new age was unveiled in 1981. At that year's Frankfurt auto show, VW displayed its Auto 2000 concept sedan. Observers were certain that Auto 2000, with its distinctive grille-free nose set off by rectangular headlamps, held clues to the next-generation Golf. When that car was introduced for 1985 as a conservative rework of the original, they said Auto 2000 instead forecast the bold look of the second-generation Passat. Wrong again.

But when the third-series Passat bowed for 1988, there was the Auto 2000's rounded form, its graceful roof pillars, its high tail, and its grilleless snout set off by rectangular headlamps. Finally, it seemed Volkswagen was willing to break from its evolutionary rut and try something fresh. The Passat/Santana/Quantum range of 1980–1988 had sold well enough—European production approached 2.2-million in nine years. But the cars were somehow anonymous. By VW's standards, this successor was downright adventurous.

The new car used a fully redesigned front-wheel-drive unibody platform: This was the Passat that finally severed all links with the Audi 80/Fox. And it broke with stodgy-engine Passats of the past by featuring a sporty 16-valve twin-cam 2.0-liter (1,984cc, 121 cubic inch) four-cylinder. Rumors soon spread about new and advanced V-6 power units, along with a four-wheel-drive option. Whatever powerplants would be used, they would have to be transversely positioned, for the new Passat discarded the longitudinal mounting of its predecessors. That meant it could not use Audi-type five-cylinder engines, which were too long.

In a subtle shift of market positioning, there was no hatchback in the new range, merely a smart six-window four-door sedan and a neat four-door wagon. Much work had gone into refining the new car's aerodynamic performance. It looked—and it was—very slippery. The coefficient of drag was reduced from the previous generation's Cd. 0.38 to a very good 0.29. Side-window glass was flush-mounted and rain channels were integrated into the roof. There was attention to underhood airflow management, even small air passages between the side mirrors and body.

Passengers had much more room than before. At 103.3 inches, the new Passat's wheelbase was three inches longer, and locating the engine transversely helped even more. The seating position was high-

Volkswagen entered the 1990s as a robust force in Europe and in many of the 100 countries in which it did business. But in the United States, where it had once sold more than 500,000 cars annually, things were desperate. VW tallied just 43,902 U.S. sales in 1993, and its market share withered to a microscopic 0.05 percent. Industry observers speculated it might pull out of America. But VW fought back with new products and American executives again talked of 200,000-unit sales years. Symbolizing this rebirth was the Concept 1 show car of 1994 (opposite). Scheduled for production as a 1998 model, it showed that Volkswagen was willing to embrace its past to shape its future.

er, for a feeling of greater driver control. And the rear suspension, still a trailing-arm, twisting-beam layout, had been repackaged to allow yet more backseat space.

At launch, all engines were based on the Type 827 four-cylinder design, which had been in use on VWs and Audis for 16 years and showed no signs of running out of development potential. In Europe, there were five sizes and tunes, ranging from 1.6 liters and 72 horsepower to 2.0 and 136, plus an 80-horsepower 1.6-liter turbodiesel. All had catalysts, for in the increasingly environmentally conscious Germany, VW was determined to be the "greenest" of carmakers.

Realizing the Passat was still a car without much of an image, VW advertised the new version as a big brother to the much-respected Golf, with all the same merits but with more space and versatility.

In the United States, VW sold off its remaining '88 Quantums, then walked through 1989 without a model in what was America's compact-car segment. The new Passat was introduced for the 1990 model year, now under the name used in Europe. It was offered in both body styles, but only with the twin-cam 2.0, which was rated at 134 horsepower at 5800 rpm and 133 pounds/feet of torque at 4400. A five-speed manual transmission was standard and VW's first four-speed automatic was optional. Base prices started at $14,770 for the sedan and at $15,885 for the wagon, which was initially available only with automatic transmission.

Taking a cue from amenity-laden Japanese rivals, VWoA sought to make its Passat as passenger-friendly as possible. Standard equipment included air conditioning, front-seat height and lumbar adjustments, a 60/40 folding rear seatback, rear defogger, tinted glass, and a tilt steering column. Among the options were anti-lock brakes ($835), a Convenience Group consisting of power windows, locks, and mirrors, cruise control, and six-speaker audio system ($1,200), power sunroof ($695), and leather upholstery ($710).

American autowriters were impressed with the car's generous interior space, cavernous trunk, and spirited handling, but they criticized the vague manual-shift action, stiff ride, and high noise levels. Standing-start acceleration was decent, 0-60 mph taking 8.8 seconds with the five-speed and about 10.5 with the automatic. Alas, the automatic's shift action was spastic and harsh, making for rather unpleasant around-town driving. With a curb weight of 2,985 pounds, an automatic-transmission sedan would average about 22 mpg in combined city/highway driving. Ladle on desir-

able options, and a Passat sedan could easily sticker for over $19,000. All things considered, it wasn't a great value against tough rivals such as the Honda Accord, which was faster, more refined, and less costly.

American VW dealers sold 21,149 Passats in 1990. They had never sold that many Quantums in a single year, and VW sales as a whole ticked upward to 129,714. But it still wasn't good. The company's share of the U.S. market had shriveled to just 1.4 percent, and by summer 1990, a nervous VW was offering full refunds to unsatisfied Passat customers who returned their new car within 30 days or 3,000 miles.

In Europe, VW was tinkering with both ends of the Passat range. It introduced a new super-economy naturally aspirated 68-horsepower diesel. And at the top, it unveiled the Passat G60, which used the same 160-horsepower supercharged 1.8-liter four and Syncro four-wheel-drive system as the Golf G60 Rallye. The Passat G60 had a top speed of 134 mph. To claw back some of the performance lost to catalysts, the most popular of the European engines, the 107-horsepower twin-cam 1.8-liter, was scrapped in favor of an eight-valve 2.0-liter with 115 horsepower and 16 percent more torque.

All this was prelude to a groundbreaking technical development unveiled on a Passat at the 1991 Geneva Motor Show: the first all-new Volkswagen engine since the 1970s. It was no ordinary engine, but a new-age design that packed 2.8 liters of V-6 into the space formerly occupied by a 2.0-liter inline-four. No automaker had attempted anything like it since Lancia had produced a limited number of V-4s for the Fulvia in the 1960s and '70s.

VW's trick was to locate the cylinder banks at 15 degrees instead of the typical 60 or 90 degrees. From the outside, the engine looked like an inline powerplant and in fact was so narrow that just a single head was needed to cover both banks of cylinders. To get the design message across, Volkswagen called it the VR6, a combination of "V," and *Reihe*, the German word for an inline design.

By interesting coincidence, VW's Audi division had recently introduced a new 90-degree 2.8-liter V-6, but it was designed for longitudinal installation; the VR6 was intended for transverse mounting, which had important implications for its future use in Golf-sized cars. VW's director of research and development, Ulrich Seiffert noted that the Passat would have to have been six inches

(continued)

It took Volkswagen seven years to deliver on the design promise made by the sleek Auto 2000 show car of 1981 (top left). Its styling cues finally were reflected in the third-generation Passat, which bowed in Europe for 1988 (other photos). The new Passat demonstrated that VW could draw on its own design history and go its own way in powertrains. Unlike the longitudinal-engine layouts of previous Audi-based Passats, the new front-drive car had a transverse-engine arrangement that was VW's alone. A station wagon was offered, but the absence of a hatchback body style was another signal that VW was refining its marketing philosophy.

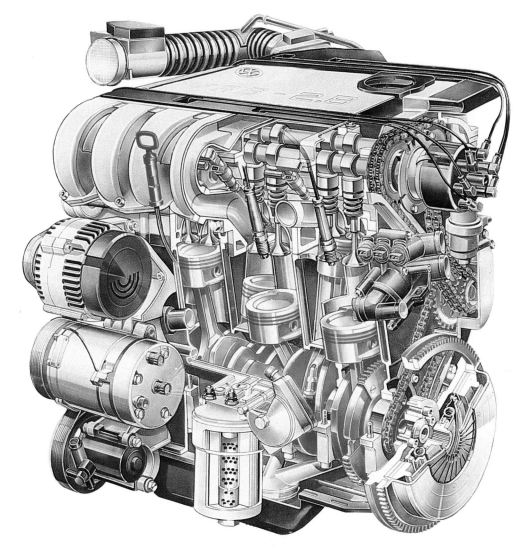

While Audi's engineers designed a conventional 2.8-liter V-6, Volkswagen's took an original tack to create their first new engine since the 1970s. The result was the VR6, a unique powerplant that packed 2.8-liters of V-6 into the space of a 2.0-liter inline-four. Its cylinder banks were set at a 15-degree vee, rather than the conventional 60 or 90 degrees. The narrow angle allowed use of a single cylinder head for both banks. There were two valves per cylinder and, despite the DOHC stamping, one overhead cam per cylinder bank. Horsepower was rated at 174. The VR6 name was a combination of "V" and Reihe, the German word for an inline design.

VW shelved the Quantum name when it shipped its new flagship to the U.S. as the Passat. It bowed for 1990 as a sedan and wagon, both with a 134-horsepower twin-cam 16-valve 2.0-liter four-cylinder engine and the same grille-free nose used on European models. The VR6 came to America under the hood of the 1993 Passat GLX, where its only change from European specification was two fewer horsepower. VW updated the car for 1995 (this page), giving it a handsome new grille. It also replaced the annoying motorized front shoulder belts with manual three-point belts and for the first time furnished driver- and passenger-side air bags.

longer to accommodate the longitudinal Audi engine.

The VR6 displaced 2.8 liters (2,792cc, 170 cubic inches) and was designed from the start to meet a variety of emissions requirements. Thus, it carried virtually the same ratings in both European and American tune: 174 horsepower at 5800 rpm and 177 pounds/feet of torque at 4200. VW said there was a minimum of 147 pounds/feet of torque from 2000 to 6000 rpm.

VW had been at work on its V-6 engine for a decade. It started with an eight-degree two-valve 2.0-liter, then tried a 24-valve 2.2, and finally tested a 12-valve 2.4. None gave the power spread of the 15-degree two-valve 2.8.

The new engine had an aluminum cylinder head and an iron block. VW labeled it a dual overhead-cam engine, though technically it was not because each cylinder bank was served by a single over-head cam. The valves were inline and had hydraulic lifters. The air cleaner was on top, in a pancake, tidying the underhood view. There was a catalyst in the exhaust system, and fuel supply was by Bosch's latest multi-point injection system.

Making the VR6 run smoothly required that VW give it a long stroke and be very clever with crank balancing. The blueprints showed an amazingly complex and seemingly cramped layout, but a longer look exposed the immense detail work that had gone into it. VW said 24-valve layouts were possible, as were diesel derivatives, so clearly this was a new corporate building-block for the late 1990s and beyond.

The VR6 came to America in the 1993 Passat, where its only change from European specifica-tions was two fewer horsepower. It was offered as an alternative to the four-cylinder engine in new Passat GLX sedan and wagon models that started at $21,130 with manual transmission; automatic cost an additional $875. GLXs included traction control as well as new six-spoke alloy wheels shod with 215/50HR15 tires (four-cylinder cars had 195/60HR14s); sedans also got a small trunk spoiler.

"The 38-horsepower boost over the base 134-horsepower four-cylinder transforms the formerly mild-mannered Passat into a deceptively quick ally," said *Car and Driver*. "Zero-to-60 times drop from 9.3 seconds to 7.7 seconds, quick enough to keep close company with the toughest Maximas and Camrys. VW claims a top speed of 130 mph, but our car's governor pulled in the reins at 121." Volkswagen listed a 8.4-second 0-60 mph time for the automatic-transmission GLX.

All Passats gained suspension revisions that softened the ride without hurting handling, but even with VR6 power, the car seemed lost among better-advertised—and faster—rivals such as the Ford Taurus SHO. Passat's reliance on bothersome motorized shoulder belts and its lack of even a driver-side air bag also were disadvantages. Indeed, Passat sales continued to slide, from a dis-appointing 12,578 in 1992, to a dismal 11,970 in '93.

The car was still strong elsewhere, however, as VW refused to force it upmarket as in-house com-petition for Audi, while at the same time wisely declining to take on real sports sedans, such as BMWs. By the mid 1990s, the Passat was being assembled at the ex-Beetle factory in Emden, and in Brussels, Bratislavia (Slovakia), Brazil, and China. With a facelift for the 1995 model year, the Passat was a settled and important member of the VW range.

While VW was at work developing the third-generation Passat, it also was busy preparing a successor to its sports coupe.

Larger, smoother, and potentially faster than the quickest Sciroccos, it arrived in Europe during August 1988 with a new name, Corrado.

This was a tricky time to launch such a machine. Sales of sports and sporting cars had fallen steadily

Successor to the Scirocco was the Corrado, introduced to Europe in 1988 (opposite top row). It was larger and heavier than the Scirocco, but was again a front-drive 2+2 hatchback. With the available 160-horsepower G-Lader supercharged 1.8-liter four, it could hit 225 kilometers per hour, or 140 mph. Corrado came to the U.S. for '90 with the G-Lader engine and ran 0-60 mph in 8.2 seconds. The VR6 was added to European models for 1992 and to U.S. Corrados for '93 (opposite bottom). Its two-valve design (this page) provided fine mid-range punch and helped cut 0-60 times to 6.4 seconds. Corrado drivers enjoyed excellent ergonomics (opposite middle left), but the car didn't survive to trade its troublesome motorized front belts for air bags. VW dropped the sports coupe from the U.S. lineup after 1994 and from its overseas roster after '95.

in the second half of the 1980s. As the British magazine *Autocar & Motor* said of VW's gamble: "It's either plugging a huge gap, or about to fall into a yawning abyss. Sales in the sub-Porsche sports coupe market are in decline across Europe and what remains is now shared by the fiercely competitive Japanese. The Corrado has been designed to plug what Volkswagen sees as an obvious marketing slot below the Porsche/Lotus division for a stylish sports coupe—a slot that's all the bigger now that Porsche has abandoned its entry level 924."

Predictably, VW was cautious. Corrado assembly would take place at Karmann's factory and at modest levels; peak annual production was targeted at no more than 20,000. Curiously, VW insisted the Corrado was not meant to replace the Scirocco, and in fact, the two did sell side-by-side in some markets until the Scirocco was finally dropped in 1992.

Similarities between the cars were obvious. Both were Golf-based (though of different generations), both had transverse-mounted engines and front-wheel drive, both were 2+2 hatchback coupes, both dipped into the Golf parts-bin for their engines and transmissions, and both were assembled by Karmann. But because it used the second-generation Golf platform, suspension layout, and 97.3-inch wheelbase, Corrado was significantly larger than the Scirocco. It was 300 pounds heavier, as well. It was longer overall at 159.4 inches, and its track was wider. The larger platform and hump-backed body shell gave Corrado more cabin space than Scirocco. In most respects, in fact, it was an acceptable four-seater, though there wasn't really a large enough space for four people's luggage.

The styling was by VW's own studio and was distinctively chunky, with more than a hint of the original Scirocco's proportions. Corrado's Cd. of 0.32 wasn't as aerodynamically slippery as some people expected; the use of a grille and exposed headlamps saw to that. So did the unique rear spoiler, which rested flush with the tailgate, then extended automatically when the car reached a certain speed—75 mph in Germany, 45 mph on cars sold in countries with lower speed limits. VW said it reduced rear-end lift by 64 percent, though it also added some measure of aero drag. The spoiler retracted at 12 mph.

European models came with power steering, four-wheel anti-lock disc brakes, low-profile tires on 15-inch alloy wheels, and Passat's robust five-speed gearbox (an automatic transmission option would follow in 1991). Among standard items were air conditioning, leather upholstery, adjustable steering column, and power mirrors.

Initial engine choices were two 1.8-liter fours, the 136-horsepower twin-cam 16-valver and the 160-horsepower eight-valve version with VW's G-Lader supercharger. Both had catalytic converters and could meet any market's current or projected exhaust-emissions regulations. All this, and a potential 140-mph top speed, made this an intriguing new car.

Driven hard, the Corrado had an outstanding chassis—better even than the Golf GTI. It handled remarkably well, put down its power without protest or wheelspin, and generally made testers long for more muscle.

Not enough power was the principal complaint when the Corrado came to the U.S. for the 1990 model year. Billed by Volkswagen as its first "full-blooded sports car," it used the supercharged 1.8, rated in America at 158 horsepower at 5600 rpm and 166 pounds/feet of torque at 4000. The $17,900 base price included air conditioning, four-wheel disc brakes, cruise control, and power windows, mirrors, and locks. Anti-lock brakes cost an additional $835, while leather upholstery added $710 and a sunroof another $695. That was a lot of money in a market crowded with flashier—and faster—new rivals such as the turbocharged Ford Probe GT and all-wheel-drive Mitsubishi Eclipse/Eagle Talon/Plymouth Laser turbos.

Car and Driver tested a Corrado that stickered for $19,750 and tipped the scales at 2,725 pounds. It turned a 0-60 mph time of 8.2 seconds and could reach 132 mph. By contrast the 145-horsepower Probe GT, which cost $17,462, did the same sprint in 7.0 seconds and had a top speed of 134 mph. The 195-horsepower Eagle Talon TSi had all-wheel drive, cost $18,500, and turned torrid 6.3-second 0-60 time on the way to a 137 mph top speed.

In its favor, the VW had a German directness about its moves. "The Corrado is less isolated than a good Japanese supercoupe, less refined, but it's fearless when pointed down a twisty blacktop," said *Car and Driver*. "What we have here is a supercoupe that doesn't care what anybody says. It's a VW and, by gawd, it'll do things its own way."

That way wasn't the popular way, and sales showed it. VW sold just 5,675 Corrados for the '90 model year, and only 4,331 during '91. The car was more popular in Europe, but never captured the market the way the original Scirocco did. VW widened Corrado's homemarket engine availability for '91 by offering the Passat's 136-horsepower 16-valve 2.0-liter. But the big news came for '92,

One intriguing Corrado feature was a rear spoiler that deployed at speed (top right). It provided aerodynamic downforce, but hampered rear visibility. Volkswagen continued to develop its entry-level Polo during the '90s. For '91 (middle), the car got a facelift, an updated interior, and revamped suspension. Pressed by a new flock of competitors, VW fully redesigned the Polo for 1995 (bottom row). Interestingly, its 94.5-inch wheelbase was identical to that of the original 1974 Golf, while its body was actually longer and it was nearly 300 pounds heavier. Though the styling was debatable, Polo III was good enough to be voted 1995 European Car of the Year. VW still had no plans to sell the car in the U.S.

with arrival of the Corrado VR6, which boasted the same narrow-angle V-6 used in the Passat, but in a higher state of tune. European models had 190 horsepower, American models had 178. This, finally, was a sports coupe worthy of the name.

Autocar & Motor called it "remarkable" and was thrilled by the 190 horsepower and 145 mph top speed: "The Corrado VR6 is the fastest front-wheel-drive production car we've yet come across.... Crack the throttle right open and the VR6 engine emits a deep-chested snarl. With the heavier V6 lump up front, you'd expect the VR6's handling to be different from that of the brilliantly behaved 16V and G60 versions. You might even expect it to be worse.... If anything, it handles even better than the four-cylinder versions. As a result, the Corrado VR6 is one of the great handling cars.... Not only does it redefine just how effective (and sophisticated) a powerful front-wheel-drive chassis can be, but it re-establishes the fact that there ain't no substitute for cubes when it comes to making small cars perform well. Very well. It's a classic, the VR6, and its talents run so deep that it takes a while for them to sink in completely."

The Yanks were just as enthusiastic about the VR6 model, which came ashore as the 1993 Corrado SLC. "Hot enough to Fahrverg your nugens," said *Car and Driver*, playing off a Volkswagen ad slogan. Though weight was up to 2,837 pounds, partly because of a fuel tank that held 18.5 gallons instead of 14.5, the 0-60 mph times were down to 6.4 seconds and top speed was an honest 141 mph. *Automobile* magazine griped about poor rear visibility when the spoiler was deployed, cited still-sloppy shift action, complained of engine noise at higher rpm, and deplored the presence of motorized shoulder belts. And it noted that the $22,210 price was steep, even if anti-lock brakes were standard. But it concluded: "If rational decision making is important to you in selecting a car, stay away from the Corrado SLC. This car appeals to a person's irrational, impetuous side. Push the throttle down, and the world along with all its problems, disappears."

Praise like that was not enough, for the tide was running against the entire sports-coupe breed. Corrado sales languished. In America, they dipped to 3,436 in '92, to 2,111 in '93, and to just 1,514 in '94. They slowed in Europe, as well, despite VW's attempts to widen the appeal of the line by introducing a simple 2.0-liter 8-valve engine. VW was forced to look at its charismatic but unlucky coupe, remind itself that the second-generation Golf on which it was based had gone out of production,

and seek an opinion from the accountants. "It's losing money, kill it," was the inevitable reply. Volkswagen didn't offer a Corrado to U.S. customers after the '94 model year. The end in Europe came at the close of '95, and no direct replacement was in sight.

Things were brighter at the ultra-practical end of VW's roster, where the Polo played on. For 1991, the front and rear ends had been reworked and made more rounded. The "coupe" got smaller rear-window glass. And all Polos gained VW's rectangular headlamps, plus big gray plastic bumpers, which made them look more substantial and somehow more expensive than before and allowed VW to claim a 10-percent reduction in aerodynamic drag. Inside was a new instrument binnacle, the heater was now governed by proper rotating controls instead of nasty sliders, and there was better integration of dials, switches, and vents.

The suspension was reworked—firmer at the front, softer at the rear—to make the car feel sportier without destroying the ride. All engines acquired fuel injection, and a more-powerful diesel joined the options list. The revamp was successful, Polo kept selling, and VW was in no rush to produce a replacement. This basic design had gone on sale in 1981, and apart from the 1991 revamp, Polo was still much the same car, and one that had been overshadowed by the Ford Fiesta, GM Corsa, Renault Clio, and the Fiat Uno and Punto. By mid decade, a renewal was long overdue.

Initial designs on the Polo III, as it was dubbed, were completed in late 1991, and after only 32 months of frenzied work, the new car appeared in the summer of 1994, ready for sale at the start of the '95 model year. It was at once familiar and unexpected. The real surprise was not its styling, which was much like the new Golf, but its size, which was quite significantly larger than before. VW's announcement that the new car would be assembled in the Seat factory in Pamplona, Spain, was also unexpected.

The '95 Polo was based on a completely new unibody platform and had fascinating dimensions compared with those of the original Golf of two decades earlier:

Model	Wheelbase (inches)	Length (inches)	Weight (lb)
Original Golf (1974)	94.5	145.8	1,654
Original Polo (1975)	91.9	137.4	1,510
Polo III (1994)	94.5	146.3	1,936

(continued)

Volkswagen's best-selling and most-important car, the Golf (bottom), was redesigned for release in Europe as a 1992 model. The sedan version (top left) was called the Vento instead of Jetta. Wheelbase was the same 97.3 inches as on the generation-two cars and overall length was up less than one inch. Styling—again by VW's own studios—was rounded and evolutionary, though the structures now met worldwide crash standards. The suspension and the front-wheel-drive, transverse-engine layout were the same. The compact size of the new VR6, however, allowed VW to add a six-cylinder engine to the traditional selection of gas and diesel four-cylinders. Demand in Germany and across Europe continued strong.

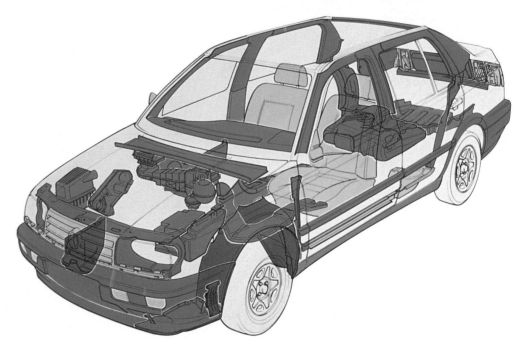

Delayed by production snafus at the Volkswagen plant in Mexico that built them, the third-generation Golf and Jetta didn't begin their first full U.S. model year until 1994. Americans again favored the Jetta (both pages) over the hatchback Golf. With sales of more than 80,000 during 1995, the Jetta was the most-popular European nameplate in the United States. A large trunk, sensible interior, a standard 115-horsepower 2.0-liter four-cylinder engine, and sub-$14,000 starting prices were attractions. Under the skin, VW loaded the car with environmentally friendly recyclable plastic, shown in shades of green in this phantom view.

As new models replace old, they invariably get larger and often move up the social scale a little. Only the reluctant downsizing inspired by the great 1980s fuel crisis halted the trend among Detroit's Big Three. In Europe and Japan, it continued, as illustrated by the Polo III. Bigger, heavier, and a lot better than the Polo generation it replaced, it was also safer, more environmentally responsible, aerodynamically smoother, and altogether more efficient than before. For those who dug around under the skin, it was clear that it also shared its platform with the new-generation Seat Ibiza, which was being built in Spain by VW's subsidiary. The two cars also shared an instrument panel. The Ibiza may only have been a sideshow as far as VW was concerned, but it had actually been launched first, in 1993. It tested many new features intended for the Polo, and gave the Spanish subsidiary the new model it so urgently needed.

Nobody called the new Polo pretty. It was sturdy, it was squat, it seemed to be diligently built—but it had the sort of shape that would be lost in a traffic jam in Berlin, Turin, Paris, or London. Furthermore, its model range had been reduced to two- and four-door hatchbacks. Sedans, sporty "coupes," and G40 supercharged engines were no longer offered. The car seemed to have put away its frivolity and versatility. The new Polo was meant to be—and was—a worthy, safe, and environmentally friendly mid-1990s minicar.

That was borne out under the hood. The small four-cylinder engines were no stronger than before—outputs in fact had not improved for years. With the added weight, the latest Polos were significantly slower than before, which was bad news for VW in a market where other makers were producing perky new cars. VW promised new 16-valve engines and a sorely needed new diesel for later years.

Though the basic mechanical layout of the new car was much as before, it had been upgraded in some important ways. Front and rear wheel tracks were wider, which promised better roadholding and stability. There was power-assisted steering on all but the most basic models, anti-lock brakes were optional, and five-speed manual transmissions were standard.

Dull or not, conventional or not, technically old-hat or not, the new Polo was clearly a remarkably well-developed design and was carefully built. At the end of 1995, a large jury of European journalists awarded it the title of European Car of the Year, which VW accepted as being no less than it deserved.

Although Volkswagen had invested heavily in new models during the early 1990s, it seemed to have lost its technological nerve. Innovation was rare, styling was heavier and less elegant, and VWs were lost among Europe's other front-drive cars. One explanation was that Volkswagen had bowed to political winds—blowing harder in Germany than in any other European country—and had elected to take the "green" and environmentally-friendly route. Instead of performance, it was safety and the recycling of components that were emphasized.

This was the climate in which VW developed and introduced its most important car of the 1990s, the new Golf. The Golf was VW's heartbeat. It had been the best-selling car in Europe for nearly a decade. VW's survival depended on a worthy successor to the 12.6 million second-generation Golfs it had pumped out all over the world.

Wolfsburg spent $1.5 billion to develop the Golf III and introduced it to Europe in August 1991 as a 1992 model. At first glance, the new car looked to be no more than a reskin of the old. It rode the same 97.3-inch wheelbase, and overall length was up by less than one inch. Golf two- and four-door hatchbacks went on sale at once. The longer four-door notchback sedan, now called Vento instead of Jetta, followed early in 1992.

Styled by VW's design studios under Herbert Schafer, the generation-three cars were slightly more aerodynamic than before, but were certainly no beauties. Dominating the nose were oval headlights with a family resemblance to those on the latest Passat. The cabin seemed to have put on a little middle-aged spread. It was an inch wider than before, and because of the very substantial rear roof pillars on both the Golf and Vento (all the better to provide a rigid cabin, VW insisted) there seemed to be less glass than before. The new dashboard was softer in shape and presented gauges and controls even more clearly. The sculpted door panels looked friendly and fresh, and features such as an adjustable steering column were new to this size VW.

The basic suspension, steering, and chassis layout was much as before, with five-speed gearboxes and power-assisted steering standard on all except the base model. Anti-lock brakes were optional across the board. The whole car was heavier than before—and capable of meeting the world's most-stringent 35-mph crash requirements.

All the familiar four-cylinder gas and diesel engines returned, and though displacements had crept up, all had been used in previous VWs with

Volkswagen struggled back to relative health in the U.S. during 1995, thanks in large measure to a renewed sense of identity. A fresh marketing campaign used Generation-X cues and the "Drivers wanted" slogan to position VW as an alternative to mundane Japanese cars. Leading the push to "emotionally reconnect" with drivers were the Jetta GLX (opposite top left) and Golf GTI VR6 (opposite middle and bottom), both of which used the 172-horsepower narrow-angle V-6. Golfs and Jettas were among the last in their class to get standard dual air bags. The safety devices arrived during the 1994 model year (opposite top right).

similar power ratings. The base European Golf now used a 60-horsepower 1,391cc unit. A 150-horsepower 2.0-liter GTI version went on sale after a brief delay to get refinement and driveability up to VW's latest standards. Finally, there was a new performance leader with the VR6 engine, here rated at 174 horsepower. There was no sign of a supercharger or of four-wheel-drive Syncro options, but VW would soon fill gaps by adding a dual-cam 16-valve 2.0-liter GTI, plus the first-ever station-wagon version of the Golf, called a Variant.

When the Vento arrived, VW tried to distance it from the old "booted Golf" image, promoting it as a separate model range. Only the larger engines were available, and it was pitched against popular European medium-sized cars like the new Ford Mondeo (Contour in the U.S.).

VW was saying through its marketing that the Golf and Jetta/Vento were automobiles that had matured, slowly and correctly since 1974. Here were cars for the real world, with such a wide choice of engines and body styles that customers could drive for economy or fun, in a gentle manner or as fast as laws allowed. VW assured the world that no VW could possibly be safer, better built, or more suited to the 1990s.

Almost at once, it seemed, a million world-market Golf IIIs were being built every year. In America, as seemed so often the case with VW lately, things were different. A prompt, smooth launch of new cars was vital, but the introduction was embarrassingly muddled. The decision-makers in Wolfsburg appeared to consider the U.S. market a low priority.

Generation-three cars were on sale for two years elsewhere while American VW dealers were left to sell leftover second-generation Golfs and Jettas. With its bread-and-butter models now obsolete, and in short supply to boot, U.S. sales of Volkswagen cars fell alarmingly. They sunk to 91,688 in 1991, then to just 73,194 in 1992, shrinking VW's share of the U.S. car market to 0.09 percent. VW's legendary reliability and durability also took a hit; the early '90s models were scraping the very bottom of independent quality and customer-satisfaction surveys.

The first generation-three Golfs and Jettas trickled into the country from VW's plant in Puebla, Mexico, in May 1993, but sales were confined to Southern California. VW dealers were now desperate for product, and sales bottomed out. For 1993, VW sold just 43,902 cars in the U.S., withering to a dangerously low 0.05 percent share of the market. This was a company that had once sold half a mil-

lion cars annually. Now its performance was comparable to that of 1956, when it sold 40,432 Beetles. Industry observers actually debated whether Volkswagen would pull out of the U.S. But the nadir had been reached, and VW's climb from near disaster had begun.

The first full model year for nationwide distribution of the Golf III and Jetta III was 1994, though early models made due with motorized front shoulder belts instead of the standard dual air bags that rivals had offered for several seasons.

Base Golfs and Jettas were built in Mexico and used the overhead-cam 2.0-liter four rated at 115 horsepower at 5400 rpm and 122 pounds/feet of torque at 122. Pre-air bag starting prices were $11,900 for the Golf. The Jetta began at $13,125 and was the model of choice among Americans, accounting for about half of the company's sales. Anti-lock brakes cost $775 extra.

The Golf GTI, which started at $19,375, and Jetta GLX, beginning at $19,975, arrived from Germany in early calendar 1995 with dual air bags, anti-lock four-wheel disc brakes, traction control, and the 172-horsepower VR6.

These were indeed more-refined, grown-up cars. Said *Car and Driver* in its review of the four-cylinder Jetta: "The nippy, zingy, adolescent exuberance of past VWs is gone, replaced by the measured responses of an adult car. There are benefits to adulthood, of course. This car will cut a quick pace through the twisties. The power steering feeds back the right information, and an accurate path comes with surprising ease. But you won't find yourself grinning much in the process." Its five-

This page: Autocratic Ferdinand Piech, grandson of Ferdinand Porsche and former chief of VW's Audi division, succeeded Carl Hahn as chairman of Volkswagen in 1992. Opposite: Following the Rabbit-based convertible as the first new VW ragtop in 14 years was the Golf III-based Cabrio. It came to the U.S. for 1995, a year after its European debut. It used the 115-horsepower 2.0-liter four and came with anti-lock brakes and dual air bags. The basket-handle crossbar again added structural rigidity and anchored the front shoulder belts. Pricey at near $20,000, its combination of room, comfort, solidity, and spirit was nonetheless unmatched for the money.

speed weighed 2700 pounds and turned a 0-60 mph time of 10.1 seconds. By contrast, the VR6 models were grin generators. They blended willing V-6 power, a supple suspension, and lively handling. Most importantly, they boasted a combination of fun and function that separated them from anything the Japanese or Americans could offer.

Automobile magazine declared the GTI, "Volkswagen's new best-in-class cult car." *Road & Track* ran a Jetta GLX to 60 mph in 7.7 seconds. "The difference between the standard Volkswagen Jetta III and the new GLX?" asked the magazine. "It's the difference between decaffeinated Diet Coke and Jolt, the cola from a few years back that bragged about having 'all the sugar and twice the caffeine.'" *Car and Driver* was even quicker with its GLX, clocking it at 6.9 seconds 0-60 mph on the way to a 136-mph top speed. Still, nobody went so far as to say that even these cars would return VW to its former sales glory in the U.S.

"The new Jetta GLX comes along at a time when Volkswagen is starving for new models," explained *Car and Driver*. "But it's a snack, not a meal. VW needs more than once nice car to keep it from imploding in the American market."

VW, of course, did have more than one nice car, and some that were much better than nice. The new Cabrio was a case in point. Throughout the 1980s, Karmann coachworks had continued to build Golf convertibles on the original Golf platform, and VW never developed a cabriolet from the second-generation car.

Apparently deciding that 14 years was long enough, VW released its Golf III-based Cabrio in Europe during the summer of 1993 as an early 1994 model. Karmann again looked after assembly at Osnabrück, and as before, there was a safety roll hoop traversing the cockpit. In the best VW tradition, the lined soft-top had a glass rear window and folded into a tall vinyl-wrapped stack, though it didn't stand as high as the previous model's. European models were made available with several of the Golf's four-cylinder engines, though not the VR6 or any of the diesels.

The Cabrio was shipped to the U.S. during 1994 as a '95 model and used the 115-horsepower 2.0. Unlike in Europe, there was no power-operated top available, though the U.S. Cabrio did count among its standard items anti-lock brakes and power windows. Base price of the four-seater was a lofty $19,975. But for refinement, design, and assembly quality, it was unmatched at that price.

VW tacitly acknowledged that the previous cabriolet had gotten a reputation as a "girl's car"—

no mystery when its own surveys showed that 70 percent of the drivers were women. But automotive journalists willingly pointed out that these women were onto something: The new Cabrio was a spacious, structurally sound, carefully built ragtop that was rewarding to drive. *Car and Driver* ran a 2,790-pound five-speed to 60 mph in 10.3 seconds. "I wouldn't mind if the woman who lives at my house bought one," wrote *Automobile* magazine's male reviewer, "just as long as she let me drive it once in a while."

By the mid 1990s, the series-three cars had achieved their sales targets. As many as one million per year were rolling out of Wolfsburg and the ex-Eastern Zone factory at Mosel, out of plants in Belgium and Mexico, and out of the Karmann works in Osnabrück. Counting all generations, VW had assembled 16 million Golfs by the summer of 1995. That was nowhere near the Beetle's production record of 21 million, of course. But by comparison, Honda had sold about 10 million Civics since its 1974 introduction.

Once they were in full supply, the new Golf and Jetta resuscitated VW's American operation. From a low of 43,902 in 1993, VW sales rebounded to 92,368 for 1994. Jetta led the way at 55,688 units, making it the best-selling European nameplate in the U.S. In June 1995, VW recorded its highest monthly sales total in five years, and sales for the year were running 18 percent over those of 1994.

Meanwhile, the early and mid 1990s saw the VW Group formulating a strategy to carry it into the 21st Century. Not only was its North American effort still not back to full health, but the removal of European trade barriers had allowed the formidable Japanese a toehold on the continent, and Southeast Asia and Latin America were emerging as critical new battlegrounds.

Controlling costs was a key. Until the 1960s, VW made just one car, the Beetle, but by the 1990s, it supported four marques, dozens of models, and an armada of factories. Admitting it was high time to make corporate sense of what had become a sprawling conglomerate, VW's braintrust attacked the problem by trimming the number of different automotive platforms. An early proposal was to use just three new platforms as the basis for every new model and derivative—and that included new Audi models. The true degree of future integration was still in flux, but one thing seemed certain: VW, Audi, Seat, and Skoda could not remain as technically independent as they had been.

For a time, Volkswagen's gaze into the not-distant future revealed the tiny Chico (above), a concept for an early-21st-Century commuter car. More ambitious was the Futura (opposite page), a Golf-sized four-seater unveiled at the 1989 Frankfurt show. The upper half of its body was a glass canopy impregnated with heat-reducing holographic filters. The gullwing doors and rear hatch could be removed to convert Futura to an open recreation vehicle. Four-wheel steering and a system of electronic sensors enabled the car to maneuver itself into a parking space at the touch of a button. Power came from a direct-injection 1.7-liter four-cylinder gas engine that was made quieter by noise-cancellation technology built into the car's audio system. Among Futura features were integrated child seats and safety belts anchored to the front seats.

(continued)

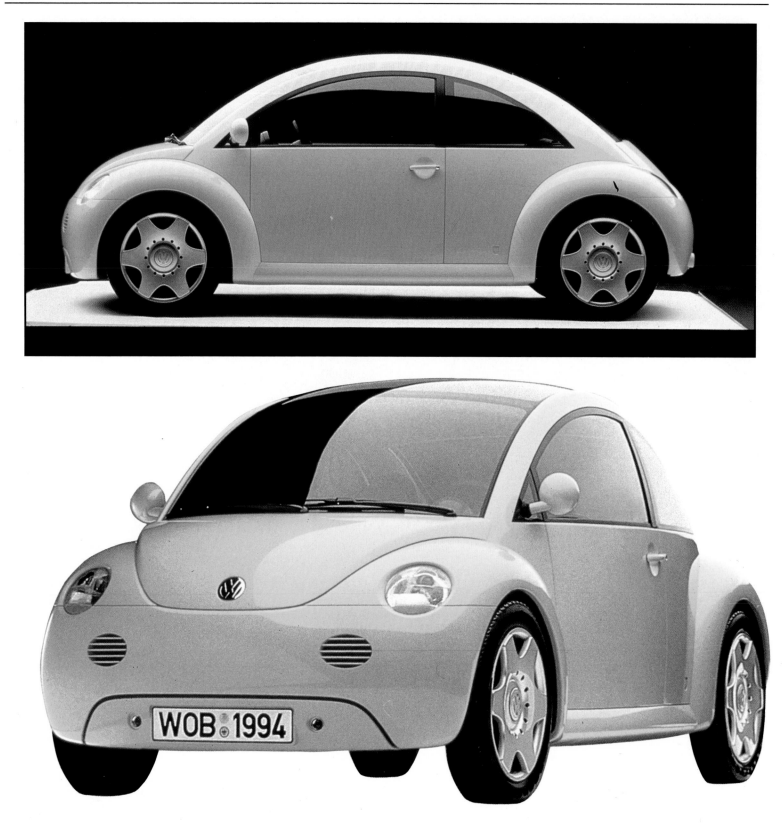

Spiritual descendent of the original Beetle was the Concept 1, built in sedan (opposite) and cabriolet (this page) form. Constructed as a 1994 show car, interest in the new-age Bug compelled VW to plan its production as a regular 1998 model. Concept 1 rode a 99.4-inch wheelbase and was engineered to accept three different high-efficiency powerplants: a turbodiesel that starts and stops depending on need; a hybrid diesel/electric; and full electric. Customer versions were expected to mirror its contours and proportions, as well as its front-engine, front-drive chassis. The show car's instrument panel (left) clearly recalled the Beetle's simple design, though Concept 1's dashboard included dual air bags.

In 1992, Carl Hahn was succeeded as Group chairman by Ferdinand Piech, grandson of Ferdinand Porsche and most recently, the tough, cost-cutting chief of VW's Audi division. Piech declared that he would not be satisfied until VW was Europe's most profitable automaker by 1997. To that end, he snared from General Motors an equally tough Spanish automotive executive named Jose Ignacio Lopez de Arriortua. As head of purchasing for GM of Europe, Lopez had gained a reputation as a fearless cost-cutter and had been recruited to work his magic on GM's American operations. But his departure from GM was full of intrigue, as he met secretly with Piech, then publicly promised not to leave GM, and finally was accused of taking confidential GM documents with him when he did go to VW in March 1993. The international controversy simmered on as Germany entered an economic recession. VW was forced to put much of its workforce on a four-day week, because of both a lack of orders and to contain wages. In early 1994, an angry Piech fired the chiefs of the Seat and Audi operations. By mid 1995, VW had reached new accords with German labor unions, its financial outlook had stabilized, and projections were of improved profits.

Platform consolidations, purchasing efficiencies, and high-profile personalities made life worth living for accountants and journalists. But it was a concept car unveiled in January 1994 that put VW back in the public eye.

Observers couldn't help but smile at the happy, yellow, egg-shaped two-door sedan under the spotlights at the Detroit Auto Show. Within 24 hours, photographs of it had been transmitted around the world. The car VW called the Concept I was genuine front-page news. And most of the headlines screamed "The Beetle is Back!"

Not exactly. This indeed was Volkswagen's proposed new model to slot below the Golf, but unlike the Beetle, it was a fully modern car, complete with front-wheel drive, dual air bags, anti-lock brakes, and full emissions compliance. In fact, it was capable of accommodating three different high-efficiency engine proposals: a turbodiesel combined with VW's Ecomatic technology, in which a computer starts and stops the engine depending on the need for power; a hybrid setup that combines diesel and electric drive; and an all-electric system.

VW insisted that it had no firm plans to put the Concept 1 into production. But it was almost immediately flooded with pleas to build it. Hundreds of potential German buyers clamored to place orders. Americans voted overwhelming in favor of the car in a VW phone-in poll. Within a year of its unveiling, Volkswagen announced that it would build both a sedan and convertible version of the Concept 1, and that the car would be introduced, with a real name, in 1998.

It was no accident that Concept 1 had its first showing in a land that never fully embraced the "new" VW. "The Americans understood the purpose of the car," VW's head of research, Ulrich Seiffert, told *Autocar & Motor* magazine. "It demonstrated that we are prepared to go back to our roots to fight for the market."

The U.S. introduction was doubly appropriate because the Concept 1 came out of VW-Audi's new design studio in Simi Valley, California. It was the work of a designer named J Mays, who directed the California studio before being named head of design at Audi. Mays said the original intention was to make a proposed electric car look friendly and familiar.

For inspiration, Mays and an assistant worked alongside a 1948 Beetle. The influence was clear; though Concept 1's 99.4-inch wheelbase was longer than that of any Beetle, the shape was unmistakable and the overall height, 59 inches, was the same. Even the simple dashboard, dominated by a single circular multi-function gauge, recalled that of the Beetle.

"We wanted to visualize what VW means.... We thought about what makes a Volkswagen and defined the values as 'simple, honest, reliable and original,'" Mays told *Autocar & Motor*.

That's pretty much the definition anyone who has ever loved a Volkswagen would use—though some would add "fun." Nobody seemed to mind that Volkswagen was looking to its past for the shape of its future. That's probably because no company has a past quite like VW's.

Designed by VW's California studio, Concept 1 rocketed Volkswagen back into popular consciousness, especially in America, which still pined for the Beetle. In October 1995, VW unveiled this evolution of the Detroit concept car. It was much closer to production-ready form, the biggest difference being a nose elongated to meet frontal-crash protection standards. At 159.8 inches, this version was nine inches longer than the original and about the same size as a Golf. The still-unnamed retro bug had seats for four and a large rear trunk. VW's official announcement of the evolutionary show car said it "illustrates the philosophy of life of its owner: individualist, lighthearted, youthful, and non-aggressive... A reinterpretation of an automotive legend [it is] a bridge between the past and future."

INDEX